📞 01603 773114
email: tis@ccn.ac.uk 🐦 @C   nstore
                                             s.com

21 DA   D0531279

Please return <u>on or before</u> the last date stamped above

A fine will be charged for overdue items

CITY
COLLEGE
NORWICH

Training to Teach in Further and Adult Education

2nd edition

David Gray
Colin Griffin
Tony Nasta

First published in 2000 by:
Stanley Thornes (Publishers) Ltd

Second edition published in 2005 by:
Nelson Thornes Ltd
Delta Place
27 Bath Road
CHELTENHAM
GL53 7TH
United Kingdom

05 06 07 08 09 / 10 9 8 7 6 5 4 3 2 1

A catalogue record for this book is available from the British Library

ISBN 0 7487 9447 6

Page make-up by Florence Production Ltd, Stoodleigh, Devon

Printed and bound in Spain by GraphyCems

CONTENTS

INTRODUCTION

Diversity is the dominant characteristic of post-16 education. Teaching and learning take place in a wide range of institutions: further education colleges, sixth form colleges, private training organisations, adult education and school sixth forms. The learner is faced with a bewildering variety of qualifications – over 17,000 of them. Many lie outside the National Qualifications Framework. Whilst about three quarters of students are over 19 and mainly studying part-time, there are more 16–19-year-olds in colleges in the further education sector than in secondary schools. Teachers in further and adult education themselves come from a range of occupations and the majority are part-time.

This diversity presents those teaching in post-compulsory education with many challenges. The new teacher will often have to teach across a range of courses, both academic and vocational, and cope with the distinct needs of school leavers and older students. She or he may have to teach and guide students taking qualifications at different levels – for example, those on foundation programmes, who will often lack basic skills in literacy and numeracy, and those on higher education programmes, such as Higher National Certificates (HNCs). This calls for a high level of professionalism.

WHO HAS THIS BOOK BEEN WRITTEN FOR?

This book has been written for those training to teach in post-16 education, primarily those teaching or intending to teach in further and adult education. Our aim has been to produce a textbook for students pursuing Cert. Ed. or PGCE courses, which reflects the diversity of further and adult education. We recognise that for most new entrants to post-compulsory education, teaching will be a second or even third career. Most will enter teaching to pass on to students the specialist knowledge they have already gained through working in other occupations or professions, for example engineering, accountancy or nursing.

We have attempted to cover the needs of two groups:

- students taking the qualification who are already teaching, as full or part-time lecturers, and are studying on an in-service basis
- students studying for the Cert. Ed. or PGCE on a full-time basis through attending a pre-service course at a college or university and reliant upon teaching practice to gain practical experience of the sector.

For both groups we have tried to provide a textbook that encourages reflective practice by covering the basic tools of teaching, learning and assessment, but placing these in a wider theoretical and organisational context. The essence of professionalism seems to involve the capability to stand back from the immediate situation and to evaluate performance critically by drawing upon a wider base of knowledge and experience.

During the last decade, there has been intense national interest in post-compulsory teacher training from government and other national agencies. In 2001 a statutory requirement was introduced for FE teachers to be qualified against national standards determined by the FE National Training Organisation (FENTO). In 2003, Ofsted published a critical survey report on ITT for FE teachers (Ofsted, 2003), which led to further changes in the national system for training that are summarised in the important DfES policy document *Equipping our Teachers for the Future: Reforming Initial Teacher Training for the Learning and Skills Sector* (DfES Standards Unit, 2004). Much of the debate in the book reflects this rapidly changing policy context.

WHAT THIS BOOK COVERS

In deciding upon the subject matter of the book we were conscious that further and adult education is a quickly changing sector and that during the first few years of a career, the new teacher will be expected to play a range of demanding roles. The following roles seemed absolutely central:

- teacher
- manager of learning/learning resources
- curriculum developer
- assessor/verifier
- student guide and tutor
- course/subject leader
- critical evaluator and reviewer
- professional developer.

These roles also reflect the main areas of skills and knowledge identified by the FENTO standards, which are critically reviewed in Chapter 11 (see Figure 11.1 on page 265).

The contents of the book reflect the approach outlined above.

- **Part 1** consists of an introduction to working in post-compulsory education. It describes how colleges and other providers are organised and funded and analyses some of the key changes which are taking place in this complex sector.
- **Part 2** focuses upon the central activities of teaching, learning and assessment. Given the stress upon independent learning and the teacher's role as a manager of learning resources, we have devoted considerable attention to the impact of information and learning technologies. There is detailed coverage of the use of the web and other forms of electronic communication. Given the fundamental importance of assessment in both general and vocational courses, this aspect is also treated in considerable detail. Where appropriate we have drawn upon educational theories, based upon the disciplines of philosophy, psychology and sociology because they add a deeper dimension to reflective practice.
- Professionalism in teaching in post-compulsory education involves an understanding of the complex context within which teaching and learning takes place. It is critical that new teachers should understand such aspects as management and organisation, student guidance and quality assurance. For this reason, in **Part 3**, you will find a detailed analysis of the wider roles played by the teacher and tutor. There are separate chapters on guidance, quality assurance and professional development.

How to use the book (our approach to teaching and learning)

We recognise that students using this book will themselves reflect the diversity of further and adult education. They will be drawn from a range of subject and occupational areas and will have a variety of prior qualifications and experience. They will also be studying by different methods: full-time, part-time and distance learning. They will, however, have one thing in common – a commitment to methods of learning which suit adults or, in other words, an approach based upon active and independent learning.

We have tried to make full use of this approach throughout the book. You will therefore find each chapter is liberally sprinkled with case studies and activities designed to engage you as an active learner. There is now a wealth of published information on further and adult education (much of it accessible through the internet). Many of the activities ask you to retrieve and analyse this information. By completing these activities, you will extend your knowledge of the sector. To give a unifying theme to the chapters, we decided to develop three case studies of fictitious institutions. These are Greybourne College of Further Education, Greybourne Sixth Form College and Greybourne Adult and Community Education Service. The first of these is a general FE college, the second a specialist 16–19 sixth form college and the third a local authority adult education provider. There are also a few case studies based upon work-based learning providers. We enjoyed developing the case studies and activities and we hope they will widen your knowledge and encourage you to learn independently.

About the authors

David Gray has taught in further and higher education, and is a senior lecturer in the School of Management at the University of Surrey. He has published in a wide range of fields including initial teacher education and information and communications technology.

Colin Griffin is a Visiting Senior Fellow in the Department of Political, International and Policy Studies at the University of Surrey, having worked in the School of Educational Studies there for many years. He has taught in adult, further and higher education, including experience at the Open University and a College of Education.

Tony Nasta has worked in further and higher education for 25 years. During this time he has served as a teacher, researcher, senior college manager, FE inspector, author and DfEE adviser.

Acknowledgements

The authors and publishers would like to thank the following organisations for permission to reproduce material: Further Education Resources for Learning (Ferl); The Further Education Funding Council (FEFC); John Wiley & Sons Ltd; The University of Chicago Press.

Every effort has been made to contact copyright holders and we apologise if any have been overlooked.

1 ORGANISATION AND MANAGEMENT

Objectives

After reading this chapter, you should be able to:

- appreciate the place of FE and adult education within the wider economic and social context
- understand the parts played by teaching and support staff in managing learning
- recognise the central role of course and subject teams in managing the curriculum
- become familiar with the ways in which further and adult education are organised and funded
- recognise the issues for teachers in responding to flexibility and rapid change.

As a teacher working in post-compulsory education, you will need to be highly adaptable because the sector is both diverse and rapidly changing. Providers of further education and training range from small adult education centres, located in the local community, to large further education colleges with several campuses and many thousand students. The last decade has been a period of turbulent change. At the start of the 1990s, colleges were still creatures of local authorities, firmly rooted in the public sector. The 1992 Further and Higher Education Act led to the incorporation of colleges and, some would argue, to a much more developed system of central control. The new millennium has been marked by yet further change as the organisation and funding of FE, work-based training and adult education has been brought together under a national Learning and Skills Council (LSC) and local learning and skills councils (LLSCs). The purpose of this chapter is to introduce you to this diversity and change and give you an idea of what it is like to work in this complex sector.

THE ORGANISATION AND FUNDING OF POST-16 EDUCATION

According to the sixth report of the Select Committee on Education and Employment (1998), in 1996–7 just under 4 million students were enrolled at colleges in the further education (FE) sector. They were taught by over 140,000 lecturers on courses offered by some 800 publicly funded institutions, with a total budget of over £3.3 billion. In terms of student numbers, the further education sector is much larger than the higher education sector. Another little known fact is that there are more 16–19-year-olds, some half a million of them, studying in FE rather than in secondary schools.

For many years the further and adult education sector has had a Cinderella image. More public and political attention has been given to schools and universities.

To some extent this emphasis has now been reversed. Both FE and adult education play a central role in lifelong learning because they offer opportunities to adults to update their skills and knowledge. Recent governments have recognised that the role of vocational education and training is pivotal to economic success. The quality of human capital, i.e. the skills and knowledge of the working population, is now regarded as the most critical asset in modern information-based economies.

In this first section of the chapter, the basic organisation and management of the main providers of post-compulsory education are described. Attention is given to colleges in the further education sector, local authority adult education and the work-based training system.

The colleges

The 1992 Further and Higher Education Act was a watershed in the development of the FE sector. It led to the incorporation of 465 colleges that were removed from local authority control. New funding councils were created in England and Wales. Colleges became responsible for managing their own budgets, estates and personnel. The 2000 Learning and Skills Act, passed by the 'New Labour' Government, consolidated the role of colleges as independent organisations, but placed a much greater emphasis upon collaboration between colleges, schools and other providers and local planning. These developments have posed a huge challenge for staff in colleges, who have had to respond to the demands of managing and working in organisations which are relatively autonomous.

Since the 1990s, colleges have responded to a national agenda based upon rapid expansion in student numbers. At the same time, colleges have been required to reduce costs because of national pressure to reduce public expenditure. Management have had to introduce new contracts of employment for staff, buy and sell major assets and ensure that colleges continue with their central function of teaching students. They have also been subject to new systems of inspection and quality control (see Chapter 10). The mantra of the 'new FE' could be summarised as 'produce more with less whilst improving quality'. Before considering how the colleges have responded to this challenge, the context will be set by giving a brief description of the main types of college in the sector.

General further education and tertiary colleges

In January 2003, the sector included 265 general further education (FE) and tertiary colleges. These varied in scale from large multi-site colleges with several thousand student enrolments and annual budgets of over £25 million to tiny rural colleges with a few hundred students and annual budgets of under £1 million. General FE colleges typically provide a wide range of both general and vocational courses, usually in localities served by schools with sixth forms. They have their historical origins in the Victorian Mechanics' Institutes and have a long record of part-time and evening education provided in response to the needs of local industry. With the decline in manufacturing, subject areas such as engineering and construction have declined, whilst courses for the service sector, for example in business and tourism, have expanded.

Tertiary colleges were originally established by LEAs as part of post-16 rationalisation to cater for the educational requirements of 16–19-year-old students. Many reformers argued that it made sense both educationally and economically to concentrate all post-16 students in one community institution. Today, most tertiary colleges have a broad curriculum which includes both academic and vocational courses. Most also have a substantial number of adult students.

Sixth form colleges

Sixth form colleges were also established by some LEAs to concentrate sixth form provision in one specialist institution. Historically they have offered one- and two-year academic courses (GCSE and GCE) for full-time 16–19-year-old students. With incorporation and the broadening of the post-16 qualifications framework, most also now provide a range of vocational courses. Some have also widened access to include adult students. In January 2003, there were 100 sixth form colleges.

Specialist colleges (agriculture, art and design and designated)

Agricultural colleges and the art and design colleges are specialist institutions which concentrate upon a particular subject and occupational area. Most are considerably smaller than general FE colleges. In January 2003, there were 24 specialist colleges. There are also specialist designated colleges in the FE sector which specialise in providing courses for adult learners. Many of these have their roots in nineteenth-century philanthropic movements whose aim was to widen access to education and training for working men and women.

ACTIVITY

Select a particular geographical area, for example the county or city in which you live. Investigate how many colleges there are within it and classify them into the types listed above. Use your college library or the college web sites to find out as much as you can about each college's mission, its range of courses and its organisation. Compare your findings with those of your colleagues on your course, who will hopefully have investigated a different geographical area from you.

LEA adult and community education

For many adults, the local adult education centre is the most accessible provider of learning. Historically many local education authorities (LEAs) have provided both 'leisure and recreational' courses for adults and courses leading to qualifications such as GCE A-levels and GCSEs. As an adult learner yourself, you will probably already be aware of the vast range of adult educational courses in your area. These courses are often located in schools and other community venues to make them accessible to adult learners.

Somewhat confusingly, many of the LEA institutions are also referred to as adult or community colleges. Their role is however quite distinct from the colleges described in the above sections. As well as receiving funding and support from the LEA, adult education institutions also receive funding from the LSC.

Over the UK as a whole, there has been a huge variation in the amount of financial support given to adult education. In some areas, LEAs have worked closely with FE colleges and schools to ensure comprehensive provision of vocational, academic and recreational courses in the community. In other areas, LEAs have provided very limited support. Historically, there has been a bias towards funding courses that lead to qualifications. However, many adults are more interested in continuing learning rather than gaining qualifications. The idea of taking examinations and completing assessments can be a disincentive.

Private training providers and the work-based route

Private training providers

A great deal of work-related training is undertaken by private training providers. These vary in size just as much as colleges. Some are tiny businesses which specialise in training for a particular occupation, such as hairdressing. Others are substantial national organisations which employ over a hundred staff and train many hundreds of people, for example the Construction Industry Training Board. Some private training is also undertaken by large national companies on an in-house basis. Many retailers, such as Marks and Spencer, have very substantial training provision in their own right.

Work-based training

Prior to 2001, a national network of Training and Enterprise Councils (TECs) existed for promoting and funding work-based training. The role of the TECs was taken over by the LSC in April 2001, which now distributes government funding for programmes designed to meet the needs of local business and industry, such as the range of apprenticeship programmes. Work-based training is funded in colleges, LEAs, voluntary bodies, such as the YMCA, and in private training providers. Usually such training is linked to the achievement of a National Vocational Qualification (NVQ). The Employment Service also plays a major role in the funding of programmes for the unemployed, such as 'Entry to Employment'.

ACTIVITY

This is a follow-up to the first activity on page 3. Using your local public library as a source or alternatively the Government's 'Learning Direct' telephone enquiry system, investigate the range of adult education courses run by your LEA. Then contact your local Jobcentre and obtain some basic information on the main types of vocational training available through work-based routes. Compare and contrast these programmes with those provided by FE.

How colleges are funded

Colleges receive income from a wide range of sources. The main sources include:

- grants from LSC based upon the funding methodology
- tuition fees for courses from individuals and employers
- funding from LSC for specific work-related training
- funding from the Higher Education Funding Council for HE courses
- grants from the European Community and from government departments
- income from residential accommodation, catering and lettings
- other miscellaneous income.

By far the most important of these is LSC income, which accounts for well over 60 per cent of the income generated by most colleges. This income is based upon a funding methodology which LSC inherited and developed when it took over the role of funding colleges from the FEFC. One of the key elements of the methodology is the link between funding and student retention and achievement.

The LSC funding system

The main features of the national funding of FE are still largely based upon the principles outlined in a historic report entitled *Funding Learning* (FEFC, 1992). Under the LEA system that existed before national funding, colleges had received funding based upon the number of students they enrolled each year. The amount of funding was not related to the real costs of learning, how many students were retained by the college or how many achieved a qualification. Many aspects of the funding developed by FEFC were maintained by LSC when it took over funding in April 2001.

Broadly speaking, the funding system (LSC, 2004) is related to the costs of supporting learners on different qualifications. It has the following elements:

- a national base rate reflecting the length of the qualification and the costs of delivery, for example full-time qualifications lasting two years will receive more funding than part-time qualifications
- a programme weighting, which reflects that the costs of running the same qualification (say an NVQ) in different subject and occupational areas – for example, a student on a construction course – will attract more funding than a student on a classroom-based programme
- an achievement uplift – funding is enhanced by up to 10 per cent for achievement or partial achievement of the target qualification
- funding is also adjusted to take into account local disadvantage, i.e. the costs of widening participation to under-represented groups and/or to take into account the higher costs of operating in particular geographical areas such as London.

Managing the funding system and the budget has become a preoccupation of managers at all levels in colleges as so many aspects of education and training are reliant upon the level of resources. Each year the Government spends over £8 billion on the LSC sector, of which about half goes to FE.

ACTIVITY

One of the most contentious issues in post-compulsory education is the differences in the way full-time students in schools and colleges are funded. Colleges complain that the funding system is less generous and much tougher because it takes into account the retention and achievement of students. Schools, meanwhile, have a funding system which is still largely based upon pupil numbers rather than a calculation of the costs of learning and achievement. There are many suggestions for reform: from colleges, government ministers and LSC. Arrange for an interview with a head of department or suitable line manager in your college and find out how the different courses that you are teaching are funded and how the system compares to the funding of similar qualifications in schools.

THE INTERNAL MANAGEMENT OF COLLEGES AND OTHER PROVIDERS

As a professional teacher in further or adult education, it is crucial to understand the wider organisation in which you work. The ways in which colleges are internally structured reflects the diversity of post-16 education. There is a world of difference between the management structures of a large FE college, a small sixth form college and local authority adult education.

In the case study below the organisation and management of three fictitious post-16 providers, Greybourne College of Further Education, Greybourne Sixth Form College and Greybourne Adult and Community Education Service, all located in a fictitious metropolitan area, Greybourne Metropolitan Borough, are compared and contrasted. There is a brief description of each institution here and details of the courses that they provide can be found in Appendices 1–3. It is important that you read these carefully as we will use these institutions throughout the book to provide a context for some of the activities. Case studies and simulations are only useful if they exemplify and help us understand some of the actual features of real situations. Hopefully, you will be able to recognise some of the salient features of real colleges in these three simplified examples.

Case Study: *Post-compulsory education and training in Greybourne Metropolitan Borough*

Greybourne Metropolitan Borough is one of six LEAs in the conurbation of Greater Astan. It is a diverse area, with pockets of social deprivation in the west and south and some generally affluent neighbourhoods in the north and east of the borough. In 1986, following a period of intense consultation with schools, colleges and parents, Greybourne LEA re-organised its post-16 provision on a tertiary basis.

Greybourne College of Further Education

Greybourne College is a general further education college which offers a broad range of general and vocational courses. It has a large GCE A/AS-level programme and offers several

NVQ and GNVQ courses. It has two campuses, one in the west and the other in the east of the borough. In 2003–04 the college had over 7,000 enrolments, of which approximately 2,000 were full-time and 5,000 were part-time. The college describes its mission as 'to widen access to learning programmes and other services for local business and the local community'. Since incorporation, the college has grown by 20 per cent in student enrolments. Most of this growth has been achieved by extending provision to adult students on foundation and level 1 courses. The college works closely with the local Muslim community in Giffinfield ward in the east of the borough. It has received some national publicity for running English language courses for Asian women in two of the local mosques. The college is the second largest employer in Greybourne with a total of 210 full-time equivalent teaching and 150 support staff. It has an annual budget of over £12 million. In 2000, a new chief executive and principal was appointed. Within two years, she had been instrumental in redefining the mission and reorganising the internal structure of the college. All teaching and some support staff are now attached to six large schools, each headed by a director of studies. Within each school, each course is co-ordinated by a course leader. For college-wide functions, there are five assistant principals. They have responsibility for managing client services, finance, marketing, college services and quality. There are also a number of cross-college units, for example the learning support unit and the design and printing centre. The internal structure is summarised in Figure 1.1. Details of the courses offered by the college are contained in Appendix 1.

The college works closely with the local major employers and the LEA. Following the publication of the Kennedy Report (FEFC, 1997b), the corporation and senior management committed the college to widening access further to under-represented groups in the local community, such as single parents and adults with poor basic skills.

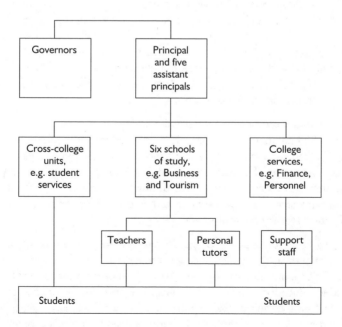

Figure 1.1 *The organisational structure of Greybourne College of FE*

Greybourne Sixth Form College

Greybourne Sixth Form College was created in 1988 on a green field site, in the north of the borough. It was originally designed to accommodate 850 students for GCE and GCSE course from the ten comprehensive schools in the area. By 2003, there were 1,500 full-time GCE, GCSE and GNVQ Intermediate and Advanced students on the roll. A new teaching block was opened to accommodate the expansion. The college has an excellent reputation, founded on its strong academic and pastoral tradition. It has been top in the local league tables for five years running. Its students' results compare favourably with schools and other colleges in Greater Astan.

The college was originally designed to provide a single sixth form for school leavers from the ten feeder schools in the borough of Greybourne. Over the last ten years, two of these schools have re-established their own sixth forms. The college now recruits students from all the adjoining boroughs in Greater Astan, many of whom are willing to endure long bus journeys each day to study at the college. Its excellent reputation for teaching 16–19 students has acted like a magnet! Following incorporation in 1993, the governors and senior management adopted a strategy of steady growth with a target of reaching 1,500 students by 2001. The college had exceeded its own growth targets each year and now faces a serious problem of how to deal with excess demand for places.

Relations between the college corporation and senior management team are good. The corporation has 16 members who between them have extensive experience of local business, university teaching, legal and accountancy practice. Their experience was crucial in enabling the college to adapt to the changes that accompanied incorporation in 1993 and the developments that have accompanied the establishment of the LLSC. The management structure is fairly traditional. There are 12 subject-based departments which manage the curriculum. Cross-college matters are co-ordinated by the principal and two deputy principals. One is responsible for strategic planning, finance and the estate. The other takes leadership of the curriculum and student guidance. Following incorporation, the college appointed a director of finance and a personnel officer. Overall, there are about 80 full-time equivalent teaching staff and 35 full-time equivalent support staff. Some of the latter, for example the technicians and librarians, work closely with teachers in supporting learning. The organisational chart shown in Figure 1.2 illustrates the internal structure. Details of the courses provided are contained in Appendix 2.

Greybourne Adult and Community Education Service

Each year, some 5,000 adults enrol on part-time adult education courses run, mainly during the evenings, at the ten secondary schools and three other community venues across the borough. The LEA prides itself in retaining an adult education service, despite the decreases in funding for leisure and recreational courses during the 1980s and 1990s. It welcomes New Labour's greater stress on co-operation rather than competition and the emphasis upon improving adult literacy and numeracy.

Over 50 GCSE, 15 GCE subjects, 20 Open College courses and a host of basis skills qualifications are offered in the adult education prospectus. There is also an extensive portfolio of recreational and leisure courses. Art and other creative crafts are immensely popular. Each adult education centre has a principal, who is funded by the authority and employed on a half-time contract. Each centre also has a part-time administrator to deal with enquiries and enrolments. There is a full-time officer from the borough responsible for co-ordinating provision. Virtually all the tutors who teach the programmes work on a

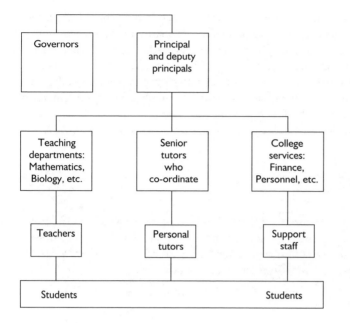

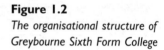

Figure 1.2
The organisational structure of Greybourne Sixth Form College

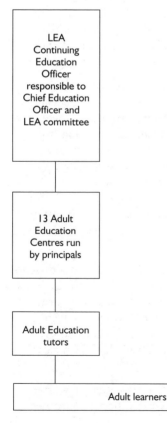

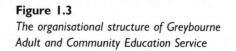

Figure 1.3
The organisational structure of Greybourne Adult and Community Education Service

part-time basis, most for only two hours per week. Some are full-time teachers from local schools and colleges. Others are local artists and other professionals who have a love for their subject and are dedicated to passing on their expertise. A major issue for the authority is ensuring a high quality of teaching, given the diversity of backgrounds from which these tutors are drawn and the wide spread of provision across a large geographical area. Figure 1.3 provides a simple illustration of the organisational structure of adult education. Details of the courses offered by the service can be found in Appendix 3.

ACTIVITY

Obtain an organisational structure for the college or organisation in which you teach or train. To what extent does it resemble any of the organisations in the case study above? How do you fit into the structure as a teacher or adult education tutor? Which staff in the organisational chart do you have the most contact with?

Course and subject teams

In this and the following section, we will analyse the roles of the different groups highlighted in the case study above: governors, senior managers, teaching and support staff. Our initial attention in this section will be to the tier of the organisation which will be most relevant to you as a new teacher in post-compulsory education – course and subject teams.

Course and subject teams have been described as the building blocks of further and higher education. Their role is central to the management of teaching and assessment. Tansley (1989) defines a course team as 'a group of staff working together to deliver a course, scheme or programme'. In higher education, course teams have a long history and are normally seen as the group of staff who work closely together to develop, teach and assess particular qualifications, for example a degree or post-graduate certificate. In further education, course teams have evolved in response to the development of multi-disciplinary vocational programmes, for example BTEC National Diplomas and GNVQ courses. Such programmes require groups of staff with different subject and occupational backgrounds to work closely together. In essence, therefore, course teams cut across traditional subject boundaries.

By implication subject teams are easier to define. They consist of a group of staff who share the same or a closely-related subject background and work together to teach and assess students. You will have noted that in our fictitious case study of Greybourne College of FE, teaching staff are organised into six large schools and within each of these it is course teams which play a central role. This organisation pattern contrasts sharply with the internal organisation of Greybourne Sixth Form College in which departments are based upon academic subject disciplines.

It would be a mistake to assume that either of these alternatives is better or worse. They have grown up as a result of different challenges and serve different purposes.

For a sixth-form college which is primarily concerned with teaching single subject GCSE and GCE qualifications, an organisational structure based upon dividing teaching staff into specialist subject departments makes good sense. This organisational pattern would not be appropriate however in a large FE college, where multi-disciplinary vocational courses are the main product.

Both course and subject teams have a range of critical functions. These include:

- course and subject development, for example preparing submission documents for validation and revalidation
- recruiting and inducting students on to the programme, for example providing advice before enrolment and at the start of the course
- organising the timetable, teaching and work experience arrangements
- providing guidance to students through tutorials and other forms of individual counselling
- liaison with support staff, for example technicians, to ensure learning is effective
- bidding for staffing and other resources to ensure the smooth operation of the course.

The way in which course and subject teams operate varies considerably from one college to another. It also depends very much on the size and type of programme. Obviously the course leader of a vocational course with 250 students is likely to have a more substantial role than the subject leader responsible for a small GCE A-level course which is externally examined. Chapter 3 provides a full discussion of some of the issues in managing assessment on vocational and other courses.

ACTIVITY

In the case study on page 8, each head of department in Greybourne Sixth Form College is in effect a subject leader. In Greybourne College of FE, each course leader has a different function but a broadly similar level of responsibility. Using your own college as an example, identify the roles and responsibilities of course and/or subject leaders. If possible, get hold of a standard job description and use this as your starting point. Once you have seen how the documentation describes the role, arrange to interview at least two course or subject leaders. Ask them how they perceive their functions and how the course team for which they are responsible operates – for example, how often does it meet and how does the course leader delegate responsibilities within the team. If your main role is as an adult education tutor, you might like to consider how the functions of course and subject co-ordination are undertaken within adult education.

Management functions, teaching and support staff

The case study illustrates that there are a range of management functions that have to be carried out throughout FE and adult education. At the crudest level, staff must be employed and paid, the estate has to be managed and, most important, student learning and support has to be organised effectively. In many respects, colleges are very similar to any other medium-sized business organisation. They offer their clients, i.e. students, a complex product, i.e. learning and qualifications, and have to marshal their human and physical resources to achieve the highest quality possible (we are aware of the dangers of pushing this analogy too far!). Most new teachers in FE and adult education find that they are drawn into managerial roles very early in their careers, usually as course or subject leaders. It is important to understand how management operates.

Key management tasks

For the sake of simplicity, management tasks can be broken down into three broad areas:

- management of the curriculum and student support
- management of financial and physical resources
- management of staff.

Management of the curriculum and student support

Given that colleges were created to teach students, this is the central activity of the majority of staff. We have already discussed the roles of course and subject teams in managing the curriculum. Two other aspects of this area need to be stressed to provide a fuller picture:

- the roles of support staff in the work of the college
- the formal structures of decision-making, such as course committees and the academic board.

Support staff

Support staff fall into two main categories:

- those directly involved in supporting learning, for example librarians and technicians
- those who have little direct contact with students and the learning process, for example those working in finance or in maintaining the college estate.

In the case study, you will have noticed that support staff at Greybourne College of FE and Greybourne Sixth Form College make up a significant proportion of the full-time employees of each college – in Greybourne College of FE, there are the equivalent of 210 full-time teaching and 150 full-time support staff. Each adult education centre in Greybourne also has an administrator to assist the principal with co-ordinating course provision.

As a new teacher or trainer, you will find that you will interact with support staff on a daily basis. For example, if you teach in any subject area involving the use of technology, you will encounter IT specialists and other technicians. Your success in teaching will be very dependent on working closely with them! You will also obviously have regular contact with the college's reprographic section and with administrators, for example secretarial staff. Another group of specialists you will encounter are staff who provide guidance and counselling to students. The role of this latter group is discussed in considerable detail in Chapter 8. Senior management, in most modern colleges, attempt to develop a whole-staff philosophy, that is they attempt to convey

ACTIVITY

Over a two-week period, for example during teaching practice or as part of your routine work as a new teacher, maintain a diary of all the contacts you have with individual staff – both teachers and support staff. Keep a simple log which describes the purpose and length of the contacts. At the end of the period, classify the individual staff into three groups – teachers, support staff directly involved in supporting learning, and other staff. Add up the amount of time you have spent with each group and analyse the frequency and types of contact. Now compare your diary and analysis with other members of your Cert. Ed. or PGCE group.

the critical message that all staff, from principal to caretaker, share in the common purpose of serving students and other customers of the college.

Formal structures for participation and decision-making

As a new teacher, you will gradually become familiar with the more formal machinery of governance and management. Under the 1992 Further and Higher Education Act and subsequent delegated legislation, every college in the FE sector is required to establish a governing body, often referred to as the *corporation*. Each college has instruments of government, i.e. a document which defines the constitution of the governing body. The corporation, which consists of a mix of internal, local community and business members, works closely with the principal and other senior managers. It is responsible for determining the educational character and mission of the college.

Day-to-day management of the college is the responsibility of the principal as chief executive, but the corporation plays a critical role in guiding the strategic development of the college. As such, it is ultimately responsible for many critical policy areas such as finance, personnel, quality and strategic planning. The relationship between the governing body and the principal is not unlike that between the board of directors of a company and the chief executive. Most governing bodies will contain both staff and student members.

In addition to the corporation, every college will normally have a formal committee system which allows staff and students to participate in decision-making. The articles of government of FE colleges, but not sixth form colleges, require the establishment of an *academic board*. The academic board normally plays a critical role in strategic planning, the maintenance of academic standards and procedures for the admission and assessment of students. The academic board will itself have a range of sub-committees, for example faculty or school boards which play a crucial role in monitoring students' achievements. At course level, it is common to establish a course committee with formal responsibilities for the assessment and examination of students.

Management structures tend to be less elaborate in LEA-managed adult education because the scale of the operation is smaller and most staff are part-timers. Within the LEA, however, the officer in charge of co-ordinating adult education will be responsible to the Chief Education Officer. She or he will also be answerable to the Education Committee, or one of its sub-committees, on which councillors will be represented. The LEA will have a stated policy on adult and community education, and will decide each year how much of its annual budget to devote to this type of provision.

ACTIVITY

Draw a simple organisational chart for the college or adult education service in which you work or have had your teaching practice. Include as much detail as you can on the line management and committee systems. Distinguish between members of the committees who have managerial roles, for example the principal, and members who are serving because of their business or community connections.

BUILDING FLEXIBILITY AND MANAGING CHANGE

There is nothing permanent except change.
Heraclitus

The last decade has been a period of turbulent change for further and adult education and no doubt Heraclitus' time-honoured dictum will apply to the decade ahead. Many contemporary commentators on the problems facing management in modern society have used similar phrases to encapsulate the challenge of change. For example, Peters, a prominent American 'management guru', encapsulates the task facing modern managers as 'thriving on chaos' (Peters, 1988).

Colleges and other providers have faced the simultaneous pressures of reducing unit costs, raising standards of student achievement and widening access to new groups of learners (FEFC, 1997b). Throughout the FE and training system, the word 'flexibility' has crept into the jargon – flexible colleges, flexible managers, flexible learning programmes, flexible access, and so on. The debate about reducing costs, raising student achievement and widening access seems to keep coming back to the concept of flexibility. Greater flexibility is seen as the method for achieving these aims.

So what exactly does flexibility mean for staff working in FE and adult education? It is possible to distinguish between three uses of the term in education and training:

- flexibility of the curriculum offer
- flexibility in the organisational structure
- flexibility in employment patterns.

A great deal of attention will be given to this interesting area, as it is an issue which you are likely to face during your career in FE and training. In analysing the meaning of flexibility we will draw on some theoretical approaches and consider how wider social changes are impacting on post-16 education.

Flexibility and the curriculum

Flexibility in the curriculum is associated with the replacement of courses by credit-rated learning programmes. Nasta (1994) contrasts the concept of a course with that of a learning programme as follows:

> *The notion of a course reflects the traditional world of further education. A course is an integrated curriculum designed by professional educationalists, usually at a national level, by awarding or professional bodies. The course is usually delivered, over a standard academic year. Most elements of the course are compulsory for students – the whole is seen as more than the sum of the parts. It is therefore unusual for the student to gain exemption from part or all of the course because of prior knowledge or experience. The pedagogical model of the curriculum is paramount – namely that there is a recognised and authoritative body of knowledge which has to be imparted by teachers to learners in a prescribed format, in a prescribed order and over a prescribed period of time.*

> *The notion of a learning programme challenges all these conventions. Entry and exit points for learners depend upon achievements both prior to and during the period of study. There are no in-built assumptions about the speed at which individuals can learn in order to gain credit towards a qualification. The delivery of learning programmes is not therefore constrained by the conventional academic year. Programmes are constructed using the building blocks of units or modules which represent discrete units of assessment. The whole qualification becomes the sum of the parts, in a form which is quite unlike the conventional course. In the learning programme, the cohesion and integration of knowledge and skills become a function of the learner's desire and ability to make connections between the different modules. The concept of the learning programme thus challenges the pedagogical model of the curriculum, which is based on the belief that educationalists need to design integrated courses to lead the learner progressively to a holistic perspective. In the learning programme, the student exercises choice, creates integration and negotiates learning outcomes. Learning becomes a partnership between the teacher as facilitator and the student as client.*

> Nasta (1994)

The key differences between a course and a learning programme are highlighted in Table 1.1 on page 16.

ACTIVITY

Turn to Appendices 1–3, which list the qualifications provided by the three Greybourne providers. Select one provider and one broad subject or occupational area, for example health or business studies. Classify what is offered into either a course or a learning programme. Give reasons for your choice.

Table 1.1   *The main differences between courses and learning programmes*

Learning stage	Course	Learning programme
Before entry	The student's choice is usually between one course or another. Each course is likely to contain a predetermined group of subjects, related to a particular occupation or profession. The student will be expected to join the course at the beginning of the academic year.	The student's choice is between different modules. These can be combined in different ways and lead to a range of qualifications in broad occupational areas. The student will be able to join the programme at a number of different points during the year.
At entry	Entry on to the course is likely to be based upon previous qualifications. The student will need guidance on the likely career implications of choosing one course, rather than another. There will also be a need for subject-based induction.	Entry on to the programme will be based upon the principle of open access. The student will need extensive guidance on module choice, based upon careful diagnosis of need and procedures for accrediting prior learning and experience. The learner will require induction into the structure of the programme and the rules governing choice of modules.
On course or on programme	The different elements of the curriculum are likely to be compulsory and delivered over a set period of time and in a set sequence. Learning styles are likely to be pedagogical. This reflects a curriculum in which there is perceived to be a body of authoritative knowledge, which has to be imparted to learners, by teachers in a traditional manner.	Student choice is likely to be maximised by the existence of modules, which the student can combine to achieve different qualification outcomes. Learning styles are likely to be based upon experiential models, reflecting andragogical principles in which the curriculum content is structured to reflect learner experience and some negotiation is possible.
At exit	At exit the successful student will attain the qualification on which she or he enrolled and progress to a particular occupation or further study.	The student will have some choice over the qualification outcome at exit. This will depend upon the module combinations completed successfully.

Some of you will probably have already encountered flexible learning programmes based upon modular and credit-rated structures. Over the last 20 years, a vigorous debate has taken place about the pros and cons of introducing credit-based qualifications in both HE and FE. This aspect of the curriculum is explored in Chapter 4.

Organisational flexibility: managing the flexible curriculum

As a professional teacher in post-16 education, you will already have encountered attempts by the college to make provision more accessible and flexible. The contrast in the institutional management structures needed for delivering learning programmes successfully, as opposed to courses, is a point that is made forcefully in the 1992 Further Education Unit (FEU now FEDA) publication, *Flexible Colleges*. A course-based college is contrasted with a learner-centred college in the following way:

> *A course-based college is organised around the needs of students, enrolling on courses that generally begin in September and end in the Summer term, with learning arranged in a fixed sequence, and assessment occurring at fixed points for the whole group. The learner-centred college by contrast provides an initial guidance, counselling and assessment to establish individual starting points, requirements and goals, and flexible access (i.e., time, place, style/mode) to learning and assessment.*
>
> FEU (1992)

Training providers and colleges committed to managing flexible learning are characterised by the following features:

- a mission and set of policies which lead to the widening of access
- the provision of resources for guidance and counselling at all the critical stages (entry, on programme and exit) of the learner's career
- enhanced market research through outreach and other activities which enable the institution to identify and respond to the needs of learners in the local community
- unit-based or modular programmes designed to accommodate the different needs of individual learners
- procedures in place for the accreditation of prior learning and experience (see Chapter 3)
- resource-based open learning centres which allow the learner to learn at a pace which suits them and develop learner independence
- information processing systems capable of tracking individual learners as they successfully gain credit for modules completed.

These themes provide much of the subject matter for the chapters in Part 2 of this book.

Three groups of staff in the institution play a key part in developing the capacity of the college to deliver flexible learning:

- the senior management team
- the programme management team
- the resource managers.

Role of the senior management team

The senior management team, usually represented by the principal and the second tier managers (refer back to case studies of Greybourne College of FE and Greybourne Sixth Form College) in the college, needs to implement curriculum policies on student access and credit, which are designed to support flexible learning across the whole institution. These are usually adopted formally by the institution through the appropriate committees of the corporation and academic board. More importantly, these policies need to be firmly embedded in the institution's culture through appropriate staff development, including support for new teachers undergoing initial teacher training. Often there is an allocation of significant human and physical resources to develop comprehensive student support and guidance services and adequate resource-based learning facilities.

Role of resource managers

The team of resource managers, often containing those with responsibility for the library and learning resources, information technology, finance and the estate, typically develop an integrated strategy for the development of all resources. The rapid impact of information technology has eroded traditional distinctions between printed and electronic sources of information. It is common for training providers and colleges to have learning workshops, in which books and periodicals are integrated with audio-visual material and on-line computer sources, through the intranet and internet. The success of such resource-based learning will depend upon how closely the resource managers work with curriculum managers in the institution to support students on individualised learning programmes. On competence-based assignment programmes, students work outside the classroom for much of their time and their achievements will depend upon how effectively the institution co-ordinates learning both inside and outside the classroom (see Chapters 3 and 4).

Role of programme managers

The programme management team is the group of staff most directly concerned with students. As a team, they are responsible for managing learning and assessment on the learning programme. On GNVQ and NVQ programmes, which are modular in character, each programme team might be responsible for managing a particular occupational route consisting of a group of related vocational units. Some units, such as the key skills units, will be common to different qualifications, whilst others will be unique to the particular qualification. Given that the delivery style is meant to allow individual students to progress at their own pace, the need for individual student guidance and support is critical to student success. This guidance is often given by staff through tutorials linked to the student's records of achievement or progress files. Such records can play a fundamental role in flexible learning programmes because they create the medium through which the student can actively plan their individual learning programme in conjunction with the personal tutor.

Flexibility and the employment of staff

About 300,000 teachers and associated staff were employed in the Learning and Skills sector (FE, adult education and work-based provision) in 2003. About a half of these were in FE (Parsons and Berry-Lound, 2004). The majority of these employees were

ACTIVITY

NVQ programmes can be managed as flexible learning programmes, in the manner described above, or run as conventional courses. If they are treated as courses, it is likely that students will all be enrolled in September and be taught as a single cohort. They are also likely to be managed by course teams based in individual college schools or departments. Where NVQs are treated as learning programmes, there is likely to be a whole-college approach to their management and some parts of the students' timetable. For example, basic or key skills will be common to different NVQ routes.

Using a college with which you are already familiar, study the organisation of NVQs across the institution. To what extent are NVQs managed as courses and to what extent are they managed as learning programmes? You may find the management structure combines elements of both!

part-time. Before incorporation in 1993, like school teachers, these staff would have been employees of the local authority. Their terms of conditions of employment were then governed by national conditions of service. For example, in FE colleges lecturers' annual teaching hours and non-contact duties were governed by a national agreement referred to as the Silver Book.

Today, employees working in colleges have contracts of employment with the college corporation. Each governing body is responsible for determining the pay and conditions of service of all staff in the college. In other words, each college has considerable discretion over the pay and other conditions under which its employees work. Many colleges have chosen to be members of one of the national employers' groups, such as the Association of Colleges in England or the Association of Scottish Colleges, which negotiate with the teaching unions and then make recommendations to governing bodies on the pay and conditions which should apply.

In the area of employment, we have witnessed a fundamental change in how staff are managed and remunerated. The era of national public sector pay bargaining has given way to a more flexible labour market. In a typical FE college, at least three groups of teaching staff are employed:

• those on full-time contracts
• those on fractional contracts
• those on hourly-paid contracts.

With the national pressure to reduce costs of provision, many colleges have increased the teaching hours of full-time staff and also increased the teaching undertaken by hourly-paid teachers. What management define as flexibility is often seen by trade unions as a worsening in pay and conditions of service. Indeed, many trade unionists would argue that the post-compulsory labour force is undergoing a process of casualisation as college managers turn to cost-cutting measures more common in the commercial sector. As you would expect, there is much controversy over these changes in work patterns and pay.

Further education has not been alone in experiencing fundamental change in organisational and employment patterns. The 1980s and 1990s were a period of fundamental change throughout the public sector. Many authorities have commented upon the crucial nature of this change. Hoggett (1987) argues that standardised public sector bureaucracy has been supplanted and replaced by:

> *new organisational and managerial forms strikingly reminiscent of the newer 'hi-tech' companies of the M4 corridor, leaner and flatter managerial structures, decentralised 'cost and innovation' centres, enlarged and more generic roles, team-working, flexibility and informality, responsive back line support to the front line staff.*
>
> Hoggett (1987)

In his classic study, *The Age of Unreason*, Charles Handy (1993) argues that the changes described above are part of a deeper revolution in the nature of organisations in post-industrial society. He suggests that many modern organisations are becoming more like 'shamrocks' than the hierarchical bureaucracy that Max Weber described. The shamrock consists of three groups of workers:

- the core, which is composed of well-qualified managers and professionals
- the contractual fringe, which is made up of individuals and organisations who deliver services on a sub-contracted basis
- the flexible labour force, mainly part-time staff which the organisation can employ to meet gaps between supply and demand.

Handy's analogy of the shamrock provides a good conceptual model for analysing changes in the nature of colleges and other post-16 providers. There is no doubt that much greater emphasis is being placed on the core of the organisation. That is on the role of full-time staff and senior managers in undertaking strategic planning and defining the vision of the organisation. The use of contracting-out expanded rapidly during the 1990s. For example, over 10 per cent of college enrolments are delivered by organisations which have a franchise relationship with the college, such as specialist private trainers, which the college contracts to deliver specialist training in the community (FEFC, 1997e).

ACTIVITY

Almost all colleges and many adult education services have a staff handbook, which contains details of the organisational structure and conditions of employment. This is usually a useful document as it gives employees details of their terms and conditions of service and other important information.

Obtain a copy of the staff handbook for the college or other organisation with which you are familiar. Study it carefully and consider what it tells you about the practices of the corporation as an employer and the extent of flexibility of the organisation. Can you spot any features which remind you of Handy's shamrock?

Review Questions

1 Classify colleges and other major post-16 providers into different types according to how they are organised and managed.
2 How does the funding system for FE colleges reward learning and achievement?
3 What is the difference between course and subject leaders? What part do they play in managing the curriculum?
4 Identify three roles played by support staff in managing learning.
5 What is meant by the term 'flexibility' in post-16 education and training? What challenges arise from managing learning programmes rather than courses?

SUMMARY

- Professional teachers in FE and adult education face the challenges of working in a context which is diverse and rapidly changing.
- The organisation and funding of post-16 education is more complex than schools and takes into account the costs of learning and the ability of colleges to retain students.
- The internal structure of post-compulsory providers reflects their different aims, objectives and communities.
- Teachers in FE work with a range of other professionals and support staff.
- Responding to the need for greater flexibility and access presents a challenge to all staff in FE and adult education.

Suggested Further Reading

Ainley, P. and Bailey, B. (1997) *The Business of Learning: Staff and Student Experiences of Further Education*, London: Cassell

Lucas, N. (2004) *Teaching in Further Education – New Perspectives for a Changing Context*, London: University of London, Institute of Education

2 INTEGRATING THEORY AND PRACTICE

Objectives

After reading this chapter you should be able to:

- identify issues in the relation between educational theory and practice
- understand what is meant by concepts such as 'reflective practice', 'practical knowledge' or 'communities of practice'
- distinguish between behavioural, cognitive, humanistic and experiential learning theory, and give examples of their relevance to classroom teaching
- provide examples of ways in which sociological research and theory have influenced education policies such as equal opportunities or access
- identify examples of value issues in education which are based upon philosophical positions.

This chapter is intended to introduce the role of theory in relation to educational practice. Whereas in the past it tended to be assumed that theory was something entirely distinct and separate from practice, nowadays the relation between them is seen rather differently. Theory used to be something that was 'applied' to practice, and it was thought of as a very abstract body of knowledge, which teachers needed to know about for its own sake. Today, theory and practice are seen not as entirely distinct, but as much more integrated. So we are able to think of theory as 'embedded' in practice, or of theory which 'informs' practice. Ideas such as 'practical knowledge', 'reflective practice' or 'communities of practice' are examples of this new relationship.

The chapter explores these themes by taking examples mainly from theories of learning, but also from sociological and philosophical perspectives, and provides examples of the various ways in which some kind of theory always informs educational practice. As a result of reading the chapter, you should be able to see specific links between these theories and the kinds of teaching aims, methods and assessments systems described in subsequent chapters of this book, together with the national qualifications system as a whole.

THE THEORY/PRACTICE ISSUE

The relation between theory and practice in education has often been fraught with problems. Generations of teachers in training have been unhappy with what they felt was the necessity to learn a lot of abstract theory unrelated to the kinds of skills they needed to develop for good classroom practice. Their concern, naturally, was that the *relevance* of theory needed to be much more obvious. Theory should be something teachers can 'use' in classroom situations.

The reasons why this came about may well be to do with the widespread assumption that somehow abstract knowledge is superior to mere practical skill, a form of academic snobbery which can still be traced in the 'pecking order' of subjects and disciplines. The relative status of academic and practical, or skills-based, courses remains an issue not only in the classroom but in education policy, as governments strive to raise the status of vocational education so that it is seen as equal to that of academic study. For example, this was a major theme of the Tomlinson Report (DfES, 2004).

ACTIVITY

As both a learner and a teacher, have you ever experienced some kind of 'pecking order' of disciplines, subjects or courses? Did some of them have a higher status than others? In particular, has it been your experience that academic study has a higher status than practical or skills-based courses? If so, what practical effects did this have on you? If your answers to the first two questions are yes, outline your own theory to explain how such a situation may have come about.

In attempting this activity, you may have been defining theory as a kind of *explanation* of what happens in the real world. But it was only *your* theory. So what if someone suggests a different one? How would you decide which is true? We need to look at how to *define* what is meant by theory anyway.

Theory, knowledge and research

We all have our theories about why something happens, but if someone disagrees with us they may simply say: 'prove it!' This is not the place to enter into a philosophical discussion of what 'proof' means, but obviously we are looking at a theory as something that can be backed up by *evidence* or research. In other words, theories belong to the world of public knowledge, rather than to the world of private opinion or subjective belief.

Theories in education belong to the realm of the human or social, and not the natural sciences, and reflect research findings about how people learn, for example, or what part education plays in society.

ACTIVITY

Good teaching practice involves teachers in using a range of teaching methods or learning activities. If you agree with this statement, and try to put the principle into practice yourself, how do you know it is true? Is it because it is true from your own experience, or because someone told you or you read it in a book? Or is it true because research has proved it?

What is called 'research-based' practice is increasingly being expected of professionals, including teachers. To be able to demonstrate 'generic' or 'underpinning' knowledge is increasingly part of what is meant by good professional practice nowadays.

This is what is meant by 'practical knowledge'. It means that research-based theory is *integrated* into our practice as teachers, and not separate from it. We know quite a lot from research about such things as:

- learners' motivation
- classroom interaction and group dynamics
- learning styles and teaching styles
- assessment and its effects
- effective management styles
- curriculum development
- classroom management
- managing change.

Perhaps you can add to this list yourself from your own knowledge and experience? The point is that there is a wealth of research-based knowledge, in the form of theory, about the practice of education in every department. And although we may always have our own theories based on our own practical experience, nevertheless it would be foolish to neglect what research evidence has demonstrated and which might help us to be better teachers. This does mean going to the sources in social science research, and this is how education theory is nowadays often conceived:

> *The body of practical knowledge . . . is a unique mixture of applied knowledge from the various social science foundation disciplines, but it is not a pure discipline in itself.*

> Jarvis (1995: 263)

Reflective practice

In the last section we considered one way in which theory and practice may be integrated, and this is through what might be called 'practical knowledge'. This could be defined as:

> *Integrating theory not 'for its own sake' but rather as a body of research-based knowledge which underpins good professional practice.*

What this means is that we are provided with a *rationale* for our teaching or organisational or classroom interaction practices, which would be relevant in any situation we find ourselves in.

However, having a rationale might seem to suggest that our practical experience counts for nothing. And, since so much of what we learn *is* from experience, we have another way of integrating theory and practice, which is that of systematic and critical *reflection* on our practice.

This is the perspective most associated with Schon (1983), who argued that professional workers in all fields 'think in action'. In other words, Schon suggested that at the heart of all professional practice there is a process of reflection, rather than a mechanical application of 'theory'. Professionals are people who learn many of their skills through the practice of them in new situations. This kind of learning is, therefore, neither wholly theoretical nor wholly practical – they deepen their own knowledge through the exercise of the skills themselves. As we shall see, this is what is implied by the idea of professionalism as a community of practice.

ACTIVITY

Take any particular classroom skill, which may be to do with motivating learners, communicating information, managing learning resources, and so on.

a) Identify the underpinning knowledge behind the practice.
b) Identify the sources of your knowledge.
c) Amongst the sources of your knowledge, try to identify your own reflection upon your professional practice.
d) Describe the kinds of methods you would employ to measure the extent to which your students have engaged in reflective rather than 'rote' learning.

The idea of reflective practice is rather similar to that of experiential learning, which we will consider later. One of the best known writers on the role of reflection in learning is David Boud (Boud *et al.*, 1985) and he has also written about the importance of reflection in the process of self-assessment of learning (Boud, 1995). The theory is that reflection, after the event, on what has or has not been learned is a major element in the learning process itself (Jarvis *et al.*, 2003: ch. 6). It follows that the facilitation of learning by the teacher requires the provision of specific practices in order to structure reflective learning on the part of the student, and you may have listed these under activity (d) above. For now, however, we can think of it as another way in which theory and practice are integrated in every professional activity. The professional is someone who is continuously developing his or her underpinning knowledge through reflection on their own (and others') practice.

Reflective practice has been adopted in the education and training courses of many professions, including that of teaching. You may have encountered it in the form of the reflective journal, which often forms a part of the assessment of professional development programmes.

Reflective learning, however, is also a feature of professional life, and professional practice itself is situated in a 'learned' environment. Traditionally, a profession has been thought of as a number of practitioners who apply a common body of theory to whatever their practice is concerned with. However, it is possible to think about this in other ways, so that a profession is a 'community of practice', in which there is no strict separation of theory from practice, but rather a shared experiential reflection upon what it means to be, for example, a member of a profession such as teaching. Thus, professions (like other social groups) consist of people who are members of a joint enterprise, sharing a body of competencies and a repertoire of language, resources and methods. Professionalism is therefore constituted by shared meanings and values in practice, as much as by a common research or knowledge base (Lave and Wenger, 1991; Wenger *et al.*, 2002). This might be brought out, for example, in the case of the kind of professionalism required for facilitating the learning of students with special educational needs.

ACTIVITY

Consider your role in relation to students with special educational needs, and try to identify as many features of it as possible which suggest that professional teachers are members of a community of practice.

We have now considered two ways of thinking about the integration of theory and practice – practical knowledge and reflective practice – and we have seen how it is possible to think of professionalism itself as a community of practice.

Practical knowledge, as Jarvis suggested, is 'applied knowledge from the various social science foundation disciplines' (Jarvis, 1995: 263). Traditionally, in the education of teachers, these foundation disciplines have been taken to be psychology, sociology and philosophy. So we must now turn to these disciplines as bodies of research and theory, and consider some examples of their contribution to practical knowledge for teachers. The most significant of these disciplines has always been psychology, and its body of research into human learning. As we shall see, however, within the discipline of psychology itself there are a range of different theories, and four of the most important of these will now be described with, in each case, an example of how they might form the basis of practical knowledge for teaching.

THEORIES OF LEARNING

None of the social science foundation disciplines present a single, unified, body of research and theory: all of them present a range of different and often conflicting perspectives. This has also proved a source of confusion for student teachers, who have sought for something more consistent and unified. Nevertheless, all of these perspectives on learning have something to contribute to our understanding of human learning. In the real world of teaching and education, no single theory could account for all our experience, nor could it serve as a basis for all of our practical knowledge.

Behaviourism and learning measurement

In some ways, recent trends in education reflect this theory of learning, with their increasing emphasis on demonstrable outcomes of learning, such as skills, competence and learning objectives. This is learning that must be objectively measurable and, by definition, expressed through changes in behaviour. Behaviourism remains controversial, since the theory originated in research into animal behaviour, rather than that of human beings. It is argued that animal and human learning are qualitatively different.

On the other hand, it is suggested that teaching as an activity cannot be justified unless it can be demonstrated in some way to have had a measurable effect in the form of learning. Behaviourism also lends clear direction for the activities of teachers, such as planning lessons, and learning and assessment methods, in the light of the intended outcomes.

ACTIVITY

For any lesson you have recently given, assess the extent to which your evaluation reflected behavioural outcomes on the part of the students in the class. Do you assume that such outcomes necessarily mean learning has taken place?

At the heart of the issue of behaviourism is the question whether learning can take place without behavioural changes being observable. Classical behaviourism would seem to deny that the learning of knowledge, values, attitudes, and so on, could ever be demonstrated unless it came out in the form of changes in behaviour.

Pavlov (1849–1936)

Although the name of Ivan Pavlov is famous for his experiments with dogs, he was not actually the founder of the behaviourist school of psychology. From these experiments came the learning theory of classical conditioning: the dogs 'learned' to salivate on the expectation of food when this was linked to the sound of a buzzer. Salivation on hearing the sound of the buzzer Pavlov described as the 'conditioned' response.

What are the implications for teaching of this theory of learning by association? Although for some there is a worrying element of mind-control to all this, Pavlov was drawing attention to the way in which learning, for humans as well as dogs, involves stimulus, association and habit. There are clear implications for teaching here, whatever philosophical reservations may be held. The classroom setting is a place where teachers have some control over the environment, and it can be a place where stimulus, association and habit have a part to play in learning. For example:

- a supportive environment acts a *stimulus* for study
- the *association* of a subject with a particularly facilitative teacher
- *habitual* expectations about classroom discipline or assessment.

Pavlov drew attention to the way in which learning is affected by external conditions, and the ways in which these can be manipulated to make it more effective. This does, however, mean that this kind of learning takes the form of behavioural effects and it fails to consider learning as a self-conscious or reflective process.

Watson (1878–1958)

J.B. Watson, like Pavlov, began his research career by studying animal behaviour. But he did begin to use the term 'behaviourism' to describe a general theory of human learning that was based upon observation and measurement: he believed that, from a strictly scientific view, we can make no assumptions about consciousness, memory and so on, except as far as these are expressed in *behaviour*. Only behaviour can be observed and measured. Learning itself was a result of conditioning into habitually acquired behaviour, through the reinforcement of the stimulus–response by frequency and repetition.

In practical terms, this means that we learn as a result of habitual association of stimulus and response, and the more frequent and repeated the association the better we learn.

As in the case of Pavlov, many have associated this kind of learning theory with behaviour modification and control. From the teacher's point of view, a student is a blank sheet on which to write, and it serves as a reminder that the teacher's role is one of controlling the environment of learning.

ACTIVITY

Taking a recent lesson you have given, try to identify ways in which you *intentionally* controlled the learning environment. This may have been through the layout of the classroom, the presentation of materials, the kinds of activities organised, or whatever. To what extent could your teaching be analysed as reinforcement and conditioning, and could you evaluate the lesson in terms of observable and measurable changes in student behaviour?

Thorndike (1874–1949)

E.L. Thorndike also began his study of learning with the observation of animal behaviour, and worked within a stimulus–response theory, adding another element to the ones we have already identified in Pavlov and Watson. This was the so-called 'law of effect', whereby the experience of pleasure or satisfaction associated with a particular situation will lead to its repetition, whereas the experience of dissatisfaction or discomfort will lead to avoidance. Put at its simplest, people are more likely to respond to stimulus when response is associated with pleasure, and less likely when it is associated with pain.

From the teacher's point of view, this version of behaviourism suggests that rewarding learning will stimulate further learning, whereas not rewarding it, or actually penalising it, will not. In other words, this amounts to a theory of *motivation*, and it has become an integral assumption of many teaching and assessment methods. The idea of *formative* assessment, for example, involves a view of assessment as reinforcing what has been learned, and motivating new directions for learning. Formative assessment is not judgemental but intended to be supportive and motivating, so it reflects Thorndike's 'law of effect' in that effort is rewarded with encouragement.

> ## ACTIVITY
> Review your understanding of the work of Pavlov, Watson and Thorndike in relation to your own teaching. Can you begin to describe it as 'practical knowledge'?

We have reviewed the work of some of the best-known behavioural psychologists, and suggested the implications for teaching. There are, of course, others, notably B.F. Skinner (1904–90), whose theory is often described as 'operant conditioning' in which the response is followed by another stimulus, thus reinforcing even further the kind of sequence suggested by Thorndike. Again, its relevance to teaching consists of the potential of reward and punishment in their effect on motivation and performance.

Behaviourism is the kind of learning theory that underpins much of the teaching that is concerned with *learning objectives* and *learning outcomes*, which are generally associated with the teaching of *skills* and *competencies*.

Learning objectives describe the changes in the learner's behaviour that the teacher intends to bring about – 'After reading this chapter you should be able to distinguish between behavioural, cognitive, humanistic and experiential learning theory, and give examples of their relevance to classroom teaching' or 'After reading this chapter you should be able to distinguish between practical knowledge and reflective practice.'

However, this remains a fairly broad definition of learning objectives. For one thing, different readers of the chapter may come to different conclusions and definitions – in other words, they may have *conceptualised* the issues differently. A stricter definition of behavioural objectives can be found in teaching directed towards assessment of *competencies* and *performance*. An example of this kind of practical theory is therefore provided by the National Vocational Qualifications (NVQs) that are described in Chapter 3.

Behavioural objectives and outcomes may be suited to certain kinds of learning, and perhaps relevant to most. But they are particularly associated with the learning of skills and with *vocational* training and education. Since not all learning in colleges is of this kind, we need now to look at the kind of learning theory that underpins, for example, the *academic* courses that they offer.

Cognitivism and knowledge

The distinction between skills learning and knowledge learning is by no means straightforward, but there is an important distinction to make between those learning theories that focus on behaviour and those that focus on cognition. By 'cognition' is generally meant knowledge and understanding. From a cognitivist perspective, behaviourists reduce learning to forms of behaviour, and ignore or deny the ways in which human beings learn to 'know' or 'understand' something. In other words, the cognitive position is that it is possible to have learned something without there being any measurable or observable changes in behaviour.

So if, as a teacher, your objective is the growth of knowledge or understanding in your students, then the cognitive theory of learning will be the basis of practical knowledge. We will look at the work of Piaget, Vygotsky and Bruner and the implications of their theories of learning for teachers.

Piaget (1896–1980)

Jean Piaget is mostly associated with the theory of childhood learning, but his work is important for the study of learning in general, because it is *developmental*. He identified the stages of cognitive development in chronological order as shown in Table 2.1.

Table 2.1   *Piaget's stages of cognitive development*

Age	Stage	
0–2	Sensorimotor	Differentiating between the self and the external world
2–4	Pre-operational thought	Beginning to classify objects
4–7	Intuition	Beginning of classification
7–11	Concrete operations	Beginning of logical thinking
11–15	Formal operations	Beginning of abstract conceptualisation

This 'stage theory', although it was derived from studies of children, and has been criticised and elaborated, remains an important basis of the cognitive theory of learning. This is because it focuses on the way people *think* and *reason*, and not simply on the way they behave. So, any kind of teaching that is concerned with the communication of information, or with getting students to think and reason for themselves, is likely to be informed by assumptions of a cognitivist kind.

ACTIVITY

In the case of your own teaching, perhaps of a range of subjects, try to distinguish between the behavioural and the cognitive outcomes that you are aiming at. For example, you may think of students researching a historical topic on the internet: this might suggest behavioural skills in the use of the technology, but cognitive skills in historical understanding.

In attempting this activity you may well have encountered some difficulty in trying to distinguish between demonstrating skill and demonstrating understanding. And although in practice this may raise problems, the system of assessment (described in Chapter 3) formally incorporates the distinction. Thus, for example, whereas NVQs are 'rooted in assessment against performance criteria linked to occupational standards', the assessment of the General National Vocational Qualification (GNVQ) includes elements of conceptual understanding. GNVQ assessment also includes a strong element of formative assessment, which we saw has its origins in the stimulus–reinforcement theories of behaviourism. The replacement of the GNVQ award by other applied vocational courses, such as BTECs or the Vocational Certificate of Education (VCE), will continue to reflect these kinds of assessment theories of theoretical and practical learning. Similarly, in the case of GCSE and GCE courses, what is tested is 'a sample of the knowledge, skills and understanding outlined in the syllabus'.

In practice, therefore, the distinctions between knowledge, skill and understanding, which are the basis for the distinction between behaviourist and cognitive theories of learning, do not have much meaning. The fact is, that forms of assessment reflect a wide range of assumptions about the nature of learning. The competence-based NVQ award comes closest to matching one particular theory, the behaviourist, but it is not really possible to generalise beyond that.

Nevertheless, teachers need to know something of the research-based theory of learning, and its varieties, as the basis of their own practical knowledge of teaching. When you read Chapter 3 on assessment and qualifications, you should be able to identify the underpinning learning theory on which both qualifications and assessment systems rest.

Vygotsky (1896–1934)

The Russian psychologist Lev Vygotsky, like Piaget, researched the ways in which children learned. But instead of thinking in terms of the stages of development, Vygotsky focused on the *development process* itself. This he saw as a complex process, much more so than Piaget's stage theory seems to suggest. The development of the individual is conceived in terms of a potential for growth, which may be uneven in the sense that the same individual may be highly developed in one area and relatively less so in another. Each developmental stage can only be understood in relation to what has gone before. Equally significant, Vygotsky took the view that, in the developmental process, the whole social, cultural and historical *environment* needed to be taken into account. Thus, it makes no sense to talk of any individual's stage of cognitive development in isolation from that of others in comparable situations.

The cognitive theory of learning focuses on the mind and the mental processes that have to do with knowledge and understanding. What Vygotsky argued from his research was that mental processes had to be understood as in some sense *social*. They have to be placed in the context of social relationships, since this is where most of our learning actually occurs.

So this is a much more social and less individual account of learning, and is of particular relevance for teaching and the classroom. In particular, this theory is one of individual *potential* for development and intellectual growth.

> ## ACTIVITY
>
> Give some examples of the ways in which teachers might use insights derived from Vygotsky's theory, focusing on:
>
> - the need to know about the student's developmental stages
> - any assumptions you might make with regard to the student's uneven progress through developmental stages
> - any assumptions you might make about the potential of students to progress to a higher developmental stage.

In attempting this activity, it was implied that as teachers we make *assumptions*. For example, we may assume that if a student is highly developed in one cognitive function, she or he will be highly developed in others. A student's potential is something we may assume rather than really know about. In such ways as these, the importance of some familiarity with the practical knowledge of learning theory is an important aspect of professionalism in teaching.

Bruner (1915–)

Jerome Bruner is rather different from the other psychologists of the cognitive school we have so far considered, because he is very much concerned with the educational implications of the theory. His research has been into educational institutions themselves, and he is particularly interested in the role of the teacher and with the principles of instruction.

For Bruner, learning is about acquiring new information. But he also sees knowledge more in terms of an *interactive process* rather than as a static body of information. In other words, learning is a kind of transaction between the learner and what is learned. It also has a transforming effect: the learning process occurs when we attach *meaning* to what we learn in relation to what we already know or believe. In a way, this denies that knowledge is objective, or 'out there': the meanings we give to what we learn are, for Bruner, cultural meanings, so that learning is an active process of fitting new learning to our already existing frames of meaning. This kind of 'cultural' cognitivism obviously has implications for the theory of intelligence, and Bruner has influenced educational psychologists such as, for example, Howard Gardner in his theory of multiple intelligences (Gardner, 1993). So according to this kind of perspective, learning is a kind of making sense. Thus, Bruner tends to reject the stage theories of learning that seem to restrict what we can learn to the stage we are at: in fact, he thought children could be taught anything so long as it was presented in a meaningful way. Bruner's name has been associated with the progressive schooling movement, because his theory of instruction involves presenting the learner with the widest possible opportunity to explore alternative meanings. In other words, learning is essentially a process of *discovery*. The idea of learning as making sense or as discovery has implications for the assessment and measurement of learning, because it challenges the conventional belief that intelligence is the kind of fixed, stable or unitary concept that behaviourism often seems to reflect.

Bruner's theory of instruction therefore defines the role of the teacher as one of getting students to learn for themselves, organising the content of the learning to maximise comprehension, and in general putting the learner at the heart of the learning process.

Although the educational progressivism with which Bruner's name was associated has been heavily criticised, the influence of this kind of cognitive learning theory continues to be considerable. Under names such as 'discovery learning', 'enquiry-based learning' and 'problem-based learning', the instructional principles that Bruner advocated remain in common use.

ACTIVITY

As a result of your understanding of cognitivist theories of learning, list the ways in which your teaching methods could be described as 'learner-centred' and try to relate these to the opportunities and constraints of the syllabuses or courses you teach.

To conclude this section on cognitive learning theory, it is possible to see what kinds of teaching it seems to underpin, in the form of practical knowledge. For just as teaching for skills or competencies seems to reflect a behaviourist theory of learning, because it is concerned with behavioural objectives, so teaching for knowledge and understanding seems to reflect a cognitivist theory. If behaviourism underpins teaching for NVQs, then cognitivism underpins more academic courses such as A- and AS-levels. In fact, courses that are intended to prepare students for higher education, which may therefore include access courses, will demand preparation for independent and critical understanding, levels of abstract conceptualisation, and so on.

You should bear in mind your understanding of the practical knowledge of learning theory when you come to read Chapter 3 on assessment and qualifications, and also Chapter 5 on teaching and learning methods. All forms of assessment and qualifications, and all kinds of teaching and learning methods, reflect theories about how people learn. When you read them, therefore, you should be able to identify elements of both behaviourist and cognitivist learning theory.

Humanistic psychology and personal growth

We have seen in the above descriptions of behaviourism and cognitivism how the study of learning, beginning in studies of animals and using the methods of natural science, gradually moved towards a more learner-centred, or person-oriented, position. We saw, in Bruner, for example, how learning is connected with human development and the context of meaning and culture: this has come a long way from stimulus–response and conditioning theory. Humanistic psychology was a reaction against what was seen as the behaviourists' reduction of human qualities, such as free will or moral choice, to merely behavioural effects.

Many teachers see their teaching as being concerned in some way with this wider view, perhaps thinking of the 'whole person' of the learner. Practical knowledge derived from learning theory suggests that learning, in fact, does involve the 'whole person'. Success or failure in learning has as much to do with personal or emotional states as it has with motivation or intelligence: we know that the barriers to learning are as likely to consist of these kinds of problems as of problems of understanding. Teachers themselves can be barriers to learning. So where does this kind of practical knowledge come from? In this section we will consider two humanistic psychologists whose work has had an important influence on teaching and learning theory: Abraham Maslow and Carl Rogers.

Maslow (1908–70)

Abraham Maslow was mainly concerned with human motivation and potential, and he is best known for his hierarchy of needs and his idea of self-actualisation. The basic idea is that all human beings have the potential for realising the best of themselves, but whether they achieve this or not depends upon meeting more basic needs, and this is where the role of the teacher comes in. The hierarchy of needs is expressed as a pyramid (Figure 2.1).

As you can see, the base of the pyramid represents the most basic physical needs, and the point our most spiritual or emotional needs.

- *Physiological needs* are basic survival needs, such as food and shelter.
- *Safety needs* are for physical and psychological security.
- *Social needs* are those for being a member of family or social group, providing friendship, or care and affection.
- *Esteem needs* are those for respect, recognition or status.
- *Self-actualisation needs* are those for complete self-fulfilment and the attainment of potential.

The first four of these needs Maslow calls 'deficiency needs', because unless they are met it is not possible to achieve self-actualisation or full potential.

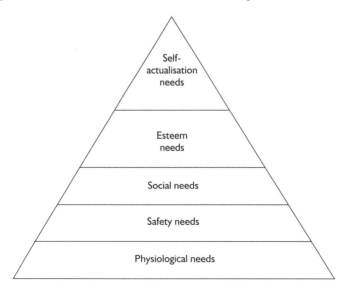

Figure 2.1 *Maslow's Hierarchy of Needs (Maslow, 1954)*

In addressing this activity, you may have been able to think of a whole range of classroom factors that may inhibit learning, from unheated rooms or unsuitable furniture to the failure to treat students as individuals with their own individual learning needs and styles.

Maslow's work has been criticised for its lack of scientific rigour, but the lessons for teachers are real enough. The skills that are needed to carry out the kinds of tasks described in Chapter 9, on recruiting, guiding and supporting students, are precisely those to do with meeting the kinds of needs suggested by Maslow as fundamental for personal development. In particular, the kind of skills needed to carry out the personal tutor role described in Chapter 9 reflect the needs of students for individual attention if they are to realise their full potential as learners.

Rogers (1902–87)

Carl Rogers, like Maslow, has had an important influence upon progressive or learner-centred educational theory. He took the ideas of self-development and self-direction in learning to a much more extreme position, and came to imply that traditional teaching actually inhibited self-actualisation or self-development because it inhibited learning itself. Much of what Rogers put forward has been absorbed in the post-school sectors of education, and the idea of the teacher's role as one of *facilitating* learning, rather than teaching subjects, has been widely, but not universally, accepted.

The most important role Rogers left to teachers was that of helping students to learn how to learn and to be aware of their own developmental processes. This is what mattered – not what was learned, but *how* it was learned. It is probably the most extreme form of learner-centred education theory, and seems almost to dissolve the teacher–student relationship entirely into that of facilitation. It gives great freedom to the students themselves to decide their own learning needs, decide the best ways of achieving them, and decide whether or not they are met. And whatever the criticism of Rogers, many of his ideas, such as learning contracts or the negotiated curriculum, have been widely adopted in some sectors of the system. If we add to this the new possibilities of flexible learner choice, modularisation and the exponentially growing possibilities for learning presented by new communication media, then it is beyond dispute that the traditional role of the teacher is changing rapidly. As you will see when you read about information technology and resource-based learning in Chapter 7, the kinds of skills needed by teachers now are much more than those traditionally required by the subject specialist. To some extent at least, Rogers' views have been vindicated in practice.

The humanistic perspective on teaching and learning, which has been introduced through the work of Maslow and Rogers, has found its most influential expression in the field of adult learning and adult education. The next section will therefore introduce this particular contribution to the practical knowledge needed for effective teaching.

Adult learning theory

The stress on development, self-direction and experience in humanistic psychology and learning theory has found its strongest formulation in adult learning theory, and nowadays this produces an even more prolific literature than childhood learning itself. In the space available, we can only consider two of its most influential forms: experiential learning and andragogy.

Experiential learning

Although it was John Dewey (1938) who first put forward the progressive idea that education was concerned with experience rather than abstract knowledge, it is the work of Kolb (1984) and Boud (Boud *et al.*, 1985) that has been most influential in associating experience and reflection with adult learning.

Kolb's own theory is usually expressed as an experiential learning cycle, as shown in Figure 2.2. This is intended to represent a general theory of human learning, and has been further elaborated (Jarvis, 1995) to include more detail of the process.

According to this kind of learning theory, all learning begins in concrete experience of the world, although experience here is fairly broadly defined. We then observe and reflect upon our experience, in a self-conscious way, and begin to generalise from it and to construct abstract concepts. Finally, we evaluate these generalisations and abstract concepts against reality by trying them out in practice. When we speak of teaching as a form of *reflective practice*, therefore, we mean that it is a practical representation of the learning cycle that Kolb proposed.

For example, suppose the concrete experience is a classroom situation where an element of small group work is sometimes organised but often proves unproductive in terms of the desired learning outcomes. Observation of the interactions and dynamics of the groups reveals differences in the ways they organise themselves. Reflection on what happens suggests a variety of reasons for this, such as the physical arrangement of furniture, the composition of the group, or the kind of task assigned to them. The repetition of this kind of experience leads to generalisation on the part of the teacher concerning the relation between group organisation and effective group learning, which in turn may lead to an abstract concept of the connection between organisation and outcome. For example, arranging groups in a

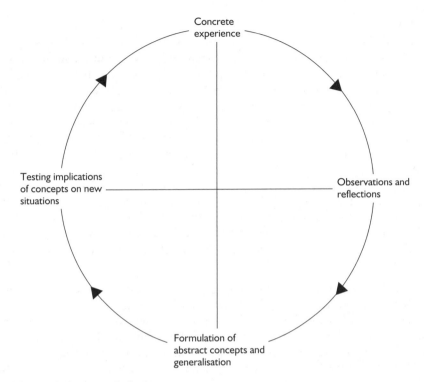

Figure 2.2 *Kolb's Learning Cycle*

Kolb, D. and Fry, R. (1975) 'Towards an Applied Theory of Experiential Learning' in Cooper, C.L. (ed.) *Theories of Group Processes*, Chichester: John Wiley & Sons Ltd, reproduced with permission

certain size, or according to a seating plan, or a mix of students, may yield certain kinds of connections. Finally, according to the learning cycle (which is the learning cycle of the teacher), the hypothetical connection between group organisation and effective learning may be tested against reality by consciously organising groups according to the principles that have been deduced from experience and reflection. This may be on the trial-and-error basis, which lies at the heart of much experiential learning.

ACTIVITY

Think of an example of ways in which your reflective practice as a teacher may embody the principle of Kolb's learning cycle. Draw the diagram with an example from class-room experience at the top of the cycle. Now re-read the section on reflective practice on page 24. You should now be able to relate what Schon says about the reflective practitioner to Kolb's learning cycle. Above all, you should be able to examine your own practice in the light of these practical theories of teaching.

Andragogy

The term 'pedagogy' is a familiar one, referring as it does to the teaching of young children. But the term 'andragogy' is usually familiar only to those concerned with the education of adults. It has to be said that pedagogy has on the whole negative connotations: it conveys a sense of traditional schoolmastering, with all the rigid discipline and control associated with the rather Victorian classroom in which it was assumed that knowledge was something to be imposed upon reluctant and infantile learners. To call someone a 'pedagogue' was to imply someone boringly and tediously trying to demonstrate superior knowledge upon everyone else: treating them, it appeared, as though they were children. One dictionary definition of a pedagogue is 'a narrow-minded pedant'. It should be said that in other countries pedagogy does not have these unflattering meanings. However, until recently, most of the learning theory arising from psychological research was concerned with the ways in which children, rather than adults, learned. Pedagogy is therefore often associated with the kinds of behaviourist theories of learning described above, with students as 'a blank sheet on which to write'.

Although he did not invent the idea, andragogy will always be associated with the name of Malcolm Knowles (1913–97). It was intended to assert that adults learned in quite different ways from children, and the theory of andragogy was intended to be put into sharp contrast with pedagogic theories about childhood learning. Although Knowles subsequently drew back from making andragogy and pedagogy mutually exclusive, his theory has been extremely influential in adult education, and he also pioneered the idea of the learning contract (Knowles, 1978; 1986).

Knowles defined andragogy as 'the art and science of helping adults learn', and it is based fundamentally upon the characteristics of adult learners as contrasted with those of children. So what are these distinguishing characteristics? Knowles formulated them into four assumptions (Knowles, 1978: 55–8):

- 'as a person grows and matures his [*sic*] self-concept moves from one of total dependency . . . to one of increasing self-directedness'
- 'as an individual matures he accumulates an expanding reservoir of experience that causes him to become an increasingly rich resource for learning'
- 'as an individual matures, his readiness to learn is decreasingly the product of his biological development and academic pressure and is increasingly the product of the developmental tasks required for the performance of his evolving social roles'
- 'children have been conditioned to have a subject-centred orientation to most learning whereas adults tend to have a problem-centred orientation to learning'.

The model of the adult learner, according to andragogy, can be summed up, therefore, as:

- self-directed
- experienced
- developmental
- problem-centred.

If adult learners have these kinds of characteristics, they will not learn effectively if they are taught as though they were children, since the model of the child as learner can be summed up as:

- other-directed
- inexperienced
- immature
- subject-oriented.

This rather stark contrast is most unlikely to find expression in reality: to say that *all* adults are experienced or problem-centred is rarely borne out in experience. Nevertheless, the implications of adult learning theory, such as that of andragogy, is that these are *assumptions* that teachers of adults need to make in their practices.

ACTIVITY

In a class of older adults, what are the implications for (a) teaching methods, (b) classroom organisation and (c) assessment of learning, according to the theory of andragogy? Suppose you have a mixed class of younger and older adults, describe some strategies you might adopt. By now, you should be able to consider your responses to these situations in terms of both practical knowledge and reflective practice.

Increasingly, mature adults are represented in both colleges and other institutions, and it is no longer possible to think of teaching in the post-school sector as almost wholly concerned with young adults in the 16–19 age range. The emphasis upon widening access to higher education, and upon lifelong learning, together with demographic and workplace trends, all suggest that the skills needed to teach adults will be required by all teachers. Reflective and experienced practitioners over the years have learned that treating adults as though they were children is a certain recipe for ineffective teaching and failed learning. Theories such as andragogy, whatever their shortcomings, should serve to sensitise teachers to the issues involved in the effective teaching of adults. Indeed, many well-established features of adult education, such as reflection, critical thinking, informal learning, and even credit accumulation and transfer, are being advocated for young peoples' learning at 14–19 (DfES, 2004). In this way, it is intended to make stronger links in the transition from earlier to later learning in life, which the concept of lifelong learning entails.

Summary of learning theories

We have now briefly introduced four broad types of learning theory: behaviourism, cognitivism, humanism and adult learning. Of course, in practice, they cannot be wholly separated from one another. But it is the function of practical knowledge and reflective practice on the part of professionals to underpin their practice by reference to this kind of research and theory. You should by now be able to identify the kinds of teaching and the kinds of courses that they may underpin. Table 2.2 suggests some links.

As suggested earlier, you should test your understanding of your practical knowledge of learning theories by considering them in relation to the teaching and learning, planning and assessment issues raised in the later chapters of this book.

Table 2.2 *Learning theories and types of course*

Practical knowledge	Types of learning	Types of course
Behaviourism	Competence/performance	NVQ
Cognitivisim	Knowledge/understanding	A-level
Humanism	Personal growth	Access
Adult learning	Reflective practice	CPD

THEORIES OF SOCIETY

Practical knowledge for teaching does not entirely consist of learning theory, although this is perhaps of most direct classroom relevance. Teaching and education can be thought of as *social relations*, and schools and colleges as *social institutions*. So the body of educational sociology also contributes to the kind of practical knowledge needed for teaching. We will consider just two examples of the kind of research and theory that underpin educational *policy*: equal opportunities and widening participation, using case studies to illustrate both. It is important to remember that teaching is carried out in a policy context, and teachers often need to know about this as much as about classroom practice itself.

Social divisions and equal opportunities

Inequalities in society have traditionally been a major focus of sociological research and theory. In educational sociology, which has mostly been concerned with schools and schooling, some of the most important research in the early days of the subject was into the relationship between educational achievement and such social factors as family, class and gender. The general effect of sociological study was to suggest that educational achievement, measured as examination success, length of schooling or the level of qualifications achieved, could be correlated with the social divisions that sociologists discovered. For example:

- There were *demographic* and *family* factors that affected educational achievement, such as family size, the position of children within the family, or the degree to which families were supportive of learning.
- There were *social class* factors that tended to privilege the children of middle-class families who, it was said, passed down 'cultural capital' from one generation to the next. On the other hand, education was the most typical source of upward social mobility for the children of ambitious working-class parents.
- There were *gender* factors that generally confined girls to certain kinds of educational routes, and to certain kinds of curriculum subjects, so that the *status* of subjects in the curriculum might be correlated with the social divisions of the school population: 'girls' subjects' and 'boys' subjects'.
- There were *cultural* and *ethnic* divisions that reflected the unequal *status* of different communities of society, and which privileged a stereotypical white middle-class male over females, working-class children and members of minority ethnic communities.

The above sketch of sociological concerns with education simply reviews some of the kinds of social divisions that continue to influence what are widely called the *educational life chances* of children and young people. In the case of adult education too this was often categorised as essentially a white middle-class pursuit, with perhaps a different kind of gender composition.

The message of sociology for education has, on the whole, been that it is as likely to *reinforce*, or reproduce, such social divisions as already exist, as it is to contribute to a more meritocratic and equal society. That is not to say that for individuals education has not represented the opportunity to rise up the social ladder in all kinds of ways through education. But it is important to remember that sociology is not concerned with individuals as such, but rather with society itself as a structure or as a system of social interaction.

There are other contributions that sociology has to make to the body of practical knowledge for teachers. Sociologists have studied classroom *processes* and *interaction* and considered the difference that teachers themselves can make to educational achievement on the part of learners. Through *labelling* and *stereotyping* of students, teachers can, in fact, exercise a very negative influence on educational achievement. What happens *within* the classroom can be as important for success or failure as 'external' factors of social division. On the other hand, the learning that occurs outside the formal education system is also very significant for young people, and this 'wider' social context is addressed in the Tomlinson Report (DfES, 2004: ch. 3) in relation to the opportunities this provides for learning about work, citizenship and community. Here again, the distinction between what is called 'human' and 'social' capital has been explored in recently influential social theory (Coleman, 1990).

On the whole, the message from sociology is one of unequal opportunities. So how could education contribute to making educational opportunities more equal, and how could education make the life chances of individuals more equal? Obviously, equal opportunities policies of colleges are intended to do this. But whether these statements of intent have substantive effect or not depends as much upon what happens in classrooms as what is happening in the wider society.

ACTIVITY

Obtain a copy of your college's equal opportunities policy, and any associated literature, and analyse it in the light of the above account of social divisions. For example, what kinds of social divisions are mentioned? The policy may, for example, mention sexual orientation or forms of disability, which have not been traditionally much studied by sociologists.

In the end, the effectiveness of equal opportunities policies depends upon the degree to which they are implemented in practice, as well as in lip-service: racism, sexism, ageism and discrimination need to be confronted. In reality, this is not always easy, but the practical knowledge of social divisions, and of the day-to-day processes of discrimination that sociology presents, should serve to support teachers in implementing equal opportunities policies.

Case Study: *Implementing equal opportunities policies at Greybourne College of FE*

Greybourne College has adopted an Equal Opportunities Policy that is intended to be incorporated into its advertising, recruitment, employment, management and classroom practices. The policy covers discrimination according to gender, ethnic origin, disability, religious and cultural belief, and sexual orientation.

In one of the classes you take, there is much larger proportion of male to female students. Over the first few weeks of the class, a culture of sexist jokes has developed amongst the male students that is expressed through the subject being studied. The female students did not, at first, appear to be offended by this, but now you feel that matters are getting out of hand, and that the female students are beginning to find it offensive. You also find it offensive, and begin to fear it is interfering with the learning progress of the class as a whole.

ACTIVITY

You do not feel you have been particularly well prepared or skilled to address this issue, but you have to face it. What are the alternatives open to you? Make a list of the possible ways of dealing with the situation, bearing in mind your awareness of the college's equal opportunities policy and the need to confront the situation without delay.

What sociologists call social divisions are at the heart of equal opportunities policies, and although a knowledge of sociology is not going to solve the problem, which is one of professional practice, it is important to understand the difference, for example, between personal and institutional racism, seeing it in terms of social relations and not just personal prejudice.

Social inclusion and widening participation

The Kennedy Report (FEFC, 1997b) made many recommendations for widening participation in further education. By widening participation is meant the more active recruitment and support for members of those social groups that sociology identifies as created by social divisions. In fact, further education has tended, like other educational sectors, to reproduce rather than challenge existing inequalities in provision:

> *There has been growth, but the students recruited have not come from a sufficiently wide cross-section of the community and there is concern that initiatives to include more working-class people, more disaffected young people, more women, more people*

from ethnic minority groups are being discontinued because they fall through the gaps in the system.

FEFC (1997b: 3)

Identification of non-participating groups is a process that we identified as the process of educational sociology, and the Kennedy Report more or less summarises the kinds of research evidence that sociology has produced over the years:

There are two ways of identifying the groups which do not participate. One way is to look at specific characteristics such as age, sex, or ethnicity . . . The other way of identifying such groups is to look at general characteristics such as levels of previous educational achievement, or levels of income, or where people live. We discovered that this method applies both locally and nationally. It also stands the test of time.

FEFC (1997b: 20–1)

The Kennedy Report was primarily concerned with ways in which the funding mechanisms for further education might contribute to widening participation. The Report was particularly concerned with the division drawn at the time between what was then called Schedule 2 and Non-schedule 2 provision created by the Further and Higher Education Act 1992. As a result of this division, the further education curriculum was divided between those programmes that lead to qualifications and those that do not, with Non-schedule 2 provision made the responsibility of the LEAs.

The Kennedy Report saw this division as creating inequalities of status between the different kinds of courses, and also as getting in the way of the aim of increasing participation: 'chaos and confusion' was the term used in the Report to describe the situation. In effect, adult learners' needs are being fitted to the system, rather than the system being geared to learning needs:

These difficulties must be significantly reduced. Collaborative inter-agency approaches should be adopted locally. Government should introduce a consistent national policy framework which recognises the richness and diversity of further education. The framework should embrace planning, funding, quality assessment, performance measurement, financial support for learners and guidance. It should also stimulate demand for learning.

FEFC (1997b: 33)

Accordingly, one of the Report's recommendations to the Funding Council was that it should:

include in the criteria for schedule 2(d) provision, any non-schedule 2 provision which is specifically planned to act as a first step towards embarking on schedule 2 provision.

FEFC (1997b: 26)

Policy for widening participation means that adequate funding of Non-schedule 2 routes is vital to help adult learners to begin again or continue as learners. Adult motivation to learn, as we have seen in this chapter, is extremely diverse, and may simply have to do with gaining qualifications or with personal development or recreation. And although the terms Schedule 2 and Non-schedule 2 are no longer applied, the crude distinction between liberal and vocational provision, on which it was based, is still very important for adult education, implying as it does that some kinds of learning are worthy of public funding and others are not. This would mean that the concept of lifelong learning, as an object of government policy, is quite narrow. As the Report says:

> *Further education, with its comprehensive curriculum, and its diversity and richness is uniquely placed to respond to this challenge.*
>
> FEFC (1997b: 29)

So what might a typical further education college be doing to meet this challenge from the Kennedy Report?

Case Study: *Greybourne College links to adult and community education*

The mission of the college is 'to widen access to learning programmes and other services for local business and the local community'. In accordance with the Kennedy Report, it is committed to 'widening access further to unrepresented groups in the local community, such as single parents and adults with poor basic skills'. Up to now, the college has sponsored the non-vocational programmes run by the Adult and Community Service, but it is actively seeking ways of strengthening the route between these and the more skills-based vocational provision. Accordingly, the college and the adult and community education service have set up a joint working party to explore the possibilities of co-operation in the areas of planning, funding, quality assessment, performance measurement, financial support and guidance for learners across the two institutions. This is in anticipation of future government policy to link these two kinds of provision more closely.

ACTIVITY

Greybourne College already sponsors the programmes run by the Adult and Community Service, and is trying to widen access to unrepresented groups in the community. List some of the ways in which you think progression from the Service's non-vocational courses to the College's more skills-based and vocational provision might be made simpler for these unrepresented groups.

Implications for teacher training

Since the publication of the Kennedy Report in 1997, there have been shifts in government policy. There is now a much greater emphasis upon the links between traditional educational sectors of schooling, further, adult and higher education: the focus of the Tomlinson Report on the 14–19 curriculum bears this out (the Report also makes quite strong links to the need to prepare young people for lifelong learning in later adult life). Also, there is a stronger stress on the importance of skills, which have tended to replace competencies as a major focus of attention. These have implications for the training of teachers.

In the first place, Lifelong Learning UK, the Sector Skills Council (SSC) for Lifelong Learning, started operating in 2005. This will be the lead body for professional development of all those working in the field of lifelong learning, and one of its tasks will be to plan a new system of initial teacher training in the learning and skills sector together with the development of sector-wide standards. In effect, the work of FENTO in establishing standards in the FE sector will be absorbed into the new Lifelong Learning Sector Skills Council. One priority is defined as the reform of teacher training in the colleges, because, unlike the schools sector, by no means all FE teachers are trained to teach. They also tend to come from diverse backgrounds.

An Ofsted survey inspection, carried out during 2002–3, found good practice, but within some fundamental weaknesses in teacher training:

- the practice–theory link needed to be strengthened
- new teachers needed more support
- subject teaching needed to be improved.

The first of these points clearly refers to the subject of this chapter, although the use of the term 'link', as we have seen, still suggests the kind of relation between theory and practice that many would reject in favour of 'integration' or some other term expressing a more complex relationship. As it stands, theory continues to sound as though it is something that is 'applied' to practice, rather than being embedded or expressed in it.

The prevailing FENTO standards, which were becoming mandatory, were judged by Ofsted to be inadequate for the purposes of those to be demanded by the Lifelong Learning Sector Skills Council. They were regarded as too wide-ranging to define the curriculum of initial teacher training, and not an 'appropriate tool' for judging the final attainments of trainees. The Report went on to suggest that 'While the FENTO standards provide a useful outline of the capabilities required of experienced FE teachers, they do not clearly define the standards required of new teachers . . . They are therefore of limited value.'

One of the driving forces behind new government policy is to address the relatively low level of basic skills of the UK population compared with those of other countries. This is the sociological basis of policy in relation to equal opportunities and wider participation and social inclusion, as these are affected by education and training. An example of this would be the Skills for Life Strategy, reflecting the findings of the Moser Report into national levels of basic skills, and co-ordinated by the National Research and Development Centre for Adult Literacy and Numeracy at the Institute of Education in London.

We have now considered some sociological underpinnings of education policy, in terms of equal opportunities and widening participation. It has become clear that practical knowledge of the kinds of social divisions and exclusions that have brought these policies into existence is needed for a full and reflective idea of the teacher's role.

Finally, there are considerations of a more philosophical kind, which also constitute a kind of practical knowledge, and we end the chapter with these.

VALUES IN EDUCATION

However much psychology and sociology might form part of the social sciences, no social activity, such as education, can be value-free, and values themselves raise philosophical rather than social scientific issues. We will consider three aspects of education that raise philosophical issues: the meaning of 'education', equal opportunities, and knowledge in the curriculum.

The meaning of 'education'

The English philosopher of education, R.S. Peters, is remembered for having defined the aims of education as quite distinct from those of, for example, training. He argued that the aims of education can only be understood with reference to what counts as an 'educated person', which itself depends upon certain social or public criteria. His definition of 'education' was that it was concerned with things that are worthwhile in themselves, and not merely a means to something else, such as employment or social status. The concept of education, he said:

> *Involves certain formal criteria – commitment to modes of thought and conduct that are regarded as worthwhile in themselves, which involve some depth of understanding, and which are not pursued with cavalier disregard for other ways of looking at the world. A curriculum is largely composed of such activities and forms of awareness.*
>
> Peters (1973: 28)

Peters' definition of education was therefore one based upon the idea of knowledge and learning for its own sake, involving the whole person rather than just a rather narrow band of skill: it was a humanistic vision of personal growth and development.

Peters has been criticised for elitism, and for the kind of distinction between education and training that is said to be a feature of the British education system. Nevertheless, his arguments, and those that oppose them, do represent a fundamental philosophical issue about the aims and meaning of education, and they cannot be lightly dismissed.

ACTIVITY

Do you think there is a meaningful distinction between education and training? Write down a definition of each term, and discover the extent to which you think there are real differences, or not. Then consider whether you would describe your own activities as a teacher as education or training, or both.

Equal opportunities

We have already seen how the concept of equal opportunities is universally adopted as a feature of education policy, and incorporated into their rules and practices by authorities and colleges. We have also seen that such policies refer to the kinds of social divisions that exist, such as those of class, gender and ethnic origin. But these divisions are not only based on sociological observation – they raise moral issues about how people should be treated, and they raise philosophical issues about justice, fairness and equality itself. Some of these issues, such as positive discrimination, raise political issues. But from a philosophical point of view, the question posed is whether or not differences between individuals should be regarded as relevant to the way they are treated. So equal opportunities policies could be regarded as a response to unfair or unjust (and morally indefensible) treatment of individuals by virtue merely of the fact that they belong to different social categories or divisions. The prevention of discrimination therefore reflects a moral or philosophical view of how individuals should be treated.

The concepts of justice and equality have been the subject of a great deal of philosophical debate, which it is not possible to pursue here. But teachers need to be aware of the philosophical and moral issues raised by equal opportunities policies, and the reasons for their existence.

ACTIVITY

In the case of the equal opportunities policy of your own college or institution, consider the moral and philosophical grounds for rejecting discrimination against the various social groups referred to in the document.

Knowledge in the curriculum

Philosophy has traditionally been concerned with the nature of knowledge, considering such issues as, for example, what is the difference between knowledge, opinion and belief. We have seen that a 'theory' of anything usually refers to a body of evidence or factual knowledge or research that justifies holding it. Our personal or subjective values and opinions are, in the end, just ours, and other people's values and opinions may be just as valid.

The curriculum of education is often associated with a body of knowledge, which may take the form of understanding, or else underpin some kind of skill or competence. We have already seen that the philosopher R.S. Peters defined the curriculum as certain 'worthwhile' ways of thought and conduct 'which involve some depth of understanding'. According to this philosophical tradition, the curriculum could be divided into various disciplines or forms of knowledge, or realms of understanding.

In recent times, this discipline-based organisation of knowledge has been largely superseded by a more integrated or flexible concept of curriculum. In fact, the modularisation of the curriculum is based upon a redefinition of educational knowledge, and again, there are philosophical arguments for and against, which are about the nature of knowledge itself.

ACTIVITY

Take any subject area in which you teach, and consider the effects of modularisation upon it as a subject. These effects may be in terms of depth, content, forms of assessment, or any other aspect you feel may raise issues about knowledge of a philosophical kind.

We have briefly considered some philosophical issues for teaching and education. Philosophy does not form a basis for practical knowledge in quite the same way as psychology or sociology, but nevertheless, philosophical issues around such things as aims, equality or knowledge will never go away, and a truly reflective practitioner will need to take them into account.

Review Questions ———————————————————————

1 Give examples of ways in which practical knowledge, reflective practice or communities of practice may help to integrate theory and practice in education and teaching.
2 What kinds of teaching methods reflect behaviourist theories of learning?
3 What kinds of assessment methods reflect cognitivist theories of learning?
4 How would you distinguish between pedagogic and andragogic practices in your own teaching?
5 Identify ways in which wider educational participation by socially excluded groups could be made easier.
6 What philosophical issues about knowledge are raised by the modularisation of the curriculum?

SUMMARY

- Theory and practice can be integrated in different ways. Ideas such as practical knowledge, reflective practice or communities of practice are examples of how the theory/practice issue might be resolved.
- Psychological theory and research in the forms of behaviourism, cognitivism, humanism and adult learning theory are all significant in how we think about educational courses, methods and assessment.
- Sociological theory and research into social divisions and social interaction contribute to our understanding of policy issues such as equal opportunities and widening participation.
- Concepts of the curriculum or the aims of education reflect philosophical issues about the meaning of education, knowledge and equality.

Suggested Further Reading

Curzon, L.B. (2003) *Teaching in Further Education*, London: Continuum International Publishing Group
A well-established textbook reviewing recent developments in FE theory and practice, and describes implications of research relevant to teaching and learning. in particular, psychological accounts of the basis of training, transfer, adult learning and so on, are outline in an accessible way.

Hillier, Y. (2002) *Reflective Teaching in Further and Adult Education*, London: Continuum International Publishing Group
This is a textbook for teacher training as well as continuing professional development, organised around the concept of 'reflective teaching', and relevant to the FENTO standards described in Chapter 11 of this book. It is based upon the analysis of typical issues and incorporates some theoretical insights together with practical exercises.

Jarvis, P. (1998) *The Practitioner Researcher: Developing Theory from Practice*, San Francisco: Jossey-Bass
This book presents an account of various ways of approaching the theory/practice issue for professionals. It reviews the main theoretical positions, and provides a more detailed account of the concepts introduced in this chapter.

Jarvis, P., Holford, J. and Griffin, C. (2003) *The Theory and Practice of Learning*, 2nd edition, London: Kogan Page
This short book sets out the basic theories of learning that underpin educational practice, relating them to current developments in education, such as self-directed learning, contract learning, open and distance learning, work-based learning, lifelong learning, etc.

Longworth, N. (2003) *Lifelong Learning in Action: Transforming Education in the 21st Century*, London: Kogan Page
Outlines the concept of lifelong learning and its impact on traditional education systems around the world. Describes the background to the development of lifelong learning as a fundamental policy shift affecting every sector of education.

Merrill, B. and Hyland, T. (2003) *The Changing Face of Further Education: Lifelong Learning, Inclusion and the Community*, London: RoutledgeFalmer
A good account of the changing policy context of the Further Education sector and its expansion under the initiatives of the lifelong learning concept. Links between the colleges and their communities are described, and the relations of Further Education to government policy initiatives under the lifelong learning banner are analysed.

3 ASSESSMENT AND QUALIFICATIONS

Objectives

After reading this chapter, you should be able to:

- recognise the functions of assessment in teaching, learning and accreditation
- make use of a range of assessment methods to enliven your teaching
- understand the processes of assessment and moderation on vocational qualifications
- understand the role of assessment as a diagnostic tool in identifying learners' needs and accrediting their prior achievements
- appreciate the formal aspects of assessment such as regulations and appeals
- understand recent debates about the reform of post-compulsory qualifications.

The FENTO standards for teaching recognise that a professional approach to assessment underpins successful learning and achievement. Designing assignments that stretch students and promote their development is a creative activity that requires great skill and understanding. To perform successfully as a teacher or trainer in post-16 education, you will need a thorough knowledge of how to assess and verify the key elements of the vocational curriculum – competencies, underlying knowledge and key skills. Processes of assessment are also closely linked to the achievement of qualifications and to the maintenance of standards. There is not universal agreement about how qualifications should be assessed, what appropriate standards are or how they should be maintained. This is evident in the annual debate that accompanies the publication of the GCSE and GCE AS- and A-level results each summer. Similar issues always arise. Are the pass rates too high? Are standards falling? Should there be a greater emphasis upon external examinations?

WHAT ASSESSMENT IS AND WHAT FUNCTIONS IT SERVES

What is assessment?

Assessment is the process by which evidence of student achievement is obtained and judged. Ecclestone (1996) points out that assessment requires two things: *evidence* and a *standard* or scale. The evidence can take an almost infinite variety of forms, from traditional examinations to projects carried out within a work-based setting.
Ecclestone goes on to explain that the standards or scales can also take many forms. All, however, will involve measuring the student against one of three things:

- an absolute criterion – 'Can this person add 2 + 2 together to make 4?'
- performance relative to a cohort or group – 'How does this person compare with others in his/her group/this year's candidates/all students?'
- the learner's own previous performance – 'Can this person do this better than they could at the start of the course/training programme?'

Basis of assessment

It is important for the teacher or trainer to understand on what basis – criterion, norm or ipsative – a candidate is being judged.

- Where the evaluation of a student is based upon an explicit and absolute standard, for example the performance criterion on an NVQ programme, this is referred to as *criterion referencing*.
- Where assessment is based upon judging the performance of students in comparison to the standards of a reference group, for example the performance of a GCE A-level student in comparison to the performance of all GCE A-level students in his/her group, this is referred to as *norm referencing*.
- Where assessment is used as a measure of an individual learner's progress over a set period of time, for example through Records of Achievement, this is referred to as *ipsative assessment*.

ACTIVITY

Choose a vocational programme with which you are familiar, for example a BTEC National Diploma, or an AVCE or NVQ programme. Check the course documentation, for example the student handbook or the awarding body's specification and regulations. Find the relevant sections on assessment and look particularly at what assessments the student has to complete to gain the award. Classify these using the three types of assessment defined above. You may find that all three types of assessment are in use on a single qualification. Once you have completed this task, discuss your findings with a colleague on your Cert. Ed. or PGCE programme.

Why assess?

Ecclestone (1996) identifies three main reasons for assessing people:

- to *diagnose* their learning needs
- to *select* them for the next educational stage or for work
- to *certificate* their achievements.

Diagnostic assessment

The function of diagnostic assessment is to identify each individual learner's existing capabilities so that realistic learning goals, for example a particular course, can be identified. This is obviously critical for many adult students, who may have left formal education some time ago and are often unsure of what course or programme to select. Diagnosis is especially important for identifying students' needs for additional learning support – for example, help with study skills or with basic literacy or numeracy. Alternatively diagnostic assessment may be used to confirm existing competencies and skills, so that the learner is not required to repeat unnecessarily elements of a course or training programme in which she or he is already competent. The section *Assessment as a diagnostic tool*, on page 69, discusses the ways in which diagnostic assessment is used in more detail.

Recruitment and selection

Assessment plays a critical role in recruitment and selection. Interviews for a job or a place on a higher education course are illustrations of this. Usually the university or the employer will stipulate what qualifications, experience and other qualities are essential for applicants. Candidates will then be compared against one another so that a selection decision can be made. The whole of the University and Colleges Admissions process (UCAS) is an example of the use of assessment for these purposes.

Accreditation

The certification or accreditation of learners' achievements by an examining or awarding body provides proof, through the award of a qualification, that the candidate has achieved a defined standard. Accreditation draws attention to the more formal aspects of assessment, such as assessment regulations, verification and academic appeals. These are explored further in the section on *The formal aspects of assessment* on page 73.

Formative v. summative assessment

Whatever the reason for assessment, as far as the student or trainee is concerned it plays a critical role in promoting learning. This is because it allows the teacher to provide feedback of a *formative* kind so that the learner gains a view of his or her strengths and weaknesses. Armed with this knowledge she or he can take practical steps to improve performance. Skilled teachers use feedback, for example in marking, to enable the learner to develop their strengths and remedy their weaknesses. Assessment also has an important *summative* function. It is used for the purpose of grading candidates studying for a qualification and for distinguishing between them for the purpose of making selection decisions.

It is common during the early stages of courses for teachers to make considerable use of formative assessment. They often do this by setting assignments that are not graded so that learners can build up confidence in their own capabilities and gain an appreciation of the standards expected of them. Towards the end of most courses, the proportion of summative assessment increases – most obviously through examination, but also through the increased use of in-course assessment.

ACTIVITY

Look back at your own experience as a student or trainee. Select one teacher or trainer who you regarded as a good assessor because they provided you with excellent feedback that enabled you to improve your performance. Try to identify three features of this good practice in formative assessment. Write these down and compare your responses with a colleague on your Cert. Ed. or PGCE course. Now consider the grades that they awarded you for your assignments (i.e. the summative assessment). Did you regard these as fair? Why? Or why not?

ASSESSMENT AND QUALIFICATIONS

The teacher's choice of assessment methods is constrained by the nature of the qualification and the regulations of the awarding body. The most extreme example of this is with courses that are entirely examined through external examinations, for example some professional courses and some GCE A-level programmes. In these, the teacher's role in assessment is to ensure that the student covers the syllabus and has practice in writing and performing under time pressure. By contrast, some vocational qualifications are deeply rooted in the workplace and the role of the teacher is to ensure that students or trainees have the necessary competence to perform in the job.

The range of post-16 qualifications

There are more than 4,500 different post-compulsory qualifications and over 150 examining and awarding bodies. The diversity of qualifications is matched by a diversity of assessment methods. Most teachers will be required to work across a wide range of these qualifications. A critical professional skill therefore is being able to adapt to a range of different assessment methods. This is one of the most demanding yet most rewarding aspects of professional practice in post-compulsory education.

In order to make sense of this complexity, it is helpful if the teacher asks three simple questions when deciding how to assess students:

- *What is being assessed?* Most qualifications contain a blend of three elements: subject-based knowledge, often referred to as *underpinning knowledge*; skills, often referred to as *key skills*; and *competence*, that is the ability to perform occupationally specific tasks in the workplace. It is the different emphasis given to these three elements by the awarding body that plays the major part in determining the assessment methods to be adopted.
- *When does it need to be assessed?* For almost all courses, the teacher will make use of formative assessment throughout the programme. Every marked assignment will contain feedback from the assessor on how to improve performance and learn from both strengths and weaknesses. The timing of summative assessment is a different matter. On most vocational courses, for example GNVQ and City & Guilds craft-based courses, there will be a mix of in-course assessments and external examinations. Where there is a significant element of continuous assessment, the course team will be responsible for phasing this appropriately over the course, to avoid the student becoming overburdened at any one time. The examining body will also obviously regulate the timing and phasing of summative assessment over the course.
- *Why is it assessed?* This is the most fundamental of the three questions. It is important that the teacher or trainer is absolutely clear as to whether the assessment is for the purpose of diagnosis, certification or selection. This will determine the nature, style and procedures for the assessment. For example, if the assessment is part of formal assessment for a qualification, it is likely that suitable procedures for marking and moderation will have to be agreed well in advance. In contrast, if the main aim of the assessment is formative, a more informal approach to assessment might be more suitable.

Assessment and the National Qualifications Framework

During the last 30 years, there have been several attempts to rationalise the UK's complex system of post-16 qualifications. The formation of the Business Education Council and the Technician Education Council in the late 1970s (later to merge and become BTEC and then Edexcel) was one such attempt. This was followed by the formation of the National Council for Vocational Qualifications (NCVQ) in 1986. Further rationalisation was accompanied by the creation of the Qualifications and Curriculum Authority (QCA) in 1997, which is responsible for the regulation of all qualifications, from nursery level to adult education, other than those awarded by universities. In the first decade of the millennium, fundamental changes are in train as a consequence of the Tomlinson reforms (Tomlinson, 2004) and the changes to the national qualifications structure through the creation of a Framework for Achievement (FfA) by QCA.

The three main post-16 qualification routes

These various attempts at reform have led to the evolution of a post-compulsory National Qualifications Framework with three main qualification routes:

- a general or academic route leading through from GCSE to GCE A-level and on to university degree programmes
- a work-based training route with National Vocational Qualifications, which incorporate occupational standards
- an applied route with qualifications designed mainly for full-time students wishing to base their studies in a broad vocational context. Examples include the Advanced Vocational Certificate in Education (AVCE), Vocational GCSEs and GNVQs.

These three routes are illustrated in Figure 3.1. In the paragraphs that follow, the nature of assessment on the main three routes in the National Qualification Framework is outlined.

National Vocational Qualifications: the work-based route

National Vocational Qualifications (NVQs) and their equivalent in Scotland, Scottish Vocational Qualifications (SVQs), are based upon occupational standards set by employers that identify what people have to do to show that they are competent in a job. The standards are determined by National Training Organisations and their successor bodies, the Sector Skills Councils (SSCs), following detailed analysis of the knowledge, skills and competencies that people in a given occupation need in the workplace. NVQs and SVQs are divided into five levels (DfEE, 1998a), which broadly equate to:

- Level 1 – foundation skills in occupations
- Level 2 – operative or semi-skilled occupations
- Level 3 – technician, craft and supervisory occupations
- Level 4 – technical and junior management occupations
- Level 5 – chartered professional and senior management occupations.

Given the strong emphasis upon work-based competencies, NVQs and SVQs are most widely used for people at work undertaking training in the workplace or attending a

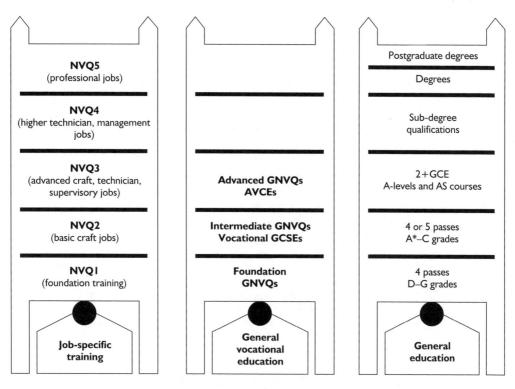

Figure 3.1 *The post-16 National Qualifications Framework*

part-time course at college whilst in employment. NVQs are usually linked to government-funded training programmes, such as the apprenticeship schemes. Generally NVQs and SVQs have had the most take-up at Levels 1–3. The impact of these qualifications at Levels 4 and 5 is smaller. More traditional vocational and professional qualifications, for example Higher National Certificates and Diplomas or Foundation Degrees, are more popular at these levels.

The NVQ assessment model is rooted in assessment against performance criteria linked to occupational standards. The candidate (i.e. the student or trainee) has to present evidence to demonstrate that she or he can satisfy the performance criteria for the award. The essential elements of assessment in this system are highlighted in Figure 3.2. As the figure shows, these qualifications are broken down into separate units of competence. It is possible therefore for a student to gain a particular unit rather than the whole NVQ. The system is essentially modular in design. As far as the candidate is concerned, the main activity is collecting and presenting evidence to an assessor to demonstrate competence against explicit performance criteria. This evidence can take many forms and the facility is available for students or trainees to gain part or all of the award by making a claim for accreditation of prior learning (APL), for example proof of a related qualification or experience in a similar occupation. The procedures associated with APL are discussed in more detail on pages 71–2.

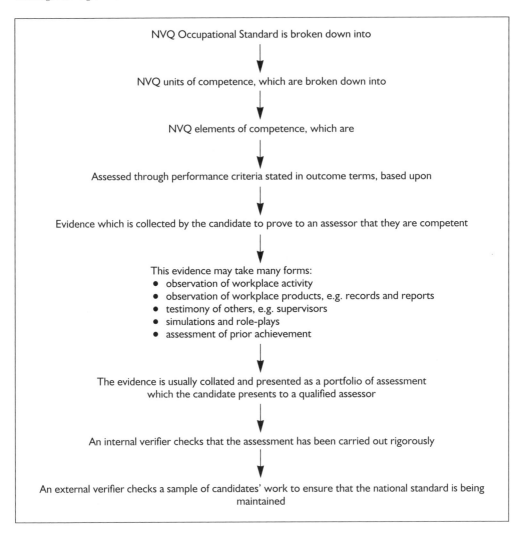

NVQ Occupational Standard is broken down into

↓

NVQ units of competence, which are broken down into

↓

NVQ elements of competence, which are

↓

Assessed through performance criteria stated in outcome terms, based upon

↓

Evidence which is collected by the candidate to prove to an assessor that they are competent

↓

This evidence may take many forms:
- observation of workplace activity
- observation of workplace products, e.g. records and reports
- testimony of others, e.g. supervisors
- simulations and role-plays
- assessment of prior achievement

↓

The evidence is usually collated and presented as a portfolio of assessment which the candidate presents to a qualified assessor

↓

An internal verifier checks that the assessment has been carried out rigorously

↓

An external verifier checks a sample of candidates' work to ensure that the national standard is being maintained

Figure 3.2 *The NVQ and SVQ competence-based assessment model*

In terms of the concepts outlined earlier in this chapter, you will quickly recognise that the NVQ/SVQ system is based upon criterion referencing. Absolute and explicit standards expressed as performance criteria are the measure for judging whether students are competent or not. Some commentators (Wolf, 1994) have questioned the extent to which assessment can ever be a totally objective activity. She has pointed out that ultimately assessment involves one group of people (teachers or trainers) making a judgement about the performance of another group (students). It is therefore misleading for those strongly attached to a criterion-referenced system to claim that assessment can be a totally objective process based upon absolute judgements.

ACTIVITY

You have been called for interview for a full-time teaching post at Greybourne College of FE. The post will require you to teach on a range of NVQ programmes in your specialist area. As part of the selection procedure, you have been asked to make a presentation about how you would guide students, new to NVQ courses, through the assessment process. You need to focus upon the following aspects:

- the use of performance criteria
- the collection of evidence for student portfolios
- the gathering of work-based evidence.

Prepare a presentation and then ask a group of colleagues on your Cert. Ed. or PGCE programme to simulate the roles of the selection panel.

Applied vocational qualifications

General National Vocational Qualifications (GNVQs) were introduced by the National Council for Vocational Qualifications (NCVQ) as a new qualification in 1992. The Government at that time was seeking to create a credible vocational alternative to GCSE and GCE A-levels for the 16–19 age group. Each GNVQ was related to a broad area of employment, for example business studies or manufacturing, and is designed to provide students with a general education so that they can progress to either employment or further study. GNVQs were available at three levels:

- Foundation Level, equivalent to four GCSEs below grade C
- Intermediate Level, equivalent to four or five GCSEs at grades A* to C
- Advanced Level (applied GCE A-levels).

In September 2000, a new award entitled the Advanced Vocational Certificate in Education (AVCE) was introduced to replace the GNVQ at advanced level. Its introduction followed a major review of 16–18 qualifications – the 'Qualifying for Success' reforms. One of the aims of these reforms was to introduce greater commonality and parity between GCE A-level and advanced vocational qualifications. This was achieved by using a common grading system (A to E) and creating a unit-based structure (based on 3-unit, 6-unit and 12-unit awards) for both GCE and AVCE qualifications. Meanwhile, changes were also afoot to replace the GNVQ at intermediate level with new vocational GCSE qualifications (VGCSEs). These were introduced, mainly for school pupils at Key Stage 4, in 2002. In fact neither advanced nor intermediate GNVQ qualifications have disappeared. The three qualifications tend to be offered in different combinations in different schools and colleges.

There are many parallels between the assessment systems used for NVQ, GNVQ, AVCE and VGCSE qualifications, as Figure 3.3 illustrates. The assessment systems are based upon criterion referencing. The awards consist of individual units specified in the form of the learning outcomes to be achieved. Like the NVQ system, therefore, the qualifications have a modular structure. Students take mandatory units, which contain the core areas of knowledge linked to the vocational area, and optional units. Students are assessed against explicit performance criteria that themselves are derived from the outcomes for each unit. There is a mixture of internal and external assessment.

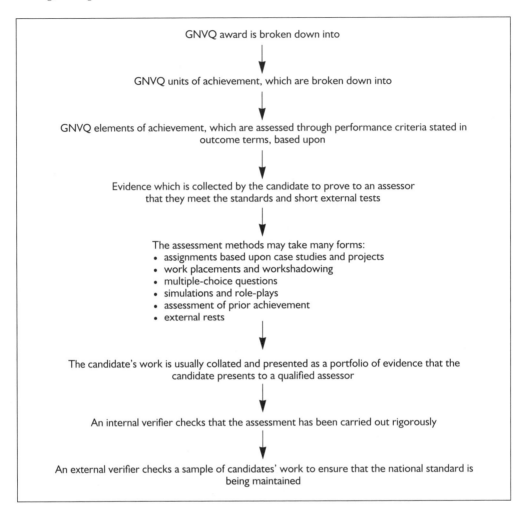

GNVQ award is broken down into

↓

GNVQ units of achievement, which are broken down into

↓

GNVQ elements of achievement, which are assessed through performance criteria stated in outcome terms, based upon

↓

Evidence which is collected by the candidate to prove to an assessor that they meet the standards and short external tests

↓

The assessment methods may take many forms:
- assignments based upon case studies and projects
- work placements and workshadowing
- multiple-choice questions
- simulations and role-plays
- assessment of prior achievement
- external rests

↓

The candidate's work is usually collated and presented as a portfolio of evidence that the candidate presents to a qualified assessor

↓

An internal verifier checks that the assessment has been carried out rigorously

↓

An external verifier checks a sample of candidates' work to ensure that the national standard is being maintained

Figure 3.3 *The GNVQ/AVCE assessment model*

To satisfy the demands of the internal assessment, each student is required to prepare a portfolio of evidence. This usually consists of a collection of assignments, projects and other assessments that relate to the performance criteria for the programme. For some units, the candidate also has to pass external tests that are designed and administered by the three awarding bodies. Students are also expected to demonstrate competence in the three key skills of Communication, Application of Number, and Information Technology. Until the academic year 2000–1, key skills formed part of the overall GNVQ award. Since then, key skills have been separately assessed. Students are encouraged to gain a key skills qualification in addition to their vocational qualification.

A positive feature of vocational assessment is the strong emphasis upon formative assessment. Great emphasis is placed on the students' ability to plan and organise their own learning. Tutors therefore devote considerable time to working with students on an individual basis to guide them and give feedback on their strengths and weaknesses. As with the NVQ system, certification can be given for individual units as well as for the full qualification.

GCE A- and AS-levels and GCSE: the academic route
General Certificate of Secondary Education (GCSE), General Certificate of Education Advanced level (GCE A-level) and GCE Advanced Subsidiary (GCE AS-level) courses are a major part of provision in post-compulsory education for both adults and 16–19 students. It is highly likely that during your career in further and adult education you will be required to teach and assess students pursuing these qualifications. They still form the dominant part of the curriculum in sixth form colleges. Many general further education colleges and adult education centres also provide a wide choice of GCSE and GCE A-level subjects for both 16–18-year-olds and adult students. In 2000 there were over half a million GCSE and GCE examination entries from colleges and other institutions funded by the Learning and Skills Council (LSC).

Both these qualifications are extremely well established in both secondary and further education and remain the main route for entry to higher education. GCSE was introduced in 1988 and, with the implementation of the National Curriculum in schools, has become the main form of assessment at Key Stage 4. GCE A-levels were introduced in 1951, replacing the single Higher School Certificate, and in 1987 were supplemented with GCE Advanced Supplementary examinations (which are now known as GCE Advanced Subsidiary), worth approximately half a GCE A-level. Given the long history of GCE A-level qualifications, there have been many changes in the regulatory frameworks governing their assessment. The most recent changes have resulted from the Dearing *Review of Qualifications for 16–19-year-olds* (Dearing, 1996) and were implemented through the 'Qualifying for Success' reforms of 2000, and further changes are in train as a result of the Tomlinson reforms (Tomlinson, 2004).

There are over 500 different GCE A-level syllabuses across some 50 different subject areas. During recent years there has been a spate of mergers between the vocational and GCE/GCSE awarding bodies. The result has been a considerable rationalisation with three large awarding bodies, for example Edexcel was formed from the merger of BTEC (the Business and Technology Education Council) and ULEAC (the University of London Examinations and Assessment Council). Since 1997 the awarding bodies have been regulated by the Qualifications and Curriculum Authority (QCA), which provides guidance on the subject content, assessment and grading of both GCSE and GCE. Prior to the formation of QCA, schools-based qualifications were controlled by the Schools Curriculum and Assessment Authority (SCAA) and vocational qualifications were regulated by the National Council for Vocational Qualifications (NCVQ). These two bodies were brought together in 1997 to form the Qualifications and Curriculum Authority (QCA).

GCSE and GCE assessment

Both GCSE and GCE A/AS-levels can be assessed through internal assessment and external examinations. Internal assessment is usually based upon coursework, which is assessed by teachers and then moderated by the examining body. The balance between the proportion of assessment through coursework and examination is set by QCA. It varies according to the nature of the subject – generally more practical subjects, for example Design Technology, give a larger weighting to coursework.

Examinations are set and marked by the awarding bodies. The consistency of the question papers and mark schemes is the responsibility of the chief examiner. Unlike NVQ and GNVQ qualifications, where the candidate is expected to demonstrate competence against all the performance criteria for the award, GCSE and GCE A-level assessment is more selective. The examination and coursework test a sample of the knowledge, skills and understanding outlined in the syllabus. Grading of GCSEs is based on an A* to G scale and grading of GCE A-level is based upon five pass grades A to E, with N representing a narrow fail and U representing unclassified performance. The main features of assessment on GCSE and GCE A-level programmes are represented in Figure 3.4.

There are some obvious points of contrast between the assessment procedures for GCSE and GCE A-level and those for NVQ and GNVQ qualifications. Assessment on GCE and GCSE courses is heavily weighted towards norm rather than criterion referencing. Each candidate's performance is assessed in comparison to the performance of the total cohort of candidates taking the examination paper. That is the main reason why so much stress is placed upon procedures for moderation and statistical sampling. Where large numbers of candidates are entered for a national examination, the reliability of assessment is crucial. This is particularly so when the results of these public examinations are of such interest to the media. It is therefore important for the examiners to work with a common understanding of appropriate standards. Hence the stress upon agreed marking schemes, clear definitions of grade boundaries and other standardisation procedures. For example, cross-marking of a sample of scripts is common and the chief examiner usually samples a selection of marked scripts to detect any bias creeping into the assessment process as a result of the idiosyncrasies of a particular marker. Essentially, the assessment system is based upon an elaborate process for refining professional judgement. In this sense it closely resembles the procedures in place for the marking of undergraduate examination papers in universities.

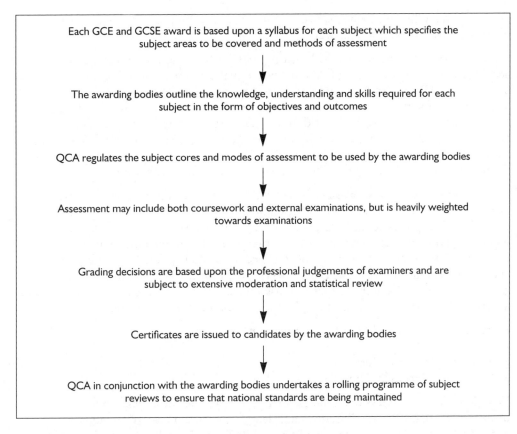

Each GCE and GCSE award is based upon a syllabus for each subject which specifies the subject areas to be covered and methods of assessment

The awarding bodies outline the knowledge, understanding and skills required for each subject in the form of objectives and outcomes

QCA regulates the subject cores and modes of assessment to be used by the awarding bodies

Assessment may include both coursework and external examinations, but is heavily weighted towards examinations

Grading decisions are based upon the professional judgements of examiners and are subject to extensive moderation and statistical review

Certificates are issued to candidates by the awarding bodies

QCA in conjunction with the awarding bodies undertakes a rolling programme of subject reviews to ensure that national standards are being maintained

Figure 3.4 *The GCSE and GCE A-level assessment model*

ACTIVITY

Obtain a copy of the GCE A-level chief examiner's most recent annual report for a subject that you teach. Read it carefully and extract comments that relate to the procedures for standardising assessment in the subject. What comments does the report make about how standards have changed in the subject and the role of the chief examiner in upholding and standardising assessment across the country?

Other post-16 qualifications

In the paragraphs above, the major features of assessment on the three main qualification routes have been described and analysed. There are, however, many other qualifications in the post-compulsory sector that you will encounter. There is not sufficient space to cover all of them in this chapter. The following may, however, prove helpful in delineating the main categories. When selecting appropriate assessment methods for them, do bear in mind the three basic questions that were discussed earlier in this chapter, namely: What is being assessed?, When is it being assessed? and Why is it being assessed? You will find attempting to answer these questions will take you a long way.

National awarding bodies, such as Edexcel and City & Guilds, are involved in the accreditation of a wide range of national vocational provision, including qualifications accredited as NVQs and GNVQs. Each awarding body has its own distinct arrangements for the assessment, control and certification of its awards. There is a range of well-established awards at different levels for both full- and part-time students. For example, Edexcel validates certificates and diplomas at First, National and Higher National levels (commonly known as BTEC First, National and Higher Diplomas and Certificates). City & Guilds provides a range of craft-based qualifications.

A large number of *professional bodies* offer their own accreditation and increasingly validate colleges to run courses and programmes across further, higher and adult education. The professional bodies were developed historically to represent their members and to protect the standards of training in the occupations that they represent. They offer a wide range of qualifications, often studied through part-time courses in general further education colleges. Assessment has much in common with the GCE and GCSE system in that it is usually based upon external examinations and a norm referencing approach. Examples of professional bodies include:

- Institute of Chartered Secretaries and Administrators
- Institute of Meat
- Chartered Insurance Institute
- Council for Licensed Conveyancers.

In addition to the professional bodies, there are a number of *membership organisations* that offer qualifications and learning programmes. Two common examples are trade unions and chambers of commerce. Some trade unions have a well-established pattern of courses for officials, for example shop stewards. Again the assessment of these is determined by the particular organisation.

Open College Networks (OCNs) are locally based and controlled networks that operate within a national framework provided through the National Open College. They offer accreditation for locally designed programmes based in the workplace, the community, voluntary organisations or colleges. OCNs award credits and certificates for achievements on recognised programmes. These are usually designed to recognise the achievements of adult learners and to consequently provide them with a qualification that allows progression into further or higher education.

Moderation and verification

Moderation and verification are procedures through which the examining and awarding bodies, in conjunction with internal assessors, attempt to maintain the standards of their qualifications. Moderators and external verifiers are appointed by the examining and awarding bodies to check that appropriate standards of internal assessment are being maintained by schools, colleges and other providers of their qualifications. They attempt to maintain standards using a variety of controls, the most critical of which is checking that teachers and work-based trainers are assessing student work to the required standard.

External examiners and assessors

On GCE and GCSE courses with a significant element of teacher-assessed work, the examining body will normally appoint an external examiner to check a sample of marked student work. Each external examiner will usually be responsible for several centres so that she or he can compare assessment on different courses and develop a feel for the appropriate standard. It is usual for the external examiner to visit the centre to meet with staff and review internal procedures for ensuring consistent assessment, especially where several markers are involved.

Internal procedures for achieving consistency include such methods as cross-marking, the use of agreed marking schemes and control via double marking of a sample of scripts by a senior teacher. At a national level, the chief examiner for the subject will arrange regional and country-wide meetings of external examiners to ensure national consistency. These qualitative approaches will be supplemented by statistical analysis of the performance of candidates, broken down by gender, age, ethnicity, region, size of centre and other criteria. Both the activities of external moderation and statistical analysis are designed to increase the reliability of assessment.

The Dearing Review (Dearing, 1996) recommended that the examining bodies strengthen their procedures for assuring consistent national standards, and QCA and successive governments have continued to apply pressure to assure standards. As discussed earlier, the GCE and GCSE assessment systems are based upon a norm referencing system. Standards are arrived at through agreement between a professional group of subject specialists. In all norm referencing systems there is an enormous emphasis upon procedures for ensuring the reliability of assessment. The attention given by the mass media to the annual publication of results is a further factor that encourages examining bodies to be assiduous and systematic.

Many teachers in FE will also be involved in assessing higher education courses, such as degrees, Higher National Diplomas (HND) and various professional qualifications. For most of these, a similar system of external examining and moderation applies. The external examiner system is a central component of degree courses, validated by the universities. Edexcel, which awards the BTEC HND and HNC qualifications, appoints external moderators to assure that standards are being maintained. Moderators and external examiners will usually visit the college on two or three occasions each academic year to meet the course team and check the standard of assessment.

Assessment and verification on vocational courses

The system designed by the awarding bodies for assuring the standard of assessment on NVQ and GNVQ programmes, based upon internal and external verification, is somewhat more complex. The general meaning of the term to verify is 'to prove to be true or accurate, to substantiate or confirm'. Verifiers are appointed to confirm or substantiate the decisions of those directly responsible for assessing students in the learning situation or workplace. Both NVQ and GNVQ programmes are weighted heavily towards continuous assessment carried out by teachers and trainers. Confirming the thoroughness of the assessment process through verification is pivotal to assuring standards.

Internal verifiers are experienced members of the teaching staff, whose role is to take an overview of assessment procedures and confirm that internal assessment is carried out rigorously and to the standards defined in the qualification. External verifiers are appointed by the awarding body to confirm that assessment procedures are appropriate and that students' work is marked to the national standard. Verification therefore is concerned with both checking that appropriate procedures are in place for managing assessment and confirming that the outcome of assessment, that is the standard of students' work, is appropriate.

ACTIVITY

You are part of a team of college and school teachers running a vocational programme for 14–16 pupils. You will be teaching a Vocational GCSE course. Your head of department has asked you to submit a teaching and assessment scheme for the year. This scheme should demonstrate how you plan to achieve:

- the sequencing of topics
- the coverage of learning objectives
- the integration of one day's work placement and
- the relationship between in-course assessment and the learning objectives.

Prepare the scheme, and then submit it to your Cert. Ed. or PGCE tutor for comments.

Authenticity, sufficiency and validity of assessment evidence

In judging decisions made by internal assessors, verifiers use three key criteria – authenticity, sufficiency and validity of assessment. As far as students on NVQ and GNVQ programmes are concerned, the main activity is collecting evidence to confirm that they have fulfilled the explicit performance criteria for the qualification. As far as teachers acting as assessors are concerned, the key function is making a judgement about the quantity and quality of evidence presented by students. Proof that students or trainees are actually submitting evidence that is a result of their own work is a fairly obvious concomitant of the NVQ and GNVQ systems, which are largely based upon continuous assessment. Indeed where there has been adverse publicity about the standard of NVQ awards this has mainly arisen in situations where private trainers have not had systematic procedures for checking the authenticity of trainees' work.

The criterion of sufficiency is the consequence of an assessment system founded upon the notion of competent performance. Competence in a task implies that the individual will be able to perform it to a particular standard on more than one occasion, in other words, that there will be mastery of the particular skill. Both assessors and verifiers have to check students' portfolios of evidence to see that a particular competence has been tackled successfully under different conditions and on several occasions. For the student and the teacher this implies collecting a lot of documentation to demonstrate sufficiency. This is one of the reasons why the NVQ and GNVQ assessment system has often been criticised for being too paper-based and bureaucratic (FEFC, 1996c).

For assessment to be valid on a vocational programme, it must relate to the work context for which the qualification is designed. On NVQ programmes, this will usually mean that the learner will have to demonstrate competence in a real work situation. Most of the awarding bodies will accept that an element of simulation is acceptable, for example through the student working in a training office or college restaurant. Usually this will have to be supplemented with real workplace evidence. For this reason, NVQ qualifications are most appropriate for students in employment or training. For GNVQ programmes, where the objectives are less job-specific, the requirement for real workplace evidence is less important.

It will be apparent from the foregoing just how pivotal and professional an activity assessment is in vocational qualifications. Colleges and the awarding bodies recognise this and training is provided for teachers and trainers involved in discharging assessor and verifier roles. Most colleges and some larger employers provide in-house training for their staff to gain special qualifications designed for assessors and verifiers.

ACTIVITY

Make use of your college library and/or the web sites of QCA and the awarding bodies to obtain details of the range of professional qualifications available for assessors, internal and external verifiers. Make a list of the main functions listed under the internal verifier qualification. Now, using your own college or training organisation as a resource, arrange an interview with one of the internal verifiers. Using your list of functions as a guide, ask them how they organise the internal verification of the course(s) for which they are responsible.

Assessing key skills

Key skills have become established as an integral part of the vocational curriculum. They have also become an increasingly important part of many academic programmes. The three skills of Communication, Application of Number and Information Technology are normally an integral part of all vocational qualifications. Teachers have to demonstrate through assessment and verification how they are including these skills in their assignments for the course. The Dearing Review of 16–19 qualifications (Dearing, 1996) and more recently the Tomlinson Review (Tomlinson, 2004) have highlighted the importance of students developing these skills. Accordingly QCA, in conjunction with the main awarding bodies, has developed key skills units from Level 1 to Level 3, which can be incorporated into different courses.

During the last 20 years, these skills have been referred to variously as core, common and key skills. The pressure for their inclusion as a compulsory element in the curriculum has come from both employers and educationalists. Employers, represented by such groups as the Institute of Directors and the Confederation of British Industry, have persistently complained about the low standards of literacy, oracy and numeracy of school and college leavers. With the current emphasis upon lifelong learning to meet the needs of a society increasingly reliant upon knowledge-based industries, the call for the inclusion of key skills as a compulsory element of the curriculum has become stronger and stronger.

Educationalists have by and large supported this view. They have often stressed the need to equip pupils and students with a minimum standard of key skills to enable them to function in a society where even the least skilled jobs are dependent upon the ability to read, write and use simple arithmetic. Successive governments have also supported the more explicit emphasis upon key skills through primary, secondary and further education. The development of the National Literacy Strategy following the election of 'New Labour' in 1997, with its targets for improving the standard of literacy of 11-year-olds, is an obvious example of the strategy to raise skill levels throughout the educational system.

Its parallel in the post-compulsory sector, namely the Skills for Life Strategy, has set demanding targets for the improvement of adult literacy and numeracy.

Key skills on the three main post-16 qualification routes

The extent to which key skills are developed and assessed varies on the three main routes of the National Qualifications Framework. As stated earlier, they are integral to GNVQ programmes. On GCSE and GCE A-level courses there has been strong encouragement from the Government, QCA and other bodies to build key skills into the 14–19 curriculum. There have also been some incremental changes in the regulatory frameworks of GCSE and GCE A-level. For example, from 1996 onwards GCSE English results have shown separately the student's level of achievement in the oral use of the language. Following the Dearing Review in 1996, the GCE A-level boards worked collaboratively to identify ways of strengthening the development of communication, numeracy and IT in the subject cores. At a local level, many sixth form and FE colleges have introduced key skills for all of their full-time students through the creative use of the National Record of Achievement and through gaining separate accreditation via such national awards as ASDAN (Award Scheme Development and Accreditation Network).

National Training Organisations (NTOs), which have been replaced with Sector Skills Councils (SSCs), are responsible for setting the occupational standards for NVQs. They carefully consider the applications of communication, numeracy and information technology to their occupational areas and then build elements of key skills into their occupational standards. For example, trainees in the hairdressing and beauty industries develop communication skills through a strong emphasis upon customer care techniques. The emphasis upon key skills is most clearly evident in Level 3 NVQs linked to the Apprenticeship Schemes that combine on- and off-the-job training for 16-year-old school leavers who decide to opt for work-based training rather than stay in full-time education. Key skills at Levels 1 and 2 are also an important part of other government training schemes such as Entry to Employment.

Assessing key skills: the main issues

Three main issues have dominated the discussion about how to develop and assess key skills:

- *Should the concept of key skills also include other areas, such as study skills, interpersonal skills and modern foreign languages?* In addition to the three central skill units, there are other optional units available, such as 'Working with People' and 'Managing your own Learning'. These focus more strongly upon interpersonal and study skills, which many educationalists argue are fundamental to student success because they are about teaching learners to learn and interact successfully with others. Other subject specialists have made a strong case for design and creativity skills to be included in the curriculum because of the need to encourage innovation and enterprise in a competitive global economy. There appears to be a general consensus that communication, numeracy and information technology are fundamental. There is less agreement about what other skills should form core elements of the curriculum.

- *Should key skills be taught and assessed separately from the rest of the curriculum or developed as a natural and integral part of the subject and occupational areas students are specialising in?* In the work situation, key skills arise in the context of everyday problems. They are almost invariably related to a specific occupational issue. In the teaching or training situation, there is also a strong case for building key skills into the subject or occupational area in which the student is primarily interested. This has been the main thrust of key skills development. There has been some concern, however, that, unless key skills are separately assessed, there will be no guarantee that students have really achieved the required standard. In 1997–8 QCA, in conjunction with the awarding bodies, developed a pilot project during which a selection of students was entered for external tests in key skills. Following this pilot, the Government decided (DfEE, 1999b) that a new award covering the three key skills would be available from the year 2001. Since then, students on different qualifications have combined key skills with their courses and gained separate accreditation for them.

- *Should students be required to take key skills units at the same level as the overall qualification, for example Level 3 key skills with a Level 3 qualification?* On GNVQ programmes there has been an automatic assumption that students should take key skills at the same level as the course on which they are enrolled. In reality, this has often proved a very demanding requirement. Level 3 numeracy, for example, is technically above GCSE standard. For students on GNVQ programmes in such areas as Art and Design or Leisure and Tourism, it is debatable whether it is essential to take Application of Number to this level. In the many Apprenticeship programmes, by contrast, the level of key skills is based upon the occupational context in which the training is taking place. Thus an engineering student would be expected to take key skills in numeracy to a higher level than a student on a hairdressing course. The latter may prove a more sensible approach, providing all students achieve a recognised baseline in all of the three main skills – perhaps at Level 2.

Case Study: *Review of key skills on the GCE A/AS-level programme at Greybourne College of FE*

Greybourne College of FE runs a large GCE A/AS-level programme for full-time 16–19 students. Over 300 students are enrolled and there is a choice of over 25 subjects. Each student has had 16 timetabled teaching hours per week with 14 hours devoted to GCE A-level teaching and two hours allocated for tutorials, key skills support and additional studies. The course leader has recently been involved in teaching on the College's AVCE programmes and been impressed by how much progress students have made through having to take key skills as part of their curriculum. She is concerned that the performance of the GCE A-level students on the key skills tests are poor and this reflects the fact that neither A-level students nor teachers take key skills seriously. The local university is keen to enter into a compact arrangement with the college under which it would give preferential treatment to GCE and AVCE applicants who have gained key skills units. There are obviously a number of practical issues to resolve, for example how to build key skills into the timetable and how to secure additional resources for the initiative.

ACTIVITY

For this activity, you will have to assume the role of the GCE A-level course leader at Greybourne College, described in the case study above. Your task is to present an initial proposal for reviewing how key skills are taught and assessed on the full-time GCE A-level programme (use your imagination here). You will have to present the case for review convincingly, as you are aware that several of your colleagues who teach GCE A-level subject regard key skills as a waste of time. Try to draw upon some comparative experience, for example from other colleges that you have encountered that successfully incorporate key skills as part of their GCE A-level programme. Once you have developed your ideas you should present them to your colleagues on the Cert. Ed. or PGCE course.

More reforms to 14–19 qualifications?

No sooner had the new AVCE, VGCSE and AS- and A-level qualifications been introduced, than a more fundamental review of future 14–19 qualifications was embarked upon, under the chairmanship of the former Chief Inspector for Schools, Mike Tomlinson. In 2004 the final report of the Working Group on 14–19 Reform (Tomlinson, 2004) was presented. This report and the many papers that were presented in its wake are an enormous resource for FE teachers. Tomlinson sought to create a more coherent framework for 14–19 learning by proposing a four-level diploma framework that can incorporate some existing qualifications (GCE, AVCE etc.) and has a number of common elements.

Diplomas would be awarded at four levels – advanced, intermediate, foundation and entry – and be based upon a common structure and components of core and main learning:

- The *core learning* would ensure that students attained minimum standards in functional mathematics, functional literacy, communication and ICT. Each young person would complete an extended project that would replace many other forms of assessed coursework. Students would also be required to develop wider knowledge and skills, for example knowledge related to being a citizen, and would be encouraged to take part in wider activities such as work experience and sports.

- The *main learning* would be based on students' main qualification goals, for example vocational, academic or applied awards or some combination of these. Over time current qualifications would be based on a unified system of credits, so that it would be possible for students to select units from individual qualifications, to combine them and still satisfy the demands of the diploma.

The Tomlinson Report adopted a different approach to viewing qualifications. Historically, qualifications have been viewed in a holistic way. If they were broken down into individual modules or units, it was the qualification as a whole that gave meaning to the parts. For example, the units making up a GCE AS-level only make sense as components of the overall award. Tomlinson argued the case for a more flexible system of qualifications, one that would allow students to combine different sorts of qualifications, for example a GCSE with a vocational module. In a more flexible system, the individual units become the critical building blocks (credits) towards a wider award – in the case of Tomlinson that is the diploma award. In its response to Tomlinson in 2005, the Government (DfES, 2005) rejected the notion of an overarching diploma that would embrace both vocational and academic qualifications. It decided to preserve GCSE and GCE awards, at least for the short term, whilst rationalising the plethora of vocational qualifications by adopting a series of 14 vocational diplomas based upon Tomlinson.

ASSESSMENT AS A DIAGNOSTIC TOOL

One of the most critical decisions made in post-compulsory education is to match the learning programme to the learner's needs. It is obviously vital that each student is placed on a course to which she or he is suited and on which she or he has a good chance of success. Assessment plays a critical role when it is used as a diagnostic tool. Each time a piece of student's work is marked, the teacher is diagnosing the positive and negative features of it in order to help the student improve performance. More often, however, diagnostic assessment is associated with some form of testing to establish the aptitudes and attitudes of individuals, before they start a course.

Ecclestone (1996) distinguishes between three ways in which teachers and managers of institutions use assessment as a diagnostic tool:

- for initial guidance to help learners to identify correctly their existing achievements and make informed decisions about which course to select
- to assess a learner's needs for different types of support, such as literacy, numeracy and study skills, through diagnostic tests and initial screening
- to recognise and accredit learners' prior achievements through a structured process commonly referred to as the accreditation of prior learning (APL).

In the following two sections the latter two uses of diagnostic assessment will be explored further. The relationship between assessment and more general student guidance and support is discussed fully in Chapter 9.

Initial screening and diagnostic assessment

It has become standard practice in many colleges and training organisations to assess students' requirements for additional learning support during induction or at an early stage of the course. The LSC, which funds all colleges and some other institutions, provides additional funding for this provision. The funding system also rewards colleges that are able to retain students and enable them to gain their target qualification. Hence, colleges have a vested financial interest in ensuring students receive all the support they need to succeed. There are other publicly funded training programmes, such as those falling under the apprenticeship programmes, that build in an element of financial support to assist training organisations in providing learning support.

Screening for basic skills

The Basic Skills Agency (BSA), a government-funded national agency, defines basic skills as the ability to read, write and speak in English and use mathematics at a level necessary to function and progress at work and in society in general. Various reports have indicated that about 1 in 5 people over the age of 16 in the UK have serious problems with reading, writing, understanding or speaking English or with basic mathematics (BSA, 1994). For example, they are unable to cope with everyday tasks such as using a telephone directory, filling in an application form, calculating their change or reading a bus timetable. Basic skills are related to key skills in that they cover literacy, oracy and numeracy. The important distinction is that students with poor basic skills have an extremely low level of capability in these areas. If we were to attempt to identify their level of achievement it would be likely to be at or below Level 1 in the National Qualifications Framework.

Most colleges and some training providers screen their full-time students and trainees to identify their need for additional support with basic skills. A wide variety of initial assessment and diagnostic assessment tools is used, including electronic instruments. Many colleges have developed their own mechanisms for screening students. For example, they customise the tests to particular subjects or occupational areas to make them more accessible to students. In some cases, colleges are now using machine readable tests that enable feedback to be available to teachers and students within 24 hours.

Additional learning support

Initial screening alone is obviously only the first step in providing comprehensive support to respond to students identified as being weak in literacy and/or numeracy. Colleges make use of a wide range of strategies in providing additional learning support for students who have been diagnosed as needing additional help. Some of these involve:

- providing specialist printed and computer-based learning materials for staff and student use, often in specialist rooms
- giving additional tuition to students, on a one-to-one or group basis
- having specialist learning support staff work with students during 'normal' classroom sessions to help them with reading, note-taking, etc.

Evidence from FE colleges (Martinez, 1998) shows a significant increase in retention and achievement rates for students who receive additional learning support of the types described above. The fictitious case study below illustrates one approach to organising initial diagnostic assessment and follow-up learning support.

Case Study: *Learning support at Greybourne College of FE*

The college introduced initial testing for all full-time students over a decade ago, using the standard BSA screening instrument. A group of specialist staff manage the screening process and mark the tests. Tutors are provided with a list showing the performance level reached by their group of students within a week of the test being administered. It is left then to the tutors to make arrangements for students identified as being 'at risk' to receive additional support sessions in the college's specialist learning support facility.

Last year, the success of this system was evaluated. The main finding was that only 30 per cent of students regularly attend the additional support sessions. Student feedback indicates that students attach a great stigma to being identified as weak in numeracy and literacy. Most have already 'failed' mathematics and English at school and have come to college because they wanted to specialise in a new vocational area.

As a result of this review, the college has refined its approach to screening and providing additional learning support. New tests, based upon examples drawn from students' vocational specialisms, have been developed. The monitoring of students' attendance at support sessions has been introduced. Early analysis shows that over 70 per cent of students are now attending and that completion rates on many courses have improved by over 10 per cent.

ACTIVITY

Using your own or teaching practice college as a resource, investigate how initial screening for basic skills is organised and what follow-up support is provided for students. Try to arrange some discussions with staff and students involved in this provision. Once you have completed this investigation, compare your findings with fellow-students on your Cert. Ed. or PGCE programme.

Accreditation of prior learning

Accreditation of prior learning (APL) is a process through which previous experiential learning or qualifications can be given credit. It is based upon the simple idea that formal education should diagnose and recognise individuals' existing capabilities and not require them to repeat learning and assessment in areas in which they are already competent. APL has been developed particularly for adult learners who bring to the learning situation capabilities derived from their experiences at work and in the community. The development of procedures to recognise adults' prior achievements accords with the strong emphasis upon lifelong learning echoed in the Government's 1988 Green Paper *The Learning Age* (DfEE, 1998c). The provision of APL by different providers is a way of linking structured educational experience with informal learning. In his classic report for the Royal Society of Arts, *Learning Pays*, Christopher Ball (1991) states:

it is a central theme ... that the best individual learning combines informal and structured experience, and is as far as possible self-directed. Teaching is like nursing, with a little care most adults can preserve their health and continue learning on their own initiative.

Ball (1991: 10)

APL has been developed most fully for NVQ programmes because they are strongly work-related, modular in design and expressed in terms of learning outcomes. It is obviously easier to assess and accredit a unit of a qualification where the outcomes can be matched against the evidence an adult learner brings from their experience outside education.

Implementing APL procedures

Where APL has been developed by colleges or training providers, there are four main stages leading to accreditation:

1 *Initial publicity and guidance* Given that APL is a process that has been designed especially with adult learners in mind, publicity is needed to draw them back into formal education and training. Where APL procedures have been developed for specialist occupational groups, such as nurses, slogans such as 'adding up the past' have been used by the awarding bodies (English National Board for Nurses, Midwifery and Health Visiting, 1992) to convey the essence of the idea. Following the initial publicity, careful counselling by staff who have a general understanding of APL procedures is needed so that students are encouraged to have their existing capabilities recognised as part of gaining a qualification.

2 *Development of evidence to support claim* As stated earlier in the chapter, assessment of NVQ qualifications is based upon the candidate submitting evidence to prove that she or he is competent against explicit performance criteria. This process also applies to candidates seeking accreditation for competencies they have acquired at work. In most colleges, selected teaching staff will assist students to develop a claim in the form of a portfolio for assessment. This will usually be based upon a combination of direct and indirect evidence. Examples of direct evidence include existing certificates or licences that prove that the learner has undergone a course of training and samples of the individual's own work. Examples of indirect evidence are based upon testimonials and references from the candidate's supervisor or colleagues at work.

3 *Assessment of claim* A member of staff trained in NVQ assessment techniques will make a decision on whether the evidence the candidate has provided meets the performance criteria for the award and is sufficient to demonstrate competence. Often the candidate will be interviewed by the assessor to confirm particular evidence.

4 *Accreditation* This will follow acceptance of the evidence by the assessor and agreement from the internal and external verifiers of the course. If the learner is successful in gaining accreditation, this will allow progression on to the next stage of the qualification without any need to undertake a taught programme.

THE FORMAL ASPECTS OF ASSESSMENT

It will be clear from the previous sections of this chapter that many aspects of assessment involve formal procedures. This is a result of the link between assessment and accreditation – the fact that summative assessment is usually followed by the award of a qualification. As a teacher or trainer, you will have to be familiar with the assessment regulations of the courses on which you teach. You are also likely to participate in assessment boards and attend meetings with external examiners and verifiers. At an institutional level, senior managers will want to ensure that the assessment carried out by staff accords with the conditions laid down by the national awarding bodies and that students are treated fairly. In the following sections, the principles governing formal assessment are first outlined; then there is a brief summary of the operation of assessment regulations and assessment boards.

Principles underlying formal assessment

Nasta (1994) identifies five key principles that form the basis of the formal procedures for assessing a course: *accessibility, consistency, comprehensiveness, external standards* and *redress*. Taken together these normally underpin the rules governing assessment. These principles are briefly described below and then related to the practical task of guiding students about assessment regulations.

Accessibility

Perhaps the most fundamental principle of good assessment is that it should aim to be transparent. This means that the learner has right of access to all information on how she or he is to be assessed. The most common way of communicating this information to the learner is through a student handbook, which is written in user-friendly language and is made available to students before the start of the course. For many providers, ensuring that assessment is accessible is a fundamental aspect of Equality of Opportunity. The greater emphasis upon openness as part of the Freedom of Information Act is another reason for making assessment accessible.

Consistency

It should be self-evident that the rules assessors use to test students need to reflect the objectives of the course or programme. It would be inconsistent, for example, for assessors to make use of a percentage-based marking system for assessing a criterion-referenced NVQ or GNVQ programme. It is important that all members of the team of teachers on a course need to agree a consistent approach to such issues as grading and the timing and nature of individual assessments. Most external validating bodies will provide detailed guidance on assessment, and it is vitally important that the team study this guidance carefully and agree a common approach.

Comprehensiveness

This assessment process and regulations should endeavour to cover all eventualities. Thus the regulations should define how students will normally progress through the different stages/components of the course or programme. Procedures governing failure, referral, late submission, absence or illness should be made explicit to students. The regulations should also make clear who is responsible for different elements of assessment, when assessments are to be marked and what rights the student and the assessors have.

External standards

For both the course team and the student it is important that assessment relates student achievement to the external standards required by the award. The assessment regulations should therefore encompass the requirements of the external validating body. The relationship between the assessment procedure and the external standards will normally be monitored through a process of external monitoring or verification, involving an external verifier or moderator, usually appointed by the validating body. It is important that the course team make every effort to create clear and effective channels of communication with their moderator to ensure that proposed assessment is compatible with the external standard.

Redress

Well-designed assessment procedures should contain precise guidance on how students can seek redress in situations where they consider there has been maladministration or injustice in the assessment process. Most of the validating bodies now require that centres clearly specify how they will handle student appeals, in a way that protects both the interests of the student and allows for neutral arbitration where conflict remains unresolved. Clearly, internal assessors will attempt to ensure that conflict is resolved long before any appeals arise by defining processes at the pre-appeal stage that avert such situations.

ACTIVITY

It is common practice for course teams to give students a course handbook, early in the course. This usually contains a comprehensive outline of the assessment procedures and regulations applying to the course. It will outline the balance between internal and external assessment, the number and types of assignments, when they are due and a host of other details.

Using your own college as an example, try to obtain two student handbooks. Compare and contrast them and then decide which you find most helpful, and why.

Assessment regulations and the student handbook

If you completed the above activity, you will have probably found that the principles adumbrated in the above section are encapsulated in the handbook. The handbook should have included a set of assessment regulations, that is rules governing the marking and assessment of student work. Assessment regulations will normally cover:

- how modules and assignments are graded
- the timetable for assignments and coursework
- conventions governing marking and the return of coursework
- procedures for dealing with non-completion, referred student work and compensation

- the role of the examinations board and how moderation and verification will be applied
- how academic appeals against marking will be processed
- procedures for investigating and deciding upon allegations of cheating and/or plagiarism
- provision to be made for students with learning difficulties and/or disabilities
- the award of credit for partial achievement.

A note on plagiarism

Plagiarism occurs when a student takes someone else's words or ideas and presents them as their own – without acknowledging the source. It includes a student:

- presenting material from books, journals or from the web as their own
- copying the work of another student and presenting it as their own
- collaborating with another student when an assignment specifies that it requires the work of an individual
- submitting substantial sections of a previous assignment as a new piece of work.

It is a growing problem, partly due to the growth of the web, from which material can be cut and pasted into a Word file in a matter of seconds. At a more serious level there is a growing 'industry' of web sites that specialise in the sale of assignments to students. Clearly, if there were no demand, there would be no supply! Hopefully, in most cases, however, plagiarism will occur at a more accidental level, with a student merely forgetting to cite the source of their material.

Plagiarism is a serious offence and a college will usually have a clear policy that both defines what plagiarism is, and the consequences for students found guilty of it. From a teacher's perspective, it is important to know the policy and to ensure that your students know it too. You should be alert to plagiarism when reading student assignments and know what the college expects you to do if you are suspicious that plagiarism has occurred. On a more positive note, it is worth stressing to students that striving to avoid plagiarism can help them to improve the quality of their work. For example, all of the following should produce a more focused and concise prose:

- avoid extensive quotes, and instead use paraphrasing or summarising
- use a thesaurus when paraphrasing to identify alternative words
- ensure that all sources are cited
- when quoting directly from a source, cite the reference accurately (for example, using the Harvard system).

ACTIVITY

Your own Cert. Ed. or PGCE course should be a model of good practice. Ask your course director for a full copy of the assessment regulations and appeals procedure. Examine them carefully and evaluate the extent to which they reflect fully the five underlying principles of accessibility, consistency, comprehensiveness, external standards and redress. Look in particular at how your regulations deal with the issue of plagiarism. Discuss your conclusions with fellow students on your course.

Review Questions

1   Identify from your own experience examples of formative, summative and ipsative assessment.
2   Compare and contrast the main features of assessment on NVQs, AVCEs and GCE A-levels.
3   Outline two uses of diagnostic assessment in post-compulsory education.
4   Give examples of how guidance on assessment is given in a student handbook on courses.

SUMMARY

- Good assessment is integral to successful teaching and learning.
- Initial assessment is critical for identifying students' needs and matching them to suitable courses.
- Skilful use of formative, summative and ipsative assessment is a central competence for teachers in FE and adult education.
- Post-16 qualifications can be differentiated by the varying emphasis placed on knowledge, skills and competencies.

Suggested Further Reading

Ecclestone, K. (1996) *How to Assess the Vocational Curriculum*, London: Kogan Page
    Provides a very full analysis of methods of assessment in post-16 education.

Tomlinson, M. (2004) *Summary of the Final Report of the Working Group on 14–19 Reform*, London: DfES.
    This is the most recent and most thorough analysis of assessment and qualifications and proposals for long-term reform.

4 CURRICULUM PLANNING AND DESIGN

Objectives

After reading this chapter, you should be able to:

- give a definition of curriculum as it relates to your own teaching practice
- identify the curriculum model or models that best describe your practice
- describe those aspects of your role that are concerned with curriculum development
- write and prepare statements of aims and objectives, in relation to lesson plans and schemes of work
- identify and distinguish the elements of knowledge, skills, competence and capability, in relation to academic and vocational curricula
- demonstrate familiarity with a range of assessment and evaluation practices in relation to various curriculum models.

In Chapter 3, the functions of assessment in teaching and learning were outlined, together with an account of accreditation within the framework of post-compulsory qualifications. In this chapter, we will be concerned with the ways in which assessment and accreditation are part of a more general process of curriculum planning and design. However, not only assessment, but teaching and learning methods, which are discussed in Chapter 5, all come within a wider framework of what could be called curriculum issues.

You could begin to understand what curriculum means by thinking of it as the way in which the aims, objectives, content, methods and assessment of learning are *mutually related* to one another. An example of a curriculum issue would be, therefore, what kind of assessment would be appropriate to what kind of qualification, or what kind of teaching methods would be appropriate to what kind of learning objective?

Although there is a vast literature about curriculum, its main meaning is concerned with *the role of the teacher in the organisation of the student's learning*. This chapter begins, therefore, by looking in more detail at what we mean by 'organisation' in this context, before going on to specific examples from the kinds of courses and qualifications described elsewhere in this book. 'Organisation' is rather an umbrella term for teachers' planning and design activities, so a consideration of general principles and concepts must come first.

GENERAL PRINCIPLES OF CURRICULUM

To begin this section, we need to address issues of the definition of 'curriculum', since teachers (and learners) often have quite different things in mind.

> ### ACTIVITY
>
> Write down your own working definition of 'curriculum', one that seems most closely related to your own experience as both a teacher and a learner.

In fact, quite a range of alternative definitions are possible. In the first place, how much did you include in your own definition? Did it include, for example, anything more than statements about aims, subjects, methods or assessment? Or did it include the management, learning and student support systems, or the institution itself? Your definition may have been relatively broad or narrow.

A broad definition

In its broadest sense, the curriculum stands for just about everything that happens in the educational setting. It describes all the elements of the learning process that the student experiences. And if we take account of the various factors that *influence* learning, or make it possible, this can obviously include buildings, staff, recruitment policy, management and support systems, and so on.

In other words, at its broadest, 'curriculum' becomes just another word for 'education', and it is probably not a very useful way of thinking about it. Nevertheless, it does draw our attention to two major features of the idea:

- Curriculum stands for an *educational*, or an educationist's, view of learning. It represents the professional role in the organisation and management of students' learning.
- It is not realistic to take *too* narrow a view of the educational process, since there are many factors involved in effective learning.

Increasingly nowadays, a much wider view of the curriculum is taken, which takes in what used to be called the 'hidden curriculum'. This simply stood for all those outcomes of learning that were wider than the merely cognitive or academic or skills-related outcomes, but which were desired by teachers, parents, employers and learners themselves. These indirect, unintentional or even accidental outcomes of the teaching and learning process are much more highlighted now by parents, employers and the government. So the 'hidden' curriculum of social, economic and personal learning has ceased to be 'hidden' and now contains the kind of personal learning needed for effective citizenship and employability. Professional planning and implementation of the curriculum therefore needs to take account of these developments, not least in relation to achievement and assessment.

A narrow definition

A common way of defining the curriculum is as the body of knowledge or skills that the teacher or the institution intends to be transmitted. The National Curriculum for schools, for example, is structured mostly around subject areas, and levels or stages of achievement, with less, but fast-growing, attention to actual teaching methods.

ACTIVITY

Reconsider your response to the first activity on page 78. Can you make any meaningful distinctions between terms such as 'curriculum', 'course of study', 'programme', 'syllabus', and so on? Consider the appropriateness of these terms in relation to:

a) your own subject area or areas
b) the provision of your own college or institution
c) the wider personal and social outcomes for learners.

The narrower definition of curriculum, therefore, usually focuses upon the formal provision of courses, together with indications of teaching and assessment methods. It reflects a view of education as the planned *intention* to bring about certain learning outcomes usually in a context of formal, or public, *provision*.

It is important to understand that the curriculum is sometimes a contested feature of education, and can be a matter of public and political concern and debate. This is because there are different conceptions of where it comes from and what it should consist of.

Ideologies of curriculum

As has been indicated, there is an extensive literature on the curriculum, and you could look into this for yourself. There is only space here to look at three examples of alternative ways of thinking about the curriculum. They all reflect the kinds of 'foundation discipline' knowledge introduced in Chapter 2, and embody philosophical or sociological assumptions about knowledge.

- Philosophers such as Hirst and Peters (1970) have argued that the curriculum represents the basic structure of human *knowledge* itself, which falls into certain divisions or categories, such as natural and social science, the arts and humanities, and so on. Each of these categories of knowledge has its own logic and forms of meaning.
- Sociologists such as Lawton (1975) have argued that the curriculum is a selection from the *culture* of society, and that this in turn means that it is related to social *class*. From such an analysis comes the idea of the curriculum as an instrument of *social control* (Bernstein, 1971–5; Young, 1971).
- Educationists such as Jarvis (1995) have explored the distinction between what has been described as the *classical* and the *romantic* models of the curriculum. Briefly, the classical model is a subject-centred or knowledge-based curriculum, whereas the romantic model is a learner-centred curriculum, shaped by the needs and choices of individual learners. We shall see later in this chapter that the vocational curriculum is moving away from its traditional form as a structured course towards a much more student-centred learning programme.

> **ACTIVITY**
>
> Taking the case of your own subject area, try to identify and distinguish between those aspects of curriculum that reflect:
>
> a) the structure of knowledge or skill involved in the subject
> b) the social or cultural values that may be relevant
> c) the degree to which you would say the curriculum is classical (subject-centred) or romantic (learner-centred).

Aims, content, methods and evaluation

One of the first, and highly influential models of the curriculum was set out by Ralph W. Tyler, and this has become known as the *objectives model*, based upon the kinds of behaviourist learning theory that were introduced in Chapter 2. Tyler posed four fundamental questions for establishing the meaning of curriculum (Tyler, 1949: 1):

- What educational purposes should the school seek to attain?
- What educational experiences can be provided that are likely to attain these purposes?
- How can these educational experiences be effectively organised?
- How can we determine whether these purposes are being attained?

This is the most familiar model, which represents the narrower, or more technical concept of curriculum, and it is the one that most educational professionals embrace, in some form or other. It is usually represented diagrammatically as in Figure 4.1.

This way of thinking about the curriculum suggests it is based upon *logical sequence* and *rational planning* on the part of the educator, so that, given the overall aims, the *appropriate* learning objectives follow, together with the methods and forms of assessment and evaluation. Theories of the school curriculum have been put forward on the basis of taxonomies (formal classifications) of learning objectives (Bloom, 1956–64; Gagné, 1977), and these remain an important source of the behaviourist approach in post-compulsory education too.

Bloom's taxonomy

The idea of constructing a taxonomy, or classification, of learning objectives grew out of the felt need of teachers to have some kind of scientific or objective way of knowing that students had actually learned something. As you may remember from Chapter 2, behaviourist learning theory is regarded as providing the clearest indication that learning has occurred, simply because it is based upon the measurement of observed changes in behaviour.

Bloom put forward three major domains of behavioural change that education may bring about, each of which was subdivided into further categories:

- the *cognitive* (knowledge, comprehension, application, analysis and synthesis)
- the *affective* (receiving, responding, valuing, organising and conceptualising, and categorising by value)
- the *psychomotor* (relating to categories of manual and physical skill).

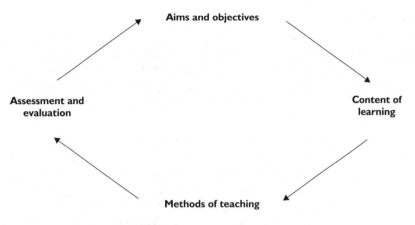

Figure 4.1 *Rational planning model for lessons*

Bloom's taxonomy has shared in the general criticism of behaviourist learning theory, and it has also been criticised because the distinctions between these domains are merely formal, and are not clear-cut in practice. Nevertheless, the emphasis upon objectives, outcomes and competencies in qualifications and assessment, means that teachers still need to produce some kind of *objective evidence* for learning on the part of their students. So Bloom's taxonomy continues to influence the whole process of writing learning objectives and lesson plans.

As you have seen in the previous chapter on assessment and qualifications, there is a wide range of assessment methods in the system of post-compulsory qualifications. But most qualifications, with varying emphasis, require the demonstration of elements of knowledge, skill, capability and competence. And as was indicated above, there is a greater reflection now of the wider personal, social and economic skills that are regarded as desirable outcomes of the learning process.

ACTIVITY

Take any course that you teach, and analyse it from the perspective of Tyler's rational planning model of the curriculum and Bloom's taxonomy of learning objectives. This means that you should be able to demonstrate the relation between aims, objectives, content, methods and evaluation, in the case of Tyler, and between cognitive, affective and psychomotor objectives in the case of Bloom's taxonomy. In terms of current policy and practice, what are the shortcomings of this rather narrow model of the curriculum?

We have already seen that, just as there are a variety of assessment methods, there are a variety of models of the curriculum. The rational planning model of Tyler, the classical or subject-based model and the romantic or learner-centred model have all been introduced. But there are other ways of modelling the curriculum.

The content model

Sometimes what has been referred to as the classical model of the curriculum is called the content model. This is because it focuses on the content of learning, that is, what things are actually learned by the learners. This is often associated in the model with knowledge and understanding, and so the outcomes of this kind of curriculum are rather broader and less tightly defined than in the case of a curriculum of behavioural outcomes.

The problem is one of how you define 'behaviour' and 'outcomes'? If, for example, you teach an academic subject at A- or AS-level, or an access course with an important element of personal development involved in it, what are behavioural outcomes for purposes of assessment? In the case of teaching literature, or history, for example, or other academic subjects, it may be that the outcomes for the learner are not behavioural but attitudinal (or affective, in Bloom's taxonomy). This means they can be measured, but not in the same way as other kinds of outcomes, such as those to do with skill or competence. This is why Bloom's taxonomy has been criticised. Many subject areas cannot be regarded as wholly one thing or the other: they involve a range of outcomes of all kinds. An outcome of learning about other cultures may be learning about oneself, but how do you distinguish between these as outcomes? Similarly, learning an applied skill in engineering may also have an outcome in learning about responsibility for health and safety. The rise to prominence of skills as major curriculum focus raises questions for all traditional models of the curriculum.

ACTIVITY

Take again the subject you considered in attempting the activity on page 80 and try to identify any learning outcomes that do not seem to be expressed in behavioural terms. In the case of such outcomes, how do you know they have been achieved? This is particularly an issue when measuring the personal, or motivational achievements of learners, where so many subjective factors are inevitably involved.

It is clear that the issue of learning outcomes is problematic, especially if the curriculum is thought of in terms of its content, or the subjects or skills or competencies that go to make it up. An alternative curriculum model focuses less upon the content or subjects, and more on the relations of teaching and learning.

The process model

This model of the curriculum sees it not as a body of knowledge or skills to be learned, but as a *process of learning*, involving learners in some kind of relationship with what they are learning, or with teachers, or with other learners. You could say that the process model is concerned not with what students learn, but with *how* they learn. So it focuses much more on the process of learning itself. This, in turn, appears to offer much more scope for achieving the kinds of personal or motivational outcomes mentioned above.

The process model gives much more responsibility to the teacher in the organisation of the student's learning. This means that it is up to the teacher to determine the appropriate aims, objectives, methods and assessment schemes in the context of the student's personal/learning needs and the kind of subject involved.

ACTIVITY

Again taking the course you considered in the last two activities, try to identify elements of the content and the process curriculum models. To what extent is the course organised in terms of subject or skill outcomes, and to what extent is it organised in terms of the students' learning processes or personal needs?

Curriculum models such as these can be helpful in organising our thinking about practice, and in directing attention to the need for reflection on the part of the practitioner. But they remain abstractions, and you may have found it difficult to make the kind of purely formal distinctions that they are based on.

However, the process model does draw attention to the roles and responsibilities of teachers for organising their students' learning.

The role of the teacher in the curriculum process

There is a great deal of central control over education, in the form of prescribed syllabuses, and also in the form of the accreditation, validation and quality assurance systems, as well as teaching methods themselves. Nevertheless, teachers both as individuals and in teams still have a great deal of responsibility for the organisation of their students' learning. This is obviously true in the classroom, but it is also true of the curriculum development process in general. The rest of this chapter will therefore be concerned with some of the most central activities in curriculum design, development and evaluation. We begin with the situation of the individual teacher in the classroom, before addressing issues for the institution or the system.

PLANNING AND DESIGNING ACTIVITIES

In planning and designing activities for the curriculum, it is difficult to distinguish between individual and institutional processes. The planning and design of individual lessons must follow the same logic as that of the curriculum itself. All of these activities require statements of aims, objectives, content, assessment and evaluation. But we will begin with the individual lesson, and the formulation of aims and objectives that each of these requires.

Aims

We saw that, in the case of both Tyler's rational planning model and the process model of the curriculum, formulating aims is a central function of teaching. In the case of Tyler, aims are a statement of the educational purposes to be attained. In the case of the process model, formulating aims in relation to individual lessons is a central aspect of the teacher's role.

Statements of aims are *general* descriptions of the *intentions* or purposes of the lesson or the course itself. It is their generality that distinguishes them from objectives, which, as we shall see, need to be much more specific and related to behavioural outcomes. Here are some examples of statements of aims:

- to familiarise students with some historical views of the causes of the First World War
- to introduce a range of current initiatives in health education at the local level
- to outline the importance of effective communication skills in retail and leisure industry management
- to develop student confidence in the use of a variety of computer-based information sources
- to encourage independent learning and the capacity for self-directed study on the part of all students
- to raise awareness of the research possibilities created by computer modelling in economic theory.

The generality of these aims is conveyed by the language used: 'to familiarise'; 'to introduce'; 'to outline'; 'to develop'; 'to encourage'; 'to raise awareness'. These aims may all be thought of as rather vague, simply because there are different ways of deciding whether they have been achieved. Individual students may achieve them in different ways, or to different degrees.

ACTIVITY

Take any individual lesson that you have recently given, or are soon to give, and write out a statement of aims along the lines of the examples provided above. In what ways is the language of your statement 'general', and how could you tell whether or not individual students have achieved the intentions or purposes you formulated for the lesson?

In carrying out this activity you may find it helpful to refer back to the range of assessment methods introduced in Chapter 3.

Although statements of aims are by definition rather general, they are not arbitrary. In other words, they must make sense in relation to the curriculum as a whole. Here are three examples of factors that may influence the way aims are formulated:

- ideology
- the qualifications framework within which the course is located
- the learning needs of students.

Ideology

The ideology describes overall values of the educational context. Thus, teaching on an access course may lead to a stress upon such things as confidence, development and personal growth, so that the aims need to reflect such things as independence in learning. Or the course may be concerned more with technical skills and competencies, in which case the aims need to reflect more vocational purposes and intentions.

The qualifications framework

If you refer to the three main qualification routes for post-compulsory education, you should be able to relate each of these routes to general statements of aims for lessons and courses. Thus, in the case of the academic route, statements of aims will focus upon knowledge and understanding. In the work-based and training NVQ route, statements of aims will focus upon skill and competence. And in broader vocational contexts, such as apprenticeship courses, statements of aims will focus upon the application of underpinning knowledge to practice. If you look again at Table 2.2 (page 40), you should now be able to relate statements of aims both to learning theories and the types of courses that reflect them.

ACTIVITY

Refer back to Table 2.2 (page 40), and write a typical statement of aims for a lesson in each of the four categories of learning and courses:

a) competence/performance (NVQ)
b) knowledge/understanding (A- and AS-level)
c) personal growth (Access)
d) reflective practice (CPD).

Needs analysis

A third factor influencing the formulation of aims, especially in relation to courses, is the learning needs of the students. In fact, needs analysis is a fundamental feature of the curriculum development process as a whole. In the classroom situation, it is the learning needs of the individual student that have to be addressed. But in developing courses and programmes, there is a whole range of other needs factors that must be addressed, such as:

- changes in the systems of qualification or assessment
- the requirement for new skills or knowledge for employment
- new groups of potential learners emerging as a result of social change.

ACTIVITY

Take any course with which you are concerned as a teacher, and make a list of the kinds of needs it is intended to address. Apart from the learners themselves, what other groups or interested parties might you include in your list? In current jargon, who are the stakeholders in the needs analysis process?

Teaching, learning and assessment

Needs analysis can therefore take many forms. It should include an analysis of existing provision, for example. Many courses are developed as a result of someone identifying a 'gap in the market'. On the other hand, it is important to take account of the available *resources* – human, material and financial – which make course development possible or unrealistic.

In reviewing these aspects of the aims of course and curriculum development, we have seen that aims are general statements of purpose or intention that are formulated against a wider background of ideology, qualifications, needs analysis, resources, and so on. Figure 4.2 shows how a model of curriculum development can be developed from the more classroom-oriented curriculum model illustrated in Figure 4.1 (page 81).

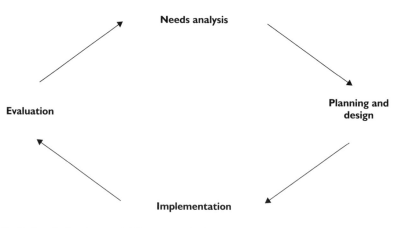

Figure 4.2 *Rational planning model for course design*

You should compare the two cycles shown in the two figures, because they represent a similar logic of development. For purposes of curriculum planning and design, the process begins with the identification of needs in relation to resources. The formulation of aims for individual classes and courses has to be put into this context. Nevertheless, aims themselves always need to be further broken down into learning objectives.

Writing learning objectives

We have already seen in this chapter that the curriculum models of Tyler and Bloom are based upon the idea of behavioural objectives, since they assume that evidence for learning can only be provided by changes in behaviour. Only these, unlike such things as knowledge, understanding and attitudes, can be objectively or scientifically measured, at least according to the behaviourist theory of learning.

If this is accepted, then it follows that we could only know whether our aims have been achieved by breaking them down into behavioural objectives.

ACTIVITY

In attempting the earlier activities in this chapter, you have already practised formulating aims and analysing them from various perspectives. Now go back to the list of six examples of statements of aims that were given at the beginning of the section on Aims above. In the case of each of them, break down the aim into a list of learning objectives that would need to be met in order to know whether or not the aim had been achieved.

Behavioural objectives

In attempting the last activity, you needed to distinguish what you understand as the aim of the lesson from the *learning objectives* into which you broke the aim down. So your objectives needed to be expressed in terms of what your students would have to be able to do. In other words, a learning objective is whatever a student can do *after* the lesson that she or he could not have done before.

For example, taking the aim 'to introduce a range of current initiatives in health education at the local level', the following might be examples of learning objectives required in order to achieve the aim.

At the end of the lesson, students should be able to:

• distinguish local from national initiatives in health education
• give examples of three local initiatives
• describe recent changes in the ways that health education is delivered.

These objectives all require students to *demonstrate* specific knowledge in relation to the general aim. But they could be broken down or subdivided even further, in order to produce more specific, sub-objectives:

• outline the main features of local health provision
• give an example of health education initiatives in schools
• identify the most important forms of health education publicity.

ACTIVITY

Taking the list of learning objectives you drew up for the last activity, consider the kinds of behaviour they required. Also, break them down further into the kinds of sub-objectives you think might be appropriate in each case.

Obviously, there is a limit to the kind of division and further subdivision of learning objectives that is possible, which is fixed by the content of the curriculum, in other words, by the amount of ground to be covered, or the requirements of the syllabus, or resources available. But looking at aims and objectives in this way reminds us that the role of the teacher is to plan the lesson as a whole, in which aims and objectives are related to both content and assessment of learning. Writing out statements of aims and objectives like this enables judgements to be made about the structure of the lesson and the appropriate kinds of assessment needed to ascertain whether or not aims are being achieved.

It is therefore necessary to be able to specify the conditions in which learning objectives are achieved or not. For example, it might be appropriate to specify a precise number of examples of health education initiatives, or forms of publicity, or types of campaign, or it might be appropriate to require students to gather information at first hand.

The essence of learning objectives based on behavioural principles is that they permit precise specifications of what students are required to be able to *do* as a result of the lesson, which they could not have done before. But, as we have seen, learning has other components as well as behavioural changes, and learning has other dimensions to it, such as knowledge, understanding and conceptualisation. The aim of a lesson may well include some grasp of general principles and their application to specific cases. Bloom's taxonomy of learning objectives included such things as knowledge, comprehension, application, analysis and synthesis. This therefore goes beyond learning facts and figures, or assimilating data, and suggests that a certain level of *understanding* is required. For example, in the case of academic subjects such as history or economics, an understanding is needed of the principles of historical or economic analysis, and not simply an accumulation of historical or economic facts.

Cognitive objectives

If we go back to the aim 'to familiarise students with some historical views of the causes of the First World War', what would be a list of appropriate learning objectives in this case?

ACTIVITY

Taking an example from your own subject teaching, try to identify the ways in which you might set out learning objectives based on *knowledge and understanding*, as distinguished from ones based upon behavioural changes.

You may have found the distinction difficult to make, because knowledge and understanding still need to be demonstrated in some way if effective learning has taken place.

Taking the example of the history of the First World War above, cognitive objectives may be of the following kind, corresponding to Bloom's categories:

- become familiar with the major nationalist movements in Europe at the end of the nineteenth century (knowledge)
- be aware of the nature of historical evidence (comprehension)
- distinguish the historical perspective from other ways of understanding (application)
- discriminate between a range of possible causes of the war (analysis)

- review the strengths and weaknesses of different historical accounts of the causes of the war (synthesis).

These are examples of objectives related to what Bloom would call the cognitive domain of learning. They still need to be expressed in words that convey student *activities*, such as listing, classifying, discriminating, arguing, justifying, and so on. But the intention of aims and objectives of this kind is to bring about knowledge and understanding, rather than simply observable changes in the behaviour of students.

The affective domain

What Bloom meant by this domain of learning was not simply knowledge and understanding but *values* and *attitudes*, and it is possible to incorporate this dimension into the formulation of aims and objectives. Specifically, this involves student activities in the realms of receiving, responding, valuing, organising and conceptualising, and categorising by value. Another way of putting all this is to say that learning involves *feelings* and *emotions* as much as behaviour, knowledge and understanding.

Getting students to adopt a certain attitude or feeling towards something they learn often enters into aims and objectives writing. For example, in the case of history, this may take the form of respect for evidence, or in the case of science subjects a respect for proof, or in arts subjects a positive valuing of alternative aesthetic responses. It is, in fact, difficult to envisage a set of aims and objectives entirely without some kind of affective dimension, unless they are wholly concerned with such things as competence or capability, and even here the context of learning may well involve some kind of value dimension. As we have seen, there are many 'affective' criteria built into present-day policy and practice, concerned with personal development, social living, citizenship, and so on.

ACTIVITY

In the case of typical learning objectives in your own subjects, try to identify and isolate those objectives that seem to you to involve some kind of affective dimension.

The National Curriculum for schools in England includes a framework for personal, social and health education, and citizenship, to prepare pupils for adult life. But it is also a good example of the way in which development may involve the construction of affective learning objectives, where attitudes and values are inseparable from the aims of the curriculum itself.

Having looked at the need for formulating aims and objectives, we now need to look at ways in which they feature in lesson plans and schemes of work.

Lesson plans

The teacher remains responsible for the organisation of learning activities in the classroom, laboratory or teaching workshop, and the individual lesson remains the basic building block of the curriculum. Whatever form it takes, the lesson must be planned in relation to the kinds of curriculum aims and objectives that have been outlined in this chapter.

There are many factors that determine the form that an individual lesson plan might take. These will be such things as:

- the position of the lesson in relation to the course as a whole
- the requirements of the syllabus in terms of ground to be covered
- the nature of the students' learning needs in relation to assessment
- the nature of the student body and range of learning styles
- time and material resources available
- links to other courses and students' learning.

You may be able to think of other factors that shape your individual lesson plans. However, there are standard ways of planning a lesson, and Table 4.1 provides a typical form. It is intended for the second of eight meetings of a class of 15 women returners on an access course, and the subject is 'The Family in Contemporary Britain'.

In particular, as was outlined earlier, learning objectives need to be specified by the teacher in relation to each aspect of the topic, and assessment evaluation would similarly need to be specific and to demonstrate in concrete terms exactly what learning had been achieved.

Table 4.1   *An example of a lesson plan*

Timing	Topic	Teacher activity	Student activity	Resources	Assessment evaluation
10 min.	Introduction: last week's video on the image of the family	Provide written questions on the video	Write answers then share in pairs and feed back	Handout from last week and question sheet	Report back (for under-standing and issues)
30 min.	Demographic family change themes: size, age, structure	Lecture with OHP statistics from Social Trends	Listen and question	OHP and copies of tables and graphs	Relevance of questions
30 min.	Our experience of change	Organise three groups and circulate	Three discussion groups: one per theme	Flip charts and pens	Report back
20 min.	Conclusion: contexting experience	Summarise points from groups and relate to demographic trends	Spokesperson reports back	Board for flip charts	Reports and evaluation form

ACTIVITY

After looking at this example of a lesson plan, try to construct what you think might be the aims and objectives of the course to which it belongs, and give examples of methods you would use to demonstrate learning.

This is just one way of constructing a lesson plan, but it incorporates the kind of detail that conveys the structure of the lesson, together with the kinds of learning activities designed to achieve the learning objectives appropriate to the aims of the course. A lesson plan should therefore reproduce the logical sequence and rational planning of student learning that is the teacher's responsibility.

Nowadays, the curriculum reflects a much wider range of elements, and a far wider range of teaching and learning activities than it once did. For example, open and distance learning, work-based and problem-based learning, flexible assessment and accreditation systems, modular courses, and so on. However, all of these continue to require the kind of planning that should underpin every individual lesson.

ACTIVITY

Take a recent lesson you have given, or one you are about to give, and compare your plan for it with the example given above. Are there any significant differences in the way you have organised your own lesson plan? If so, what are the circumstances that might make such differences necessary?

When student teachers are observed in the classroom, however, they will be required not only to have prepared their lesson plan, but also to have worked out a rationale for it in terms of such things as:

- the course in which the lesson occurs (for example, level or qualification)
- the nature of the student group (for example, A- or AS-level, or skills-based)
- the stage in the course reached by this lesson (introduction, revision)
- aims and objectives (behavioural, cognitive)
- resources (time, teaching and learning aids)
- assessment and evaluation (continuous, examination, project or other skills).

A lesson plan is meaningless unless it is contexted in this way. Nevertheless, there are some basic, common requirements, such as the content or ground to be covered in the lesson, the appropriateness and variety of teaching and learning activities, feedback and assessment systems, and so forth.

Just as an individual lesson needs to be planned along the lines of needs analysis, aims, objectives, methods, content, assessment and evaluation, and so on, so does a course of study itself. A *scheme of work* is therefore a statement of intention and organisation relating to the course as a whole, and it is therefore a major document of curriculum development.

Schemes of work

Whereas a lesson plan is intended for the teacher to plan a particular class or session, a scheme of work is intended to convey information about a course as a whole to the students likely to attend it. Table 4.2 shows an example of the kind of course structure into which the lesson plan at Table 4.1 might fit. It is organised according to the same kinds of activities, resources and assessments as the individual lesson plan itself.

Table 4.2   *An example of a scheme of work*

Week	Topic	Teacher activity	Student activity	Resources	Assessment evaluation
1	Introduction: the image of the family	Introductions: aims, methods, perspectives	Introductions: Group work	Introduction to resources video	Negotiation of student roles
2	Demographic changes	Lecture and organise groups	Written answers Group discussion	OHP and handout of tables, graphs	Questions and reports back
3	Changing roles and structures	Lecture on 'role'	Buzz-groups and presentations	Handout and reading for next week	Feedback on lecture
4	Work and the family	Lecture on the patterns of work	Examples for group discussion	Flipcharts and handouts	Discuss progress
5	Consumption lifestyle and the family	Present case studies	Discuss case studies in groups: feedback	Flipcharts and video	Evaluate video
6	Changing family Roles of men	Lecture: chair presentations	Syndicates report flipcharts	Handout: possible visiting speaker Materials for next week	Interesting speaker?
7	Politics of the family	Introduce theme: prepare debate	Organise form of the debate	Arrange room: e.g for next week	Assess the debate
8	Alternative family	Scenarios: return to 'image'	Buzz-groups: plenary discussion	Media examples	Evaluation forms

So there are common principles underlying both lesson planning and designing courses or schemes of work. The next sections outline the kinds of general principles that underpin the planning of both individual lessons and schemes of work.

Contextual factors

These relate to the general background of your planning and design activities, but it is important to bear them in mind, because they may well determine whether or not a course runs, or whether a lesson is successful. They also represent the kinds of factors that affect decisions about the validation or revalidation of your courses. Here are some broad categories:

- *Needs analysis* This should include the organisational, management and institutional context in which a course is located. Colleges represent a wide variety of educational provision, catering for a wide range of subjects, qualifications and students. So you need to consider whether a course belongs in the kind of institution you belong to, or whether it would be inappropriate for some reason or another.
- *The general philosophy or ideology of the institution* For example, Greybourne College of FE, Greybourne Sixth Form College and Greybourne Adult and Community Education Service represent different sectors and types of educational provision, not just different organisational and institutional sites. They exist for a different balance of vocational, academic and personal learning needs.
- *The qualifications and assessment framework*, as described in Chapter 3. Schemes of work have to be related to this framework, in terms of key or core skills, progression levels, assessment practices, and so on. They need to provide information about how the course will be assessed in relation to the qualification or learning outcomes it is intended to produce
- *The kinds of students being catered for*, in terms of their numbers, whether or not the range of learning needs is great, whether there are special learning needs to be met, or what kinds of support might need to be provided. The students on the course may all have fairly common needs, but there may be diversity in terms of their general programme at the college, and therefore it may be necessary to be aware of other courses that they may be following or that may be relevant.
- *Management, communication and information systems*, especially with regard to college policies such as equal opportunities or inclusive learning, are relevant to the design of a course. For example, in terms of validation and revalidation of programmes for qualifications. This, in turn, may need liaison and co-operation with outside bodies representing employers or professions.

Aims, objectives and methods

These have already been introduced as fundamental to the planning of lessons, but they are also necessary for the construction of the scheme of work. Thus, it is important that a scheme should convey the balance of kinds of learning objective that it is intended to meet, such as behavioural, cognitive, affective or personal growth. These in turn need to be related to the various teaching and learning methods to be used on the course. For example, demonstrations and practice in the case of psychomotor objectives, case studies in the case of applied vocational courses, individual project work for adults on access courses, literature reviews for A- or AS-level work, and so on.

Content and structure

This is one of the most obvious features of any scheme of work, since it is concerned with the ground to be covered in a subject or topic area. It may be fairly prescribed by a syllabus, or by students' existing levels of knowledge, but nevertheless, the teacher has the responsibility to *organise* and *sequence* the course as a whole, so that the direction is clear from lesson to lesson. This means that the *order* in which topics are treated needs to make sense: the same ground should not be covered twice unless there is a good reason for this, such as recapitulation or revision. Thus, in the case of the example from the history of the First World War, students would need to have been introduced to the nature of historical evidence, as distinct from other kinds of accounts, at an early stage.

Resources

Schemes of work need to reflect what is, and is not, available by way of resources. This may include a whole range of things, from the availability of time and staff, to material equipment, marketing expertise and funds. The layout of the classroom itself, for example, may or may not be conducive to certain kinds of methods: raked lecture theatres make group work difficult, work placements need outside contacts, some assessment schemes are more costly than others in staff time, and so on. Thus, a scheme of work needs to reflect what is *possible* in terms of resources, as well as what is *desirable* in terms of effective teaching and learning.

Assessment, feedback and evaluation

Schemes of work need to convey information about ways in which learning will be assessed from class to class, and at the end of the course. They also need to convey some idea of what channels exist for students to communicate relevant concerns arising from their progress on the course. At the end of the course, the teacher, as well as the students, should be in a position to *evaluate* the course in terms of strengths and weaknesses, so that it can be further developed in the future.

ACTIVITY

Take any scheme of work for which you are responsible, and check it against the general points made above: context, aims, objectives and methods, content and structure, resources, assessment and evaluation.

We have now reviewed some general principles of curriculum planning and design, together with some theories and models of teaching and learning that underpin them. These will be put into the context of recent developments in the next section. But before turning to them, it may be helpful to consider them in action. At this stage, look back to the case study on the *Review of key skills* in Chapter 3, pages 67–8, before going to the one that follows here.

Case Study: *Course development of the GCE A-level programme at Greybourne College of FE*

The proposal to build key skills into the full-time GCE A-level programme has been accepted. But this was largely because students who have completed a key skills programme are likely to be given preferential treatment by the local university. Several members of staff teaching GCE A-level continue to be sceptical about using time for key skills because they think it could be better used for teaching the academic content of their courses.

It has been accepted that the three key skills of communication, numeracy and information technology should be taught and assessed as an integral element of the GCE A-level programme. It was also agreed that the level of the three main skills should be that of Level 2. This development would be evaluated in two years time to find out whether GCE A-level students' progress had improved in line with that of students on other programmes, such as applied vocational courses.

ACTIVITY

Taking one of the subjects you yourself teach, prepare a typical lesson plan, and a scheme of work in which it might belong, and in each case demonstrate the integration of key skills. You should bear in mind the three issues raised in the discussion of key skills in this context: the *appropriateness* of the main skills, ways of *integrating* them, and the *level* at which they should be taught and assessed. You should also remember the general principles of lesson planning and course design that were outlined above.

DESIGNING THE VOCATIONAL CURRICULUM

In this section, we will review some of the most important implications of the development of the vocational curriculum within the framework of the changing assessment and qualifications system. This means considering developments such as the focus on skills and competence, credit-based learning, modular systems, and the accreditation of prior learning.

In Chapter 1, a distinction was established between a course and a learning programme (see Table 1.1, page 16). The idea of a *course* was basically one of a programme of study designed and determined by educationalists, whereas that of a learning *programme* is a much more flexible and learner-centred idea, in which students themselves choose the pace, structure and content of their own learning in modular and credit-based provision:

> *In the learning programme, the student exercises choice, creates integration and negotiates learning outcomes. Learning becomes a partnership between the teacher as facilitator and the student as client.*
>
> Nasta (1994: 23)

In this section, therefore, we will be looking at the typical elements of the vocational curriculum as a *learning programme*, beginning with the modular structure.

Modular structure

The use of self-contained and accredited *units* or *modules* of learning, rather than the traditional course structure, is one of the most important elements in the transition from curriculum to learning programme. Most vocational awards are structured along these lines, as are awards accredited as NVQs and other applied vocational qualifications.

The idea of building a learning programme along modular lines has long been a feature of the North American education system. Here it is linked to credit-based units of contact hours, grade points and credit accumulation, which permits a great deal of choice on the part of students to construct their own programme of learning from a wide choice of courses. It also breaks down barriers between different types of learning, and makes possible the combination of vocational and academic courses of study. Each module or unit carries a rating in terms of its level in relation to others in the system, and credit gained may be transferred within and between different courses and institutions. In the UK, the modular credit system has been largely adapted as the basic structure of degree-level work. A typical definition of a module will therefore consist at least of the following elements:

- a credit *rating* (10, 15 or 20, for example)
- a statement of student *contact* hours (class attendance plus private study)
- a statement of the *level* achieved on successful completion.

In practice, and in higher education especially, the definition can be further refined, to provide more complex ways of defining modules so that they permit maximum flexibility whilst retaining quality assurance in matters of assessment and accreditation.

As has been seen, this system of modularisation has emerged from the North American pattern, and has been widely adapted in UK higher education. So designing a modular curriculum along these lines means starting with individual modules and regarding them as relatively free-standing or self-contained. In the vocational sector, the tradition has been to modularise existing accredited courses, which is quite a different thing, since it means simply subdividing up what was once a complete course into smaller units of study. It was this rather mechanical process that sometimes made modularisation controversial, raising the kinds of issues about knowledge that were mentioned in Chapter 2. But modularisation does not have to take this form:

> *An alternative approach is to start from the modules and make them the critical building blocks of the curriculum; in other words, to start the process of curriculum design with the parts rather than the whole and to offer learners much greater flexibility about the qualification outcomes that different collections of modules can lead to.*

> Nasta (1994: 82)

It has sometimes been assumed that modularisation is more suited to some subjects than others, and this is particularly true of liberal arts or recreational courses for

ACTIVITY

You have been presented with two different ways of designing a modular course, one based on breaking down traditional courses into a number of modules, and the other based on designing individual modules and allowing students to construct their own learning programme from them. Now consider this distinction in relation to your own involvement with modular courses. Using the key modular features of credit, contact and level, try to locate your own modules in the two alternatives described.

adults, in which assessment of learning outcomes has seemed inappropriate or actually resisted by the learners themselves.

Case Study: *Proposals for modularisation and accreditation in the Greybourne Adult and Community Education Service*

Because of the decrease in funding for leisure and recreational courses, there has been a proposal from the borough to extend the system of modularisation and accreditation to courses that at present are not credit-rated.

This has been justified on the grounds that it would help to extend integration with other educational providers in the borough, and also enable credit transfer and progression, which in turn may help to make a better case for the funding of liberal arts, leisure and recreational courses. It is argued that all learning is, in principle, capable of accreditation, and that long-standing adult students should have recognition of their achievement and possible acceptance on the associate degree programme of the local university. Many courses are already accredited for qualifications, in any case.

Students and teaching staff on these courses are deeply divided, and there is opposition from students on the grounds that they 'do not want to go back to school'. Staff also feel that modularisation and accreditation would be completely contradictory to the spirit of their subjects and their teaching.

ACTIVITY

In relation to your own subject area, list the kinds of differences modularisation and accreditation makes, or would make, in relation to:

a) the teaching methods involved
b) the assessment of students' learning.

Modularisation has become virtually universal in higher education, but there are consequences for some kinds of teaching that have proved controversial. In the case of the vocational curriculum, however, the advantages for a system directed towards relevant employment skills seem much more obvious.

Credit-based learning

We have seen that modularisation is one of the prerequisites of a flexible learning programme, because it provides a way of accrediting learning in units of credit without regard to the traditional divisions between vocational, academic and other kinds of courses. This permits learners to build for themselves a learning programme that is flexible, in that they can 'pace' it for themselves, and also capable of being put together in different places or at different institutions. The credit accumulation and transfer system (CATS) has therefore become a major factor in the design of the vocational curriculum.

A credit framework for all post-compulsory education means that students do not have to choose courses from any single accrediting or examining body, since a common system, or agreed framework, creates bridges or interfaces between traditional qualification routes. It also permits students to move freely across traditional institutional divisions of further, higher or continuing education. Modular structures and credit-based learning both reflect assessment of learning in terms of *outcomes*, such as subject knowledge, skills, competence and capability.

Learning outcomes

Whatever the nature of the module, it has to be expressed in terms of learning outcomes, which may take a range of forms. We have seen, earlier in this chapter, that such outcomes can be expressed in behavioural, cognitive and affective terms. All of them represent the statement of intention on the part of the curriculum designer to bring about measurable changes in the learner. In terms of the vocational curriculum, skills, competence and capability are the aims and objectives of classical curriculum theory.

In the case of NVQs, work-related outcomes are the basis of the accredited qualification, and these are further broken down into units of competence together with performance criteria that determine the assessment and range statements that put the performance into an appropriate work context. Competence, in this context, therefore, means the ability to perform work roles.

Capability, as a learning outcome, has in the past been developed within the accreditation systems of the Royal Society of Arts (RSA) Examinations Board. And this means a rather broader concept of competence, one that is contexted in specific situations, and not simply the ability to carry out a particular task or operation:

> *Capability is viewed as an all-round human quality that involves the integration of knowledge, skills, competences and any other relevant personal attributes.*
>
> Nasta (1994: 64)

In other words, capability was something more to do with responsibility and initiative *in employment*, and takes into account factors of personality.

Skills assessment has always been at the heart of the vocational curriculum design, and they feature as major learning outcomes of both NVQ and other applied vocational qualifications. As with modules themselves, there are further subdivisions of skills, by type and level, such as key or core skills, or transferable skills. All of these types of learning outcome need to be associated in curriculum design with appropriate assessment systems, in which a range of authorities, such as employers, professional bodies and trainers, are involved.

ACTIVITY

In relation to curriculum design in the area of your own subject, in what ways can the learning outcomes for assessment be classified according to the above examples: knowledge, skill, capability, competence? Give examples of how these might relate to one another in a vocational curriculum or learning programme.

Assessment of prior learning

This has also become much more a feature of planning and design in the vocational curriculum, and as a process of assessment it was introduced in Chapter 3. As with modular systems, it is a development that had its origins in the much more flexible higher education system of North America, where it has been particularly associated with access on the part of unqualified adult learners into the formal education system. In fact, as far as adults are concerned, it is often more likely to take the form of the assessment of prior *experiential* learning (APEL) than that of the assessment of prior learning (APL), since the latter generally refers to prior *certificated* or *accredited* learning. Obviously, the difference between APL and APEL has major consequences for assessment. For example, it is extremely important to distinguish between *experience* and *learning* in using AP(E)L for admission, remission of credit, or advanced standing, or whatever.

Nevertheless, the increasing number of adults participating in vocational courses, particularly in Continuing Professional Development (CPD), together with the stress upon lifelong learning policies, makes it essential that curriculum planning and design incorporates such routes. There is no reason why AP(E)L should not be incorporated into the development of modular learning programmes, and subject to the same processes of accreditation and quality management.

ACTIVITY

Critically assess the possibilities and limitations of AP(E)L accreditation in courses for which you are responsible or with which you are involved, and give examples of the kinds of prior learning that might count for assessment in relation to any particular course.

A Framework for Achievement

The curriculum themes just introduced, such as modular structures, credit-based learning, outcomes and prior learning assessment, are all coming to the fore in the development of national systems for the 14–19 sector. In this respect, they are belatedly following a long-established pattern in adult and higher education, which have been more systemic.

Following the development of the National Curriculum for schools, the object of policy is increasingly to simplify the existing complex and overlapping system of assessment and awards, focusing much more on the individual learner and strengthening the vocational and skills element.

The Qualifications and Curriculum Authority (QCA) has therefore published a Framework for Achievement 'recognising qualifications and skills in the 21st century'. The implications for the curriculum are significant in the shift from a focus on learning towards skills and achievement. For some providers, this will 'pose challenges to programme structures and will impact on their current approaches to teaching and learning'.

Many of the emerging curriculum principles described above are represented in the Framework for Achievement, in the form of standardised units, levels and values of credit-based learning. The overall system is intended to reflect credit accumulation and transfer between mutually recognised providers in both the education and employment sectors. This would enable learners to follow their careers according to a flexible pattern, integrating all aspects of their academic and vocational learning.

The Framework for Achievement, together with other related policy developments such as apprenticeship schemes, represent major shifts in the emphases of the curriculum: from learning to achievement, from courses to credit, and from provision to learner-centred programmes.

ACTIVITY

Describe any implications of a Framework for Achievement curriculum, and the shifts in emphasis described above, for your own work as a teacher or trainer. In particular, what do you see as the challenges it may pose to programme structures or to current approaches to teaching and learning?

CURRICULUM EVALUATION

The functions of assessment and evaluation are often confused, and they have much in common anyway. But it is usual to restrict the meaning of assessment to that of individual students' learning outcomes, and evaluation to that of the course or learning programme itself. Obviously, individual teachers need to be concerned with both.

In the first place, evaluation is an institution-wide quality assurance function. A course will be validated for a specified length of time, and a course team responsible to the validating body for its evaluation as a programme of learning.

The process of course evaluation has been described (Nasta, 1994: 132–9) as focusing on three dimensions:

- *Quality* This is the focus upon the effectiveness and success of the course from the points of view of students and staff.
- *Accessibility* This focuses upon the ways in which the course is meeting or failing to meet the needs of the client group for whom it was intended.
- *Validity* This is concerned with whether or not the course remains relevant to the occupational context for which it was designed, which means whether or not it continues to satisfy the needs of the industry or employers.

This model for course evaluation is developed in the context of the vocational curriculum, but it could be adapted as a framework for any course. The first dimension, quality, applies by definition to all courses or learning programmes. But evaluation by way of accessibility or validity could also be made in the case of access or A- or AS-level courses:

- An access course could be evaluated in terms of the appropriateness of its organisation and teaching to the needs of adult learners.
- An A- or AS-level course could be evaluated in terms of its relevance to a particular examinations board.

ACTIVITY

Using the model described above, conduct an evaluation of any course with which you are involved or are responsible for. You might also make a list of the kinds of actions needed to bring it up to the necessary quality standard prescribed by an accrediting body.

Review Questions

1 Explain the definition of 'curriculum' as 'the role of the teacher in the organisation of the student's learning'.
2 What are the basic features of the objectives model of the curriculum?
3 What, if any, is the relevance of Bloom's taxonomy of learning domains to today's vocational curriculum?
4 What are the most important distinctions to observe when writing statements of aims and statements of objectives?
5 List the most important principles to observe when devising schemes of work.
6 To what extent do you think that modularisation and accreditation are appropriate for every possible form of learning?
7 Is it possible to separate course and curriculum evaluation from college-wide quality frameworks?

SUMMARY

- There are a range of possible definitions and models of the curriculum, focusing on different aspects of content and process.
- Lesson plans and schemes of work represent the role of the teacher in curriculum processes of planning and design.
- Aims and objectives can be analysed in terms of Tyler's rational planning model and Bloom's taxonomy of learning objectives.
- The vocational curriculum is based upon modules, learning outcomes, credit-based learning, competence, skill, and the accreditation of prior learning.
- A model for curriculum evaluation focuses upon dimensions of quality, accessibility and validity.

Suggested Further Reading

Huddleston, P. and Unwin, L. (2002) *Teaching and Learning in Further Education: Diversity and Change*, London: RoutledgeFalmer
Describes the changing Further Education environment and the increasingly diverse nature of its curriculum and widening range of students; covering funding, structure, curriculum, assessment, teacher training and professional development. Also investigates research base for the wider social, economic and political context. Includes practical activities and incorporates a reflective perspective.

Kelly, A.V. (1999) *The Curriculum: Theory and Practice*, 4th edition, London: Paul Chapman
This is a well-established standard text on curriculum, and provides a comprehensive account of the fundamentals of theory and practice.

Nasta, T. (1994) *How to Design a Vocational Curriculum*, London: Kogan Page
A practical guide for schools and colleges, which covers issues such as validation, design and assessment, and reflects the changing vocational curriculum away from courses towards learning programmes.

Neary, M. (2002) *Curriculum Studies in Post-Compulsory and Adult Education: A Teacher's and Student Teacher's Guide*, Cheltenham: Nelson Thornes
A practical account of the concept of curriculum, covering aspects such as planning, development, modules, change, research, competence, outcomes and evaluation. It includes exercises and is based on a problem-solving perspective.

5 Teaching and Learning Methods

Objectives

After reading this chapter, you should be able to:

- identify the range of teaching methods available
- describe a set of criteria for selecting appropriate teaching methods for different audiences
- apply these criteria so that appropriate methods are utilised
- use selected methods to maximum effect
- select strategies for overcoming barriers to learning.

When thinking of teaching methods, many people will often think of the lecture as the most widely used and dominant approach. This may be because they themselves were lectured to (or at) when studying in further or higher education. Alternatively, it may be because they have heard many teachers in the 14–19 sector referred to as 'lecturers' (although other terms such as 'instructor' are also becoming common). As Jarvis (1992) points out, however, there is an expectation in society, and amongst learners, that teachers should have 'all the answers'. These answers, it is believed, should be provided in a didactic manner so that learners can acquire knowledge. But, as Jarvis cautions, this means the teacher often provides one interpretation to multi-faceted issues. Learners should have the freedom to make their own choices, and teaching methods should facilitate this. Above all, learners should have the opportunity to actively participate in the classroom, in a way that is more than just responding to the teacher's questions. Recent government reforms also now insist on the importance of learners being provided with differentiated learning experiences that meet their individual needs. This chapter, then, will examine the broad variety of teaching methods at the teacher's disposal.

What do we mean by teaching methods?

It is important at the outset to be clear about what constitutes a teaching *method* as opposed to teaching *media*, *aids* or *resources*. A teaching method comprises the adoption of a general approach or technique that determines the type and frequency of interaction between teachers and learners. Teaching media, such as overhead projectors, televisions and computers, are examples of the kinds of tools available when using a teaching method. Some media, of course, may tend to be used with certain teaching methods; so, the overhead projector is most often associated with use in lectures, presentations or more didactic forms of method than, say, with more student-centred work. Nevertheless, it would be a mistake to draw any strong conclusions from this.

There is such a vast array of teaching methods available that it is important to use a classification scheme to give a discussion of such methods some coherence. We could, for example, use a scheme that contrasted technical against non-technical types of method. It is perhaps more appropriate, however, to view teaching methods through a more pedagogic prism – the relationship between teacher-centred and student-centred methods. In the following section, we will look first of all at the more didactic, teacher-centred approaches such as the lecture, and then at more student-centred methods on both a group and individual basis. These are summarised in Table 5.1. It should be noted that, today, the emphasis in 14–19 education is on student-centred methods, and Table 5.1 shows that there is a considerable array of such methods at the disposal of the teacher.

Table 5.1 *Summary of teacher-centred and student-centred teaching methods*

Teacher-centred methods	Student-centred methods
Lectures (page 104)	Seminars (page 114)
Practicals/demonstrations (page 109)	Role-playing and simulations (page 115)
Discussions (page 110)	Brainstorming (page 115)
Mentoring (page 111)	Buzz-groups (page 115)
The tutorial (page 114)	Snowballing (page 116)
	The debate (page 117)
	Fishbowl (page 117)
	Resource-based learning (page 117)
	Projects (page 118)
	Virtual learning environments (page 118)

Which teaching methods should we use?

In this section we will look at each teaching method in some detail, examining its advantages and disadvantages. For the sake of convenience, we will categorise teaching methods into: teacher-centred methods and student-centred methods.

Teacher-centred methods

Lectures

According to Bligh (1971), the lecture is as effective as any other method in presenting information, but not more effective at promoting active thought or changing student attitudes. Nevertheless, the lecture is still an important part of a teacher's 'armoury'. A lecture can comprise, typically, a one-hour, unbroken discourse to a large audience, with little or no opportunity for interaction between the lecturer and students. In 14–19 education, however, it is more likely that the lecture will take the form of a shorter 'lecturette', probably given as an introduction to a teaching session, or perhaps to summarise a topic.

A possible structure for a typical lecture is given in Table 5.2. It is important to remember that your audience is likely to comprise a broad spectrum of people, ranging from those who may be quite familiar with your topic, to those who have yet

Table 5.2   *Outline structure for a lecture*

1   Statement of aims/objectives
2   Outline of the structure of the lecture
3   Statement of problem/theme/concepts
4   Explanation of problem/background to the theme/definition of concepts
5   Possible solutions/elaboration of theme/elucidation of concepts
6   Analysis and validity of solutions/evaluation of theme
7   Recapitulation of problem/theme/concepts
8   Summary/conclusions

to grasp its basic concepts. Hence, stating the aims and objectives of the lecture, and defining problems, themes and concepts, can lay down an 'entry level' into the subject for all the audience. Building from basic concepts, providing plentiful examples and case studies (especially those that relate to the experiences of your audience), and providing alternative solutions can aid understanding and help listeners into *thinking* about the subject.

Whether you are delivering a formal lecture to an audience of 200 or ten, it can be a nerve-wracking experience – particularly if you are new to the method. Even wizened presenters feel 'the butterflies' as they walk into an auditorium packed with expectant faces. The key is to control your nerves and to channel this energy into enhancing your performance. To achieve this, you need to:

- master your material
- take control of yourself
- organise your lecture environment
- engage with your audience.

Master your material
Teaching in the 14–19 sector, it will often be the case that you will have to teach subjects you are, at first, only marginally familiar with. It may be that your own study of the subject was sometime in the past, or it was a minor element in previous academic qualifications. Suddenly, you have to *teach* it, and you fear that your own ignorance is about to be displayed in public! What do you do? A sensible approach is to:

- begin your preparation, if possible, well in advance
- read around the subject as extensively as possible, particularly looking at alternative perspectives, if they exist
- organise your material.

For the latter, a useful approach is to brainstorm the subject, say, by jotting down the core issues on to cards, then rearranging these into a logical order. Another method is to produce a spider diagram, as in Figure 5.1. Here, the starting point was 'The origins of the French Revolution', but, by producing the diagram, the sections and sub-sections of the material emerge for later elaboration into lecture notes.

Having organised your structure, you are then set up to produce the notes that will provide you with the basis of your presentation, visual aids and notes/handouts for students. Ensure that these notes are sufficiently comprehensive for these purposes.

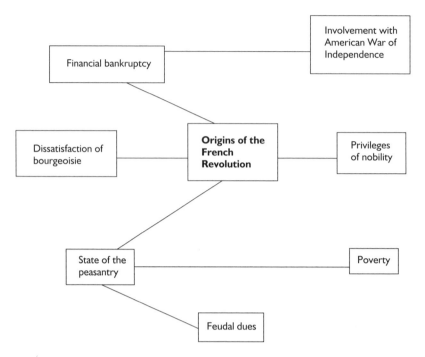

Figure 5.1 *Spider diagram showing how a subject can be brainstormed into a structure*

Take control of yourself
The key to self-confidence is thorough preparation. You have already prepared your material. Now you need to practise, practise, practise. The best place to do this is the lecture theatre or room you will deliver your lecture. This will accustom you to the physical environment and provide as close a simulation of the experience as possible. As a busy teacher, however, this may not always be practical.

Wherever you practise, deliver the presentation aloud rather than in your head. This allows you to *listen* to your choice of words, and to evaluate your own pace and delivery, tone, intonation, etc.

You may consider reading, verbatim, from your lecture notes. Every nervous lecturer has been tempted to do this. Yet, far from you taking control of yourself, this approach ensures that the material takes control of you. All spontaneity and, probably, enthusiasm will be lost, with the result that a barrier will be created between you and your audience. The ideal form of prompt is the use of visual aids, which can be used to provide:

- the structure of the lecture (for you and your audience)
- graphics/illustrations for clarity and interest
- definitions of key concepts.

In producing, say, slides for use with an overhead projector, remember the three Bs – big, bright and bold. Do not be tempted to cram all you want to say on to the overhead itself – the image will be too cluttered and the print too difficult to read. If using a computer to produce the overhead (and normally you should!) then use a minimum of 24 point text. The use of images is also helpful in adding interest and clarity of instructional message (see Chapter 6).

Organise your lecture environment

If you are presenting in a raked lecture theatre there is little you can do with the seating arrangement (apart from booking a different room!). In rooms with more flexible arrangements, plan the seating in a way that fits the purpose of your lecture. If your delivery is to be didactic then rows of desks or tables may be appropriate; if, however, you aim to achieve some interaction with your audience, you may choose a more 'democratic' seating arrangement such as a square or horse-shoe (see Figure 5.2).

Whatever arrangement you select, you must ensure that all learners have a clear view of both you and your visual aids. This is just one reason why a visit or practice in your lecture room is so important. You may need, for example, to reposition the projector or the projection screen so that learners' viewing is unimpeded. Also, ensure that there are adequate facilities for student note-taking, such as desk or table space. Finally, student information processing will not function efficiently if their physiological needs are not met. So the room must be at an adequate temperature, with sufficient light and fresh air. Note that inadequate light may induce student slumbers (particularly in sessions just after lunch), while excessive light may make overheads difficult to read. Judicious use of light switches and curtains or blinds will enable a balance to be struck.

Case Study: *Learning from a disastrous lesson*

I had been on my first teaching practice for two weeks, but had only done some ordinary classroom teaching and some one-to-one sessions with individual students. I had been asked to give a one-hour lecture during week 3 to about 40 students on the Hotel and Catering HND programme. I must admit I was really nervous about the prospect of doing this, but felt I couldn't say 'no'.

I spent, literally, hours and hours preparing for it. Although I know the subject, budgeting, fairly well, the idea of teaching it sent me into a panic. On the day of the lecture itself, I felt physically sick. When I went into the lecture theatre, all I could see was a sea of faces, and they all appeared to be looking at me!

The lecture itself was a complete disaster. I had prepared some overheads, but realised after five minutes I had forgotten to use them. I also realised that I was speaking far too quickly and that there was a stirring in the audience. After about ten minutes, I could hear some students starting to talk to each other. I felt that I had 'lost it'. Then, because I had gabbled my way through the presentation, I finished with 20 minutes to go. Luckily the students themselves saved me. The one sensible thing I did was ask if there were any questions. After a pause, lots of hands went up, and I was able to clarify lots of points I thought I had explained. The students seemed to concentrate more on this part of the session, and both them and I seemed more relaxed with each other. One or two even thanked me as they left! But next time, I will try to stay calmer and to pace the whole thing better.

(Student teacher at Greybourne College of FE)

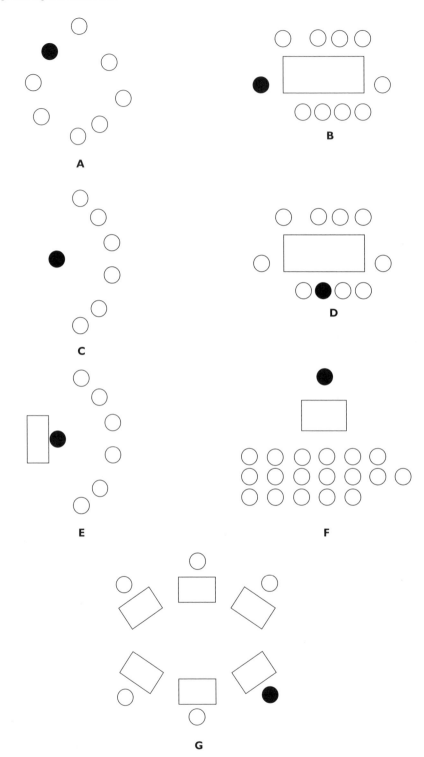

Figure 5.2 *Possible configurations of seating arrangements*

ACTIVITY

Take a topic on which you are going to present a lecture. Prepare the structure of the material by brainstorming, then flesh out the detail into some lecture notes. Prepare a set of visual aids and include some prompt notes for your own use. Go to the room you will be using (or a similar one), and organise the environment to meet the needs of your students (and the lesson). Then, practise the lecture (aloud), eliciting feedback either by using a video recorder or by getting a colleague to observe your performance. (Note: if a busy timetable makes this impracticable for most sessions, at least rehearse the lecture aloud at home – when taking a bath is an ideal opportunity, but remember to put your notes in plastic covers!)

Engage with your audience

We have seen that your engagement with your audience will be enhanced if you speak naturally rather than reading from notes. Interpersonal communication works best when you are able to make eye contact with your audience (and particularly if you 'scan' regularly, to make eye contact with most of them). Use of 'body language' is also important. A teacher, for example, who stands rigidly behind a podium, is unlikely to 'reach out' to the audience, or to engender any sense of common bond or purpose. Hence, the layout of the room can also be important; if you want to achieve more interaction with your audience, you can influence this by the careful planning of seating arrangements (see the activity above).

The use of the voice is also of importance. You need to ensure that your voice is audible, especially to those sitting at the back of the classroom. A factor that can often be forgotten, however, is the *tone* of voice. A monotone delivery, devoid of changes in rhythm or emphasis, is guaranteed to send a classroom of students to sleep! Try to put some variety and 'colour' into your voice. If you are not sure how you sound, evaluate your voice projection as part of the previous activity.

Practicals/demonstrations

Practical sessions or demonstrations are most often used for the teaching of skills such as carrying out a scientific experiment, or in types of vocational training such as hairdressing, nursery nursing or sports science. It is usual for the teacher to demonstrate how the skill should be performed, and then for the students to emulate the activity either individually or in groups. Gagné, Briggs and Wager (1992) suggest that in any activity that requires the rule-learning of processes, it is important that learners have ample opportunity for practice of the skill and for feedback on their performance.

From the teacher's perspective, this can pose problems when teaching classes of 20 or more students, especially when one or two students have particular problems with the skill and require detailed help. Nevertheless, it is important that, as a teacher, you observe most, if not all, students performing the skill so that you can be satisfied they have mastered it. This is especially significant if the skill provides the basis for higher-level skills to come. If you are teaching on NVQ/SVQ courses, it is a requirement that student skills are assessed and a written record kept while they are on their work experience placement.

It is always wise to be reflective on the way in which we teach skills, and the fact that we may become blasé about the faults and imperfections we ourselves acquire. Rapid changes in the world of work mean that our skills can soon become outdated. For those training in pre-service, during your early teaching, you may be allocated a college mentor with whom you can ask for guidance and feedback on your transmission of skills. For those training in-service, you might be required as part of continuing professional development to undertake a week of work-based experience within your professional field, so that your skills are kept up-to-date.

Discussions

Guided discussion

Guided discussion involves the Socratic method, often referred to as step-by-step discussion. The teacher uses a series of questions (some of which may have been pre-prepared) to guide the students' discussion along a desired path. Use is made of the students' existing knowledge, which may be implicit but not recognised by the students themselves. This is an approach that is more common when we are dealing with older, more mature students who bring a degree of knowledge and experience with them. It is essential, however, that students are sufficiently prepared in advance for discussion sessions, so that they can contribute, otherwise the lesson will be one-sided and dominated by the teacher. An atmosphere must also be created where participants feel free and encouraged to participate.

One of the problems with the guided discussion is that it may soon stray on to issues and pathways that had not been planned. The skill is knowing when to allow and encourage this and when to draw the debate back towards more anticipated pathways. Another difficulty is that some members of the group may tend to dominate proceedings while others remain silent. The teacher's art is to act as a conductor, setting issues in motion, aiding the discussion through posing new questions, recapitulating throughout the discussion and bringing the session to an end, noting points of agreement and disagreement.

Case Study: *How* not *to facilitate a classroom discussion*

I had been teaching this particular set of students for about five weeks, so I thought I had got to know them quite well. The problem was they weren't particularly friendly, at least towards me, and didn't seem to want to say much when I tried to get a discussion going. On this particular day, I tried to provoke some argument, and to my surprise it really took off. The problem was that one of the class quickly turned the discussion round, from how the media handle topical events to football. A heated debate followed with virtually all the class taking part, including the girls. This was the first time I had got the class talking, so I decided to take a 'back seat' and see what happened. Unfortunately, the classroom door was open and several staff walked by and I am sure heard what was going on. I wrote up in my learning log afterwards that, on reflection, the students had taken advantage of my naivety. I had allowed the discussion to continue because I wanted them to like me more. Unfortunately, the learning objectives of the session were completely forgotten.

(Student teacher at Greybourne Sixth Form College)

ACTIVITY

Join together with four fellow learners on your professional development programme. Take it in turns so that in each session, two of you take part in a discussion or debate, someone facilitates (guides the discussion) and someone observes. Those that are discussing an issue need to prepare themselves to talk for about ten minutes. This will work best if the facilitator is provided in advance with some of the material, so intelligent questions can be prepared and themes for the discussion anticipated. It is the task of the observer to note how well the facilitator intervenes in the discussion. Questions to consider might include:

- Did the facilitator allow the discussion to flow when possible?
- When the discussion flagged, was the facilitator able to inject new life into it?
- Was the facilitator able to move the discussion into new, uncharted, yet relevant waters?
- When the discussion veered off the subject, what did the facilitator do, and was this the correct decision?

After each session, change roles so that all group members have an opportunity to take on each part. When you have completed the role-play, consider what you have learnt about the skills needed for guiding a discussion.

Controlled discussion

While guided discussion involves significant elements of student participation, controlled discussion is much more teacher-centred and didactic. The teacher sets out the main purpose and themes of the session and talks about them, encouraging the students to interject with questions or comments. The problem with this method is that, unless students are very confident, or are, perhaps, mature adults with plenty to say, the teacher will tend to dominate. The threat of this can be reduced if student chairs can be placed in a circle or semi-circle, and if the teacher tries to maintain eye contact with the class (see next Activity).

Mentoring

Mentoring is moving up the Government's agenda in terms of its importance. There are many different interpretations of mentoring, but here we will take the Megginson and Clutterbuck (1997: 13) definition as 'off-line help by one person to another in making significant transitions in knowledge, work or thinking'. In the context of 14–19 education, mentoring can be undertaken between one member of the academic

ACTIVITY

Look at Figure 5.2 (page 108). In each arrangement:

a) With which students would the tutor be likely to have (i) the most, and (ii) the least interaction?
b) Which of the seating arrangements makes it (i) most, and (ii) least, difficult for the tutor to withdraw from the discussion and to encourage direct interaction between students?

staff and another, between a teacher and student or between an external member of the community and a student. Each relationship, however, will encompass different objectives.

In terms of the academic to academic relationship, mentoring is often used as a means of easing the passage of those training to teach and new members of staff into the profession. During this period the mentor may help them with improving their teaching performance, give advice on career development, act as a counsellor in times of difficulty, and share expert knowledge. For those undertaking initial teacher training, the trainee will begin with an Individual Learning Plan (ILP) and professional development record that provides the basis for establishing personal development objectives. The trainee and an appointed mentor will discuss the ILP on a regular basis in the knowledge that these developmental objectives may change over time. In addition, the mentor may:

- provide an expert introduction to the subject or vocational area that the trainee is going to teach
- arrange for the trainee to observe classes in their specialist area as well as other classes
- provide advice about planning, teaching and assessment methods and activities
- provide access to the relevant syllabi, schemes of work, assessment schedules and resources, including on-line resources
- give regular support and advice, including some informal observation and feedback
- formally assess a specified number of teaching sessions in accordance with the teacher training institution's requirements.

Sometimes the mentor will be the teacher's line-manager, subject expert or experienced teacher, but often a more independent person will be selected to take on this role.

There is also a definite government 'push' to give those undergoing workplace (in-service) teacher training access to subject-based mentors, that is, experts who not only have the basic teaching skills, but experience in teaching the trainee's specific subject. Newly qualified teachers may have a mentor for the first two years of their appointment. It is acknowledged, however, that the nature of 14–19 sector means that many specialist subjects have only one teacher. In this case, teachers should be paired with an experienced colleague in a related subject. Mentors should engage in regular observation of the trainee's lessons and offer constructive feedback. The mentor is also likely to be a member of the team that assesses the trainee's progress. Trainees should also have the opportunity to regularly observe the mentor teaching in order to gain from this evidence of 'good practice'. From the mentor's perspective, performing this role may allow them to build evidence towards the achievement of Advanced Practitioner status.

Mentoring of students is also of increasing importance in the 14–19 sector. The mentor may not be the teacher, but someone in the student's own work placement, who is concerned with excellence in practice. Hence, the FE teacher and mentor both have a common purpose (the transition of the student into expert professional practice) but will have different roles. The former may tend to be more concerned with professional theory and the latter with how this becomes integrated into practice. But this is a generalisation and, in reality, the teaching institution and place of professional practice will develop a policy that details the precise interface between the teaching and mentoring roles. Some of the experience of mentoring in the schools sector is now being imported into the 14–19 sector. A number of recommendations on mentoring in schools are detailed in Table 5.3. While some of the criteria here relate to the policies for setting up mentoring schemes, they illustrate the kinds of areas trainee further education teachers might have to understand and implement.

Table 5.3   *Good practice points for mentoring (adapted from Miller, 1998)*

Area	Good practice points
Setting objectives	Decide on the key objectives of the mentoring scheme. Choose a model of mentoring and student criteria that fit the objectives. Develop success criteria for each objective.
Raising attainment	Ensure that there is a coherent relationship between business and community mentoring, staff mentoring and other raising attainment strategies. Ensure that mentors are well briefed on GCSE coursework and deadlines. Collect monitoring data on mentored students.
Motivating students	Use falling motivation as a key student selection criterion Develop indicators to judge the impact of mentoring on motivation. Provide regular, systematic feedback to mentors on students' motivation and attainment.
Work-related and careers	Encourage mentors to develop students' work-related knowledge and skills. Advise mentors to help students explore a wider range of education, training and career opportunities.
Improving practice	Establish monitoring, review and evaluation strategies at the beginning of a scheme. Ensure that channels of communication are good. Ensure that mentors receive appropriate feedback on student progress, taking into account the confidentiality that students expect.

Tutorials

While this term is used for a number of different teaching situations, its main use in 14–19 education is to describe meetings of either a small group or an individual with a tutor, usually for the purpose of discussing an assignment or questions raised by the student(s). In individual tutorials the student may come along to discuss problems with a particular subject or assignments.

Another purpose of the tutorial is for the pastoral care of students. As was mentioned in the Introduction, the 14–19 sector is recruiting students of a much wider range of educational backgrounds and abilities. Hence, it is important that personal support is available where students can raise difficulties and receive remedial help on a one-to-one or small group basis. Sometimes, student problems will include complaints about the teaching methods of a particular member of staff. In the latter case, great diplomacy will need to be exercised. If a student is struggling with a subject, there is a natural tendency to blame the teacher, whether there is an element of justification for this or not. Where complaints are made against an individual member of staff, it is often wise to ask if the student has aired these grievances with the teacher concerned; if this has not been done, ask the student to do so. If the problem continues, you will need to seek advice on the appropriate procedure. There may be a college staff handbook, which can help.

Whatever the content or issues arising from a tutorial session, it is essential that tutors maintain a meticulous record of tutorial discussions. This enables an audit trail of progress and advice to be maintained so that any objectives or actions emerging from the tutorial can be assessed.

Student-centred methods

Seminars

A seminar is a group discussion in which either a student or guest speaker presents a topic or thesis, usually of a provocative or controversial nature. The advantage of using the seminar method is that it can provoke high levels of analysis of a theme, involving the ability to develop a sustained argument, to uncover inconsistencies in assumptions, and to present alternative viewpoints to a case. This can be thought-provoking both for the presenter, especially if she or he is a student who has prepared the material, and for the audience. One of the essential ingredients of the seminar is time in its preparation. The presenter ought to be given ample opportunity (several weeks) to prepare the session, and receive frequent guidance from the teacher. If the seminar is to achieve one of its objectives of provoking discussion, then the rest of the class also needs preparation time, including an outline/summary of the seminar paper itself. As with all teaching methods, consideration needs to be given to seating arrangements, especially if the intention is to promote debate and discussion amongst participants.

Like all teaching methods, of course, the seminar has its drawbacks. As a teacher, you are largely reliant on the preparation and skills of someone else – in most cases a student. Unless you are especially fortunate in selecting someone with well-tuned presentation skills, it is quite likely that the seminar presenter will be nervous and prone to read from the seminar notes. You may have to prepare yourself to intervene to summarise the main issues and to provoke questions and discussion.

Role-playing and simulations

Role-play is 'a brief episode acted from someone else's life or from the role for which an individual is being prepared' (Jarvis, 1992: 128). It is ideal, then, when the essence of the learning situation is to enable students to learn a specific feeling or behaviour by taking on the role of others. A typical example would be getting a group of students studying aspects of customer care to take the part of the service providers and customers (an example of a simulation of real life experience). By experiencing the different roles, important lessons can be learnt *by the students themselves* rather than being told them by the teacher, and these issues can be used as the central focus for later discussions. Hence, role-plays, if successful, can act as a powerful motivating force as well as encouraging active student participation.

It should be noted, however, that great caution needs to be exercised in selecting and using this technique.

- Not all students feel comfortable acting out a role, and some may be positively hostile to it.
- The outcomes of role-play can be difficult to predict and may not be congruent with the original lesson objectives; furthermore, role-plays may often be time-consuming to prepare and enact.
- Sometimes a role-play may produce an emotional crisis in one of the participants, which, unless the teacher is a trained counsellor, may be difficult to cope with.
- There is the issue of transfer; even if the role-play is enjoyed by participants, the connection between the activity and the real world may not be obvious to all.

In practice, it is important to conclude a role-play with a debriefing session in which participants can 'stand outside' their roles. This means they should be given an opportunity to discuss the role-play itself and the events and characters within it. This not only provides an opportunity for learning issues to emerge, but allows students to dispense with their roles.

Brainstorming

Using this method, class participants are encouraged to articulate solutions to a problem, which are recorded, usually by the class teacher. The essence of brainstorming is the production of a sufficient quantity of ideas, irrespective of the quality, so, during the initial phase, participants should be discouraged from criticising the ideas of others. Once a range of ideas is produced, a second phase can then be initiated during which the ideas are evaluated (with some being rejected) and, perhaps, ordered into priorities or categories.

Buzz-groups

Buzz-groups are formed by dividing the class up into small groups of about two to six members to discuss a particular theme or topic. In some cases, all groups will discuss the same theme; in other situations, each group will be given its own topic. Groups will discuss the issue for a short period of time, say half an hour, and then report back to the class in a plenary (whole group) session. During the period that students are discussing their solutions, the teacher, without being intrusive, should 'tour' the groups, listening to the discussion to ensure that all groups are 'on task'. This is an opportunity for members of a group to ask for further clarification of the problem or to request feedback on a line of thought. Care must be taken to facilitate the discussion rather than dominate it or offer pre-packaged solutions. If the students are sufficiently mature and confident, they may be provided with resources such as overhead transparencies and pens to produce a short presentation. Alternatively, they may report back verbally with a student or the teacher scribing the results on a chalkboard, whiteboard or flipchart.

When setting up buzz-groups it is often useful to note the learning styles of participants. Using Honey and Mumford's (2000) classification scheme of activist, pragmatist, reflector and theorist, it is often wise if each buzz-group contains a balance of students so that all learning styles are present. A group containing only reflectors, for example, might feel uncomfortable at this kind of exercise and also be very slow in producing results. If the buzz-group method is to be used frequently with a group, it might be wise, therefore, to discover individual learning styles through the use of a learning style questionnaire.

ACTIVITY

Obtain a copy of Honey and Mumford's (2000) learning style questionnaire and get a class to complete it. Make a note of each student's preferred learning style, and discuss the implications of learning styles with the class. Then undertake an exercise involving group activities, ensuring that someone with each of the learning styles is represented in each group. Evaluate the activity with the class in terms of whether the learning objectives of the exercise were achieved, but also address the issue of whether using a balance of learning styles within the groups was helpful.

Snowballing

With this method, each individual in the class works on their own solution to a problem or set of ideas about a proposition. After a set period, they work in pairs to reach a joint conclusion; thereafter, pairs are formed into fours, again, each group discussing and synthesising the ideas to produce an agreed set of results. Each group then elects a rapporteur to report back the group's collective findings.

This method can be useful for breaking down barriers, and Jarvis (1992) recommends that it is used as an ice-breaking exercise towards the beginning of a course. One of the dangers of this method, however, is that groups take too long in coming to their final conclusions. It is important, then, that the tutor controls the timing of events and engenders a sense of urgency into the proceedings. A useful accompaniment to the snowballing method is each group transcribing their ideas on to flipcharts that can then be hung around the classroom. In the plenary sessions, it can be valuable to point to the consistencies and disagreements in the groups' findings, so that essential themes can be drawn out for emphasis or further discussion.

Debates

The debate is a valuable teaching method when contrasting viewpoints need to be presented. The extent to which a debate 'works', however, is often dependent on the extent to which the session is organised. Of considerable importance is a chairperson who understands the rules of debate, and who has sufficient personality to control the audience if opinions get heated. Of equal importance is selecting speakers who are able to expound the arguments coherently and with commitment. It is vital, then, that speakers are given ample time to acquaint themselves with evidence on which to build a case. All participants, speakers and audience, need to be briefed if the rules of debate are to be adhered to. The debate will usually proceed with:

1 proposer for the motion
2 proposer against
3 seconder for the motion
4 seconder against
5 questions and opinions from the floor
6 summing up against the motion
7 summing up for the motion
8 the vote.

While students will often be keenly interested in who has 'won' the debate, the teacher needs to be conscious of the lessons to be drawn from the exercise. Hence, try to draw out and summarise the main learning points from the debate. If the debate has been successful in terms of arousing interest and passions, you may have to use your communication skills (gaining attention, for example) in order to facilitate this summary.

Fishbowl exercises

With this method, a small number of participants (say, two to four) sit facing each other in the centre of a room; it helps, then, if the chairs are arranged in a circle. The rest of the class sit around the perimeter of the room, again, probably in a circle. The group of people in the centre of the class discuss an issue or proposition, whilst the others must remain silent and observe. If someone in the outer circle wishes to participate, they must join the inner circle; this is usually done by tapping one of the inner circle on the shoulder (provided they are not speaking) and exchanging places. The person in the inner circle must always concede their place when requested.

This method can be effective in encouraging people to participate in discussions. It is usually prudent, though, to set a limit on the length of the fishbowl exercise, so that time is left for summarising and reflecting on the issues that emerged during the discussion.

Resource-based learning

Resource-based learning (RBL) is becoming an increasingly important aspect of 14–19 education, in part, because NVQs/SVQs and other vocational qualifications place such a central emphasis on student-centred learning. RBL is examined in more depth in Chapter 6, but suffice to say here that the teacher should be able to:

• direct students to the learning resources available for each topic
• produce materials to an appropriate standard where these are not available.

Whether RBL is a feature of a particular course, or not, strategies for using resources (such as libraries and the internet) should be taught or encouraged at the start of all students' courses. Knowledge of the range and depth of library resources available, and methods of accessing them (through the Dewey system, for example) should constitute a central element of student induction to a college or course.

Projects

Projects have at least the potential to stimulate thinking at the highest cognitive level, such as analysis, synthesis and evaluation, and in some subjects may require the application of practical skills. The integrative nature of the skills needed in project work may be motivating for some students, but still requires careful strategies from the teacher's perspective. Students, for example, may need guidance on selecting a topic that is both motivating for them, but also within their capabilities. Hence, a project should be challenging but not so demanding that it cannot be achieved within the limitations of resources and timescales. Help may also be required in planning the project, carrying out any research, logging data and analysing and presenting the results.

Take care not to become *so* involved that you end up doing the project for the student! Your role should be that of a facilitator. In terms of teaching objectives, one of these should be that the students should complete the project with an enhanced set of transferable skills for the future.

Virtual learning environments

With distance learning students, but also with some of those who are face-to-face, it is becoming increasingly common to communicate with such students through a computer-mediated environment. This communication embodies not only information messages (the date the next assignment is due, for example) but also important teaching and learning sessions. This communication could be on a one-to-one basis in the form of a tutorial, or, using a virtual learning environment (VLE), a forum in which the tutor and, potentially, a limitless number of students exchange information and ideas. Many colleges use Blackboard, WebCT or a similar VLE to do this. VLEs are dealt with in more detail in Chapter 7, so here we will only discuss some of the essential features of computer-mediated communication as a teaching method.

With one-to-one communication it is important to remember that many of the key features of human communication (tone and intonation of voice, use of body language, etc.) are not present (see page 123). This can pose problems for both teacher and student since the only channel of communication, the written word, has to carry all the message's meaning. This is particularly problematic if the teaching session involves distance learning students, some of whom the teacher may never meet. Particular care needs to be taken in developing a 'warm' and supporting atmosphere with the student right from the start. It can help to use an informal mode of address.

We have looked at a wide variety of teaching methods. But which ones should we select? The next section offers some suggestions.

MATCHING METHODS TO LEARNERS' NEEDS

It is probably the case that, like all teachers, you have your favourite teaching method, or at least one with which you feel most comfortable, and use most frequently. It is important, however, to utilise teaching methods that accord with the learning objectives of the teaching session, and the needs of learners. We have seen, however, that we have quite a wide range of methods at our disposal, so how is one better than the others?

The work of Gagné, Briggs and Wager (1992) may help here. The authors classify what they call 'learned capabilities' into five learning outcomes, namely:

- verbal information/knowledge
- intellectual skills
- attitudes
- motor skills
- cognitive strategies.

Intellectual skills are hierarchical in nature, involving (working from the bottom) discriminations (how to discriminate between similar examples of a concept), concrete concepts ('book', 'ship', 'Aberdeen', etc.), defined concepts ('justice', 'happiness', etc.) and rule-learning, and problem-solving. The primary difference between rule-learning and problem-solving is the complexity of the task. Rule-learning involves the execution of a basic set of procedures, whilst problem-solving may involve utilising an array of such rules in novel circumstances that the learner has not previously encountered. Clearly, this is a higher level of learning and calls for flexible ways of thinking and the transfer of previously learned skills to new situations. Table 5.4 provides an illustration of typical ways in which these learning outcomes manifest themselves in human activity.

What has this to do with selecting valid teaching methods? Let us take some examples.

Verbal information

According to Gagné, Briggs and Wager (1992), verbal information can include the learning of labels (for example, the name of an object), facts (for example, grass is green), and organised knowledge (such as a series of events in history). Clearly, one could use buzz-groups or fishbowl exercises to disseminate verbal information to a class. Since these are student-centred activities, the verbal information would have to come from the interactions between students themselves. But in these circumstances what control does the teacher have over what emerges from the discussion? Obviously, very little. Since, presumably, one of the purposes of disseminating verbal information is that it provides the bedrock of later learning activities, teaching methods can be used that transmit this information in a more direct and focused fashion. Lectures, for example, are, traditionally, ideal settings for the transmission of verbal information (as well as higher levels of learning). Similarly, tutorials and seminars could be used, or resource-based learning materials such as study guides or multimedia programs.

Table 5.4 *Learning outcomes and examples of performance*

Capability	Examples of performance
Verbal information	Stating the reigns of English monarchs Recounting the events of a journey
Intellectual skills	Studying photographs of various buses to understand the concept 'bus' (concept-learning) Demonstrating how to turn a declarative sentence into a question (rule-learning) Planning and executing the assembly of laboratory equipment to carry out a unique experiment (problem-solving)
Attitudes	Choosing to re-read and edit an assignment Choosing to complete additional reading for a project
Motor skills	Riding a bicycle Hammering a nail into a board
Cognitive strategy	Using a similar-sounding English word to remember a French word Using an acronym to memorise material

Intellectual skills

Concept-learning involves more than just being able to name an object (a characteristic of verbal information); it involves knowing the *meaning* of that object – that is, being able to identify examples and non-examples that help to define and delimit the class. Try, for example, to describe the concept 'tree'; the characteristics of being a tree might revolve around issues of colour, size, physical composition, etc. We all have our own mental maps of what 'treeness' is. What, then, is a Japanese bonsai? Does it equate with the mental map of a tree that you were considering? In teaching concepts, we could easily make use of some of those teaching methods we selected for verbal information. Since, however, an element of discrimination needs to be used (to delimit the boundaries of the concept), we could use a technique that allowed us to explore the pre-conceptions and mental maps of learners. Both guided and controlled discussions, for example, could be used so that we could explore where individual learners placed the boundaries of a concept and whether they were right.

For higher-level intellectual skills such as rule-learning, we could demonstrate the practical application of a rule (or set of procedures) as part of a lecture or practical demonstration. Note, however, that the rule must be demonstrated at a pace that suits the slowest learner, or else some learners will fall by the wayside. Effective rule-learning should allow the learner to practise the procedure themselves and to receive feedback on their performance. This is difficult to achieve in a lecture environment, but may be more possible in a practical session, which follows a demonstration. Provided they are well designed, some multimedia programs can be useful in teaching rules, because they are infinitely patient, allowing the learner to repeat the tutorial element of the program and to practise the rule, often through on-screen simulations. While, in principle, methods such as buzz-groups and brainstorming *could* be used to teach rules, they would, in practice, be exercises in discovery learning (discovering what the rule is!) and be inefficient in the use of time – presuming they would get to a definition of the rule at all.

Attitudes

It is widely recognised that positive attitudes towards the learning of intellectual skills are of prime importance. The selection of teaching methods, then, must focus not only on the content that must be taught, but also the attitude of learners to the delivery of that content. In teaching an intellectual skill the use of the lecture format, seminars or even a debate may all be equally valid, but one of these methods may be favoured by a particular group of learners above all others. There may be other circumstances when teaching objectives actually include the teaching of attitudes themselves – for example, being particularly meticulous in measuring compounds during an A-level chemistry experiment, or being attentive to children's needs during an applied vocational course in childcare. Attitudes are difficult to influence if the teaching method is teacher-centred. Ideally, a method should be adopted that allows the learner to witness, and perhaps personally explore, positive manifestations of a role. Hence, the use of demonstrations (in the case of the chemistry experiment) or role-play (in childcare) can all be effective.

Motor skills

Motor skills cannot be learned merely by hearing a description of them or by viewing a demonstration (although either might serve as an introduction). As Gagné, Briggs and Wager (1992) point out, motor skills can only be learned by repeated practice. Indeed, even after a motor skill has been acquired, continual practice will still often bring improvements (witness the work of musicians and athletes).

We have seen in this section, then, that the selection of teaching methods cannot be done according to any fixed formula. What is essential, however, is that methods chosen must reflect the desired learning objectives, and that the needs of discrete groups of learners are taken into account.

Cognitive strategies

Cognitive strategy is 'thinking about thinking'. Such strategies tend to be idiosyncratic, with learners for example adopting their own personal approaches to thinking. Cognitive strategies can, however, be actively taught, but learners may wish to select from the strategies that suit their personal cognitive processes.

Case Study: *Planning for discussion does not always achieve it*

A lesson was observed in which the stated objective of the student teacher was to get the students to analyse business problems using supply and demand theory. The planned teaching method was a discussion. Unfortunately, the entire hour appeared to be taken up with the student teacher explaining some of the elements of supply and demand theory, and expounding on how the theory could be used to analyse specific economic issues. Both approaches were entirely valid because the students needed to understand the theory in order to apply it; by observing the student teacher solving problems using the theory, they could also learn much about its application. But at no time were the students allowed the experience of solving a problem themselves. The teacher spoke in unbroken monologue for the first 20 minutes of the session and then asked for contributions. Needless to say, the students by this stage were firmly in passive mode, and none were forthcoming.

(Lesson observation at Greybourne Sixth Form College)

ACTIVITY

Plan a teaching session by stating your learning objectives, then assign each objective to one of Gagné, Briggs and Wager's (1992) learned capabilities. Then consider, carefully, which teaching method is most suited to delivering each capability. Do not forget the importance of encouraging positive student attitudes towards learning.

COMMUNICATING EFFECTIVELY IN THE CLASSROOM

What do we mean by communication?

All the teaching methods we have discussed involve the teacher and students in a process of communication. But what, precisely, do we mean when we use the word 'communication', particularly in a teaching context? In brief, communication is the transmitting and sharing of information through a shared system of signals or symbols. These signals can involve any of the senses: sight, sound, smell, taste or touch.

Learning, of course, can occur *without* communication. Jarvis (1995), for example, distinguishes between primary and secondary learning experiences. Learning from primary experiences takes place when an individual experiences situations directly, without the mediation of someone like a teacher. Learning, then, can take place, and frequently does take place, independently of educational institutions. Secondary experiences, however, most frequently occur within an educational context, and this takes place through the communication of meaning. Figure 5.3 illustrates a model of communication between a teacher and student. The speaker encodes the meaning of something in words, the words are spoken (or transmitted, say, through a visual aid), the receivers decode the meaning. Communication, however, is more complex than Figure 5.3 suggests. Each receiver brings their own biography to the listening experience; a communication may produce different interpretations, and different meanings to each learner, depending on what prior knowledge or attitudes they possess. Hence, from a single communication, different learning amongst individual listeners may occur (including, because of misinterpretation of the message, non-learning).

The significance of communication

All students (and teachers) bring their past learning histories with them into the classroom. Hopefully, most of these will be positive, but the ones that concern us here

Field of experience of teacher   **Field of experience of learner**

Figure 5.3 *A simple model of communication*

are those negative experiences that are too quickly recalled, and that cloud our responses to new learning experiences. Someone, for example, who hated mathematics at school, may respond with 'I'm no good at maths!' to the most simple of arithmetic tasks. A negative self-image may be very hard for the teacher to break.

Problems of information transfer are other reasons that may constitute a barrier to learning. Information theory suggests that a message may be distorted by 'noise'; in the case of a radio message this could include background sounds, but in the classroom it could include any kind of distraction. This could include noise itself (an aircraft passing overhead), or a draughty window or an overheated room. But noise can also include a lack of clarity in the signal itself, in the teacher's monotonous speaking voice, or an explanation which is contradictory or delivered too quickly.

Communication in the classroom

In some ways, this section attempts to integrate some important themes found in other parts of this book. A significant proportion of teaching and learning takes place in the classroom, and this cannot occur unless communication between teachers and learners (and between learners themselves) takes place. It is essential, then, that teachers are aware of, and cater for, some of the elements described next.

Gaining attention

Gagné, Briggs and Wager (1992) suggest that there are nine 'events of instruction' that form the basis of teacher–learner interaction (see Chapter 6). The first of these is gaining attention, because without this communication cannot occur. It is important to note that this does not encompass gaining the attention of *some* of the students in the class; it means gaining the attention of *all*. It is often naively assumed by those new to teaching that students will fall silent and become attentive the moment a teacher enters the classroom, but, sadly, this is rarely the case. As we will see in Chapter 6, there are practical strategies that can be employed to capture student attention and to retain it. Essentially, though, if a positive and task-orientated rapport has been established with a class, students may focus on the teacher more readily. An experienced teacher may also sense the mood of a class when entering the room, and decide how to handle the first 'engagement' with the students; if the students are boisterous, this could include demanding attention and using body and voice expressively. If the students are already focused on learning, then the first engagement may be more relaxed and informal.

Language

Language, of course, lies at the very heart of the teacher–learner communication process. Teachers need to ensure that the amount of language they use (i.e. how much they talk) is kept within proportions. We have all experienced teachers in the past who did not know when to shut up! Numerous research studies on classroom discourse, for example, have shown that, despite their claims to the contrary, teacher talk dominates classroom interactions, including unbroken monologues and teacher-led questioning.

Language register (for example, words, phrases, sentence structure) should also be considered. Words should be used that connect with the age, ability and experiences of each class of students. Hence, it is important not to patronise and 'talk down' to a mature class of adult learners, or to use complex, technical language and jargon with students who have difficulty with basic literacy skills.

The pronunciation of words also needs to be considered. This, of course, is a problematic area because accepted notions of how to pronounce words can change over time and between different parts of the country. It is usually sensible, however, to avoid using slang words or phrases, unless this is appropriate within the context of the lesson.

Differences also exist between the spoken and written word. The written word is governed by the rules of grammar, and care should be taken that learning materials are grammatically correct. Since modern word processing applications contain both spelling and grammar checking tools, this should not be problematic. Writing words on a chalkboard or whiteboard, however, can often induce the strangest of spelling aberrations in teachers. Therefore, prepare yourself so that you can both spell and describe the meanings of difficult words or concepts. Hopefully, you will build such a friendly working relationship with your classes that if, on the rare occasion, you do make a slip, the students will not be shy in pointing out that misspelt word on the overhead. Remember to thank them for their observation!

ACTIVITY

Consider your own use of language in the classroom. Tape record, say, 20 minutes of classroom activity that includes sufficiently large segments of your own verbal contributions to merit analysis. Later, analyse the tape for your own language delivery. Was the tone and register appropriate for this particular class? Were understandable words chosen? Did you avoid jargon? Was your language neutral, avoiding cultural stereotyping? How can your use of language be improved? If your analysis of the tape leaves you with unanswered questions, get feedback either from teaching colleagues or tutors.

Non-verbal behaviours

Non-verbal behaviour involves the transmission of communication signals through visual rather than verbal messages. We often 'say' much more with our hands, arms and facial gestures than we, ourselves, realise. Teachers who are nervous may stand behind a desk, fidget with a pen, tap their feet, fold their arms or avoid eye contact. Effective communication, of course, involves avoiding all of these pitfalls. Good communication involves being aware of our non-verbal behaviour so that we stay relaxed, and use our body language to reinforce the verbal message so as to build a rapport with the class.

DEVELOPING INCLUSIVE LEARNING

Given the growing diversity of 14–19 students in terms of backgrounds and abilities, developing inclusive learning strategies is important for all teachers. Policies and processes for the development of inclusive learning have also been set out by the Special Educational Needs and Disabilities Act (2001), often just known as SENDA. The Act requires that all educational institutions make reasonable adjustments to ensure that all disabled people are able to participate equally in all aspects of educational involvement. Under SENDA, disability is defined as physical or mental impairment that has a substantial and long-term effect on the ability to carry out normal day-to-day activities. This includes both visible and hidden disabilities or illnesses. Colleges, then, have to make 'reasonable' adjustments to a range of activities including enrolments, teaching, student support and assessment. This means that the needs of disabled people have to be considered in the design of the curriculum, the production of learning materials and during course review. Above all, this consideration needs to *anticipate* the enrolment of disabled students. In other words, curriculum design should not start after a disabled person has enrolled on a course. Designers should anticipate that this enrolment will take place, and plan accordingly.

Curriculum planning means that teachers must examine the potential barriers that may exist for a disabled learner. This means evaluating course outlines and learning outcomes and reflecting on whether these are achievable for disabled learners. It may be necessary, for example, to offer alternative exercises, or provide alternative ways for disabled learners to demonstrate their knowledge and skills. Inclusive practices in teaching disabled learners might include:

- providing learners with a copy of your lesson plans, handouts and presentation materials in advance of the session
- providing learners with subject glossaries or information on where they can be found (such as web sites)
- providing all of the above in an electronic format, making the information easier to adapt to individual needs
- working with the learner and his or her support worker as a team.

Teachers also need to be aware of how classrooms need to be adapted to meet the needs of disabled learners. Ferl (2004) makes some useful recommendations including ensuring that:

- there is sufficient space in the room, especially for wheelchairs
- rooms are well signposted
- a person is available to guide a visually impaired learner, particularly for the first lesson

- lighting is sufficient and appropriate
- computers have large monitors and software programs' accessibility options have been enabled.

ACTIVITY

Take a look at the FerlFirst web site at: www.ferl.becta.org.uk/

Ferl provides resources for staff working in the post-compulsory education and training sector, particularly in making use of Information and Learning Technology (ILT), but also has some very useful reports, documents and web links on inclusive learning.

The development of inclusive strategies

For most students attending a college of further education this is a period when new skills are being learnt, but it is also a period of transition towards adulthood. As Griffiths (1994) points out, this transition takes place at two levels:

- through changing self-perception as the student matures into a new environment
- as a result of society's changing perception of the student as an independent young person.

The problem for young people with severe learning difficulties is that they do not make this transition and remain transfixed in a childhood role: dependence, passivity and childlike behaviour patterns. Yet further education can assist in the process of transition. Indeed, further education opportunities for those with learning difficulties increased quite substantially during the 1990s. Many 14–19 colleges now offer a broad range of courses to a wider range of learners, sometimes in conjunction with social and health services and with voluntary organisations (see profile of Greybourne College of FE in Appendix 1).

Most full-time courses for students with severe learning difficulties in colleges attempt to promote core skills that include:

- self-care – shopping, travelling, cooking; being able to learn from mistakes
- skills for employability – basic literacy and numeracy and communication
- opportunities to develop adolescent and adult relationships
- opportunities to develop adult self-concepts – personal autonomy, economic self-sufficiency.

In terms of teaching, it is important that emphasis is given to the issue of transition (to adulthood), so that skills are developed that are relevant to independent functioning, within an integrated community setting. This may mean that, in terms of curriculum choices, less emphasis might be given to subjects such as music, art and drama – until such time as the learner has made the transition to adult status. Clearly, teaching methods need to be adopted that are geared towards promoting enabling strategies amongst students. This means the use of student-centred methods that assist towards independence of thought and action, personal autonomy, as well as the development of basic skills.

Strategies for specific inclusive learning areas

It is not the place here to give a full and comprehensive guide on how to make your teaching inclusive to students across the entire range of disabilities – there are specialist books available, some of which are highlighted under Suggested Further Reading. What we will present here are three common examples of disability that will demonstrate some of the issues raised and how inclusive teaching strategies address them.

Dyslexia

The term dyslexia is used to describe a broad range of specific learning difficulties, most of them associated with reading, writing and spelling. It is primarily a difficulty with the automatic processing of language-based information, especially the written word, and is possibly genetic in origin. It is not related to academic ability and affects somewhere between four and five per cent of the population. While boys and girls are equally prone to dyslexia, three times as many boys as girls receive additional teaching in schools for their dyslexia. Dyslexia can be associated with :

- persistent spelling difficulties even with simple words
- slow, inaccurate reading
- problems with basic numeracy, such as difficulty in memorising and recalling sequences of numbers
- difficulties in reading aloud, and in pronouncing unfamiliar words
- poor organisational and time management skills
- poor spatial orientation, such as knowing left from right
- short-term memory problems so that students may have difficulty with immediate recall, and the sequencing of ideas or events
- visual distortion, such as having difficulty in reading text of a certain colour.

By the time they reach further education, many dyslexic students may already have been diagnosed as such, but this is not always the case. If a seemingly able student is having reading difficulties or if there is a large discrepancy between their ability and achievement, then dyslexia could be the cause. If you think that this is a possibility, it may be prudent to call in a professional diagnosis.

As a general approach, teaching dyslexic students should be structured, so that reading and spelling make sense, thorough so that weaknesses in memory are compensated for by over-learning, and active to generate interest. In terms of specific strategies, when teaching dyslexic students it is advisable to:

- provide an overview when introducing a new topic so students know what to expect – highlight the main argument and the key points
- leave notes on the board for as long as possible – dyslexic students take longer to copy
- create neat blackboard presentations and use several different chalk colours for different elements of the presentation
- provide photocopied summary notes to reduce the amount of writing dyslexic students have to do
- give examples to illustrate a point
- encourage students to word process coursework

- assess students' work positively – ticks provide encouragement – and use print rather than joined-up handwriting
- ensure the teaching of good study skills
- get students to evaluate their study skills strategies
- provide a list of key vocabulary for the topic
- seek opportunities to praise and to provide positive feedback.

Dysphasia

Dysphasia is a speech disorder that affects not only the powers of expression by speech, but also the powers to comprehend the spoken or written word. Learners suffering from dysphasia may have difficulty in recognising and understanding letters or words, remembering and understanding lengthy sentences, or remembering details from long stories or documents.

When *writing* a student may have difficulty with:

- spelling
- grammar
- forming letters
- sequencing of ideas.

When *reading* a student may have difficulty in:

- recognising and understanding letters or words
- remembering and understanding long sentences
- recalling detail from long passages of text.

When *speaking* a student may have difficulty in:

- thinking of the correct words to say
- forming grammatically correct sentences
- explaining what they mean clearly.

Teaching students with dysphasia means that it is important to communicate in a quiet, relaxed, non-distracting environment, and address the person clearly without raising your voice. In terms of specific strategies for generating understanding:

- get the individual's attention before speaking
- speak slowly using short sentences
- use words that will be familiar to the learner
- avoid discussion about complex issues
- check that the person has understood what you have said
- repeat or rephrase the sentence if necessary
- do not jump from one subject to another.

Attention Deficit Hyperactivity Disorder (ADHD)

ADHD is a neurologically based dysfunction that both affects academic performance and results in impaired self-regulation and impulsiveness. It may be diagnosed by a medical practitioner or a child psychiatrist, often leading to the prescribing of medication. ADHD is found across the ability range and is much more common in boys. Students with ADHD can exhibit a number of challenging behaviours. In terms of academic performance these may include:

- reading problems resulting from problems in concentrating and focusing
- poor organisation and time management
- poor note-taking and writing skills
- difficulty in turn-taking.

One result of this is that students may become highly frustrated, and lose confidence and motivation. They may also become confused about what they are meant to do, or just procrastinate in attempting tasks. They may also exhibit inappropriate social skills or spend too much time socialising with their friends. Inappropriate social skills may include exhibiting disruptive and destructive behaviour. Children and young people with ADHD may also become depressive, anxious and obsessive.

In meeting the learning needs of students with ADHD, teachers should:

- limit distractions as much as possible, particularly areas where there is movement around the classroom
- keep classroom activities well organised, short and with varied pace to maintain attention
- consider language problems and listening difficulties
- be aware of potential relationship difficulties with other college staff and fellow students
- ensure that classroom rules are understood and applied consistently
- give plentiful warnings of impending changes, such as changes to timetables, rooms, new members of staff, etc.

ACTIVITY

Take a look at the following web site, which provides practical advice on helping ADHD students with issues such as problem-solving, social skills, impulsive behaviour and non-compliance: www.btinternet.com/~black.ice/addnet/manage.html

Make a list of the strategies that you find most useful.

Table 5.5, below, provides a list of some of the many web sites that offer help and resources for a wide range of disability groups.

The following case study shows, however, that, despite professed good intentions, some colleges need to go further than their 'equal opportunities' rhetoric. It relates the experience of a student teacher who 'shadowed' a wheelchair-using student for a day around Greybourne College of FE.

Case study: *Equal opportunities policies – theory and practice*

Paul was the college's only student who used a wheelchair, a fact that he found disappointing. He thought that the college didn't do enough to actively look for, and recruit, people like himself. Paul had made his own enquiries around a number of local colleges but had chosen this one because it was the nearest to his home.

Table 5.5 *Disability organisations and their web sites*

Disability organisation	Web site
Action for ME support	www.afme.org.uk/
Adult Dyslexia Association	www.futurenet.co.uk/charity/ado/adomenu/adomenu.htm
Autism/Aspergers Syndrome	www.users.dircon.co.uk/~cns/index.html
British Deaf Association	www.signcommunity.org.uk/
British Dyslexia Association	www.bda-dyslexia.org.uk/main/home/index.asp
The Dyslexia Institute	www.dyslexia-inst.org.uk/
Federation of Deaf People	www.fdp.org.uk/
MENCAP (for people with learning disabilities)	www.mencap.org.uk/
Royal National Institute for the Blind	www.rnib.org.uk
Patient UK – Dysphasia and Aphasia	www.speakability.org.uk/index.htm
ADHD Information Library	www.btinternet.com/~black.ice/addnet/libmain.html

(Source: adapted from FerlFirst web site)

In following Paul around the college that day I was stunned at just how unfriendly the college was for those with physical difficulties. While there were lifts, they were often very crowded with students hurrying to lectures. Paul said that it was in essential places such as the library that he found most difficulty – especially getting access to books. He had to get a member of the library staff to get books for him that were out of reach. One of the most irritating features for Paul was the problem of simply getting through doors. The new teaching block, for example, was fitted with heavy, unyielding fire doors, with no thought for people with disability who had to navigate through them. Paul, however, had a solution. He gave each door a mighty kick!

Overall, although he found the college staff friendly and helpful, he would not recommend the college to any other disabled people, simply because the design of the place was so bad.

(From a student teacher's learning log, Greybourne College of FE)

ACTIVITY

Locate your college's equal opportunities policy, and, if the college has been inspected by Ofsted, read the inspection report (this may be available, at least in summary form, on the Ofsted web site: www.ofsted.gov.uk/reports/). Evaluate the extent to which inclusive strategies are being planned and implemented. Hint: when looking at a report on-line, in your web browser go to Edit/Find and type in the word 'Inclusive'.

Review Questions

1 Why do you think that the 14–19 sector is placing more emphasis on student-centred teaching?
2 Identify four ways in which a lecture can be planned effectively.
3 What strategies can be planned for ensuring that a class discussion is student- rather than teacher-centred?
4 In what ways can strategies, aimed at encouraging inclusive learning, help *all* learners?

SUMMARY

- Teaching methods involve the use of a general approach or technique that determines the type and frequency of interaction between teachers and learners.
- Teaching methods can be classified into teacher-centred, or student-centred.
- In selecting methods, care must be taken to consider planned learning objectives and particularly the type of learned capability.
- Communication includes both verbal and non-verbal interaction between teacher and student and between students. Consideration needs to be given to gaining and maintaining student attention, and to the uses of language in the classroom.
- Where severe barriers to learning exist, for example amongst those who have severe learning difficulties, strategies for inclusive learning need to build skills that encourage student independence.

Suggested Further Reading

Farrell, M. (2003) *Understanding Special Educational Needs: a Guide for Student Teachers*, London: RoutledgeFalmer.
Provides a clear description of the fairly complex legislation and how good practice can be facilitated.

Jaques, D. (1991) *Learning in Groups*, 2nd edition, London: Kogan Page
A valuable resource for understanding how groups function, and how tutors can unleash the potential of a group.

Reid, G. (2003) *Dyslexia: A Practitioner's Handbook*, Chichester: John Wiley and Sons, Inc.
Provides practical material on approaches to teaching as well as the implications for teachers of recent legislation.

Rogers, J. (1989) *Adults Learning*, 3rd edition, Milton Keynes: Open University Press
First published in 1971, this book provides a sound, if a little dated, approach to the teaching of adult learners. It includes advice on giving lectures and using case studies, role-plays and simulations.

6 DEVELOPING LEARNING MATERIALS FOR RESOURCE-BASED LEARNING

Objectives

After reading this chapter, you should be able to:

- decide when the use of resource-based learning materials is justified
- apply basic criteria for designing resource-based learning materials, including course structure, teaching approaches and readability
- organise a programme that includes resource-based learning materials as the primary delivery mechanism
- demonstrate how to produce such materials to professional design and typographical standards.

Colleges are increasingly employing resource-based learning (RBL) in order to promote independent and student-centred learning. Educationalists see such an approach as having advantages in allowing learning that is self-paced. Yet RBL will not meet student expectations if the materials produced are not of the highest quality in terms of instructional design, layout and reproduction. This chapter will group resource-based learning approaches into three broad categories, recognising that there will be overlaps between them (see Figure 6.1):

- *independent learning* – covering situations where the learner has frequent access to a teacher, either working on the materials in class with help immediately available, or working at home with relatively frequent class sessions
- *distance learning* – the learner in this situation is learning primarily on his or her own, with limited or infrequent access to the teacher. In an extreme situation, the learner never sees the teacher, and communicates solely by written or verbal messages
- *manuals and users' guides* – the learner is on his or her own, solely dependent on the materials at hand.

WHAT DO WE MEAN BY RESOURCE-BASED LEARNING?

The three approaches outlined above have been chosen as the focal points for this chapter because they constitute points on a continuum of learner support. It is recognised that RBL materials can include a wide variety of instructional media, including video, multimedia and the web. These, however, are dealt with in more detail in Chapter 7. For practical reasons, it is likely that you will probably, in most cases, be designing text-based RBL materials, so these are the focus of this chapter. It is also recognised that, in many cases, you will often need to produce learning resources on a more modest scale (handouts, overheads, etc.). The issues discussed in this chapter will help with these.

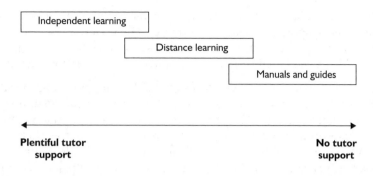

Figure 6.1 *The degree of tutor support for independent learning materials, distance learning, and manuals and guides*

Independent or individualised learning

Over the past 25 years, independent or individualised learning strategies have received considerable attention in school-based and 14–19 education. There are a number of features of independent learning materials that aim to cater for the individuality of learners. These include:

- encouraging self-paced learning
- allowing for flexibility in when and where learning takes place
- providing frequent feedback and individual attention when needed
- incorporating an emphasis on learning for mastery, thus eliminating competition among learners and replacing it with competition against a set standard of performance.

What do independent learning materials look like? Typically, they tend to be highly structured readings (such as handouts or study guides) containing activities to be carried out, plus questions, with places to record observations, data and answers. For independent learning materials, activities and some written work may typically be carried out in the classroom, particularly if there is a practical aspect to the exercise, such as a science or engineering laboratory investigation. At other times, such materials may be used for independent study in a special room or area (sometimes located in the library). These go under various names such as open learning centre or learning resource unit.

Distance learning

Distance learning can be distinguished from independent learning by the characteristic that distance learning assumes that you, the teacher, are at a distance from the learner for most, if not all, of the time. This has a number of consequences for the structure of any learning materials and implications for the assumed characteristics of successful learners.

First, materials are prepared and produced ahead of delivery time, usually consisting of written matter, but they may also consist of learning activities delivered through other media, such as audio or video tapes, 35 mm slide, pictures or maps, television programmes, or multimedia learning courseware. Whatever the medium, the course itself must be self-contained and provide unambiguous instructions to guide the learner without the support of a teacher or trainer. Open University materials provide typical examples of the type of materials that learners encounter, consisting of study guides, CD-ROM or web-based programs that direct the learner to different media.

The question obviously arises: for whom is distance learning most appropriate? While there is no simple answer, one can be assured that it is not an appropriate medium for everyone. The Open University, for example, despite the quality of its courses, has a high dropout rate and many students find the courses very demanding. While some of this may be attributed to the academic nature of the courses, working in isolation for the majority of the time does require a considerable amount of perseverance, self-regulation and self-confidence. Colleges that adopt this route for teaching need to consider carefully the ways in which distance learning students can be supported. This might mean more than simply requiring a student to meet with their personal tutor. It might involve the establishment of a regulated system for personal contact, including meetings, telephone support and e-mail communications.

Manuals and guides

Whereas distance learning entails infrequent contact with a tutor, teacher or trainer, learning solely from manuals typically eliminates a human instructor completely. Consequently, a manual intended to serve as a self-contained learning resource must be clearly, accurately and precisely written. Even seemingly small transgressions such as incorrect labels on diagrams, errors of fact, missing steps in procedures, and other inaccuracies seriously undermine a manual's usefulness. At the same time, excess information and irrelevant exercises may test the learner's patience.

DECIDING WHEN TO USE RESOURCE-BASED LEARNING

Resource-based learning, and particularly distance learning, has been used for many years in commercial and industrial settings where the need to train large numbers of people has justified the often heavy design and start-up costs. RBL, however, is now increasingly popular in 14–19 education because of the flexibility it offers as well as the potential for teaching larger numbers of students. The decision to use RBL, though, should be taken as much on educational as on economic grounds. Furthermore, in deciding to use this approach, you should consider the knowledge and aptitudes of the students who are your intended users. Anderson, Brown and Race (1997) also warn that a positive attitude towards RBL needs to be inculcated in the college and that both students and staff may need training in its use. Let us now look at the situations in which the uses of RBL might be justified.

Learner characteristics

To succeed, your learners must be intrinsically motivated and possess significant amounts of independence and initiative. They must be 'self-regulating' individuals. Let us look at the traits required in more detail.

Learned capabilities

As we saw in Chapter 5, these comprise intellectual skills, cognitive strategies, verbal information, motor skills and attitudes. In principle, RBL materials can be used to deliver learning that involves any learned capability. It is probably most effective, however, in the teaching of verbal information, intellectual skills and cognitive strategies. This is because concepts, procedures and problem-solving skills can usually be taught, at least in part, by a text-based medium. This is less so with motor skills, which usually need a practical demonstration of the skill. Attitudes can be discussed in text, but entrenched attitudes are notoriously difficult to change, and may require more personal, experiential forms of learning such as role-play or buzz-groups (as discussed in Chapter 5).

General abilities

It is vital that RBL materials are designed to match the literacy and numeracy levels of the target audience. It is also essential that students possess good study habits. Since key skills are becoming a central element of the 14–19 curriculum, it is more likely (but by no means certain) that most students will possess these, or at least begin to acquire them.

Aptitude for learning

RBL materials can be designed for all levels of learners. While it is important not to make the materials too complex for some learners, equally those learners with high aptitudes must be stimulated and 'stretched'. Students with special educational needs will also have particular requirements that will have to be taken into account.

Personal traits

For some learners the positive motivation to succeed is outweighed by the negative fear of failure. Learners who fear failure have a tendency to persist longer on difficult tasks they have no chance of completing. They also have a tendency to choose such tasks as opposed to simpler ones. In a classroom it would be possible for the teacher to see when this was happening and to guide the learner towards more accessible tasks. With RBL this is obviously not so easy. It may be prudent, then, to counsel such students (to the extent that they can be identified in advance) on to programmes that contain a greater element of personal contact and support from tutors.

Convenience

Many people, and adults in particular, do not have the time or opportunity to study full-time at their local FE college. RBL, then, allows these people the flexibility to study at a time and place convenient to themselves. Indeed, research by Calder and McCollum (1997) concludes that the flexibility of using this approach was one of the prime reasons that adults in FE liked it.

Individualised learning

Since course materials are sent to a variety of students in different locations, it is possible to individualise the pace and content of the study materials. This can be achieved by providing a variety of routes through the content, including alternative entry and exit points.

Quality

Another advantage of RBL materials is that, in principle, the quality of instruction can be improved by assigning the best subject matter specialists and educationalists to their production. Certainly, the Open University, for example, has developed a well-earned reputation for the professional quality of its open and distance learning programmes. In contrast, with live instruction, the quality of the presentation will depend, in large part, on the individual skills of the tutor.

Economies of scale

One of the principal advantages of resource-based learning is that it can be used to instruct large numbers of students. This is significant when there is limited capacity in existing educational institutions, but pressure to teach more students. In teaching large student volumes, it is possible to achieve economies of scale where fixed costs can be spread, resulting, overall, in falling average costs per student.

THE SYSTEMATIC DESIGN OF RBL MATERIALS

One important issue associated with RBL is whether to use or adapt existing resources or to design them 'from scratch'. Following the advice of Anderson, Brown and Race (1997), it is important to avoid the 'Not invented here' syndrome, that is, looking too critically at materials that have at least some potential for use. What is essential is that you check any stated learning aims or objectives contained in the materials to see if they match the learning outcomes your students need to achieve. You could even try out the materials yourself, or trial them with a group of students. In many cases, however, you will have to either adapt or produce your own materials, and the remainder of this section assumes you will be doing this.

To ensure that resource-based learning materials meet quality requirements, they should be produced according to a system. Figure 6.2 suggests one such structured process.

Stage 1: Planning

Analyse learner needs

Before the process of course design and production can begin, you need to establish a clear picture of your target audience – its size and composition in terms of aptitudes, key skills, knowledge, etc. What do they know, and what do they *need* to know?

Set aims/objectives

As with good practice for the design of any instructional session, set out clear and well-formulated aims and objectives. As noted in Chapter 4, without objectives that are constructed in measurable, behavioural terms (for example, the students will be able to define, describe, calculate, analyse, etc.) you will be unable to later evaluate whether these learning outcomes have been achieved.

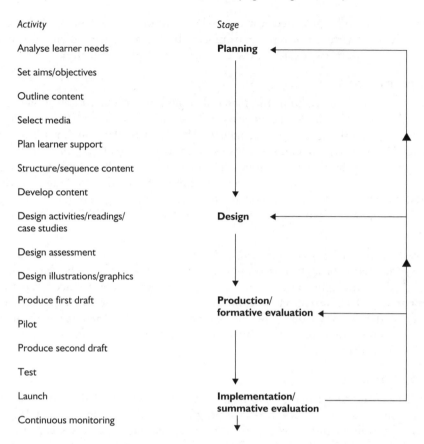

Activity	Stage
Analyse learner needs	**Planning**
Set aims/objectives	
Outline content	
Select media	
Plan learner support	
Structure/sequence content	
Develop content	
Design activities/readings/case studies	**Design**
Design assessment	
Design illustrations/graphics	
Produce first draft	**Production/ formative evaluation**
Pilot	
Produce second draft	
Test	
Launch	**Implementation/ summative evaluation**
Continuous monitoring	

Figure 6.2 *Systematic process for the design of resource-based learning materials*

Outline content

At this stage, it is enough to have an overview of the broad areas you intend to cover. Establish the parameters of the topic so you know what you intend to include and what will be discounted.

Select media

We have seen (in Chapter 5) that media should be chosen on the basis of an analysis of the learned capabilities to be delivered. It may be the case, for example, that text-based materials are simply inadequate for teaching a particular behaviour or motor skill.

Plan learner support

This stage is so often omitted when planning RBL materials, yet it is vital for a programme's success. If you meet with and teach your learners regularly, you may decide to design independent learning materials. In this case, some of the student support may be designed into the materials, but you will be able to provide some of the support face-to-face. With distance learning materials support will have to be planned into the materials themselves. You will also have to decide how additional support, if any, is to be provided, for example, by tutorials, a telephone help-line, or perhaps through a virtual learning environment. If students have individual learning plans, you might want to consider how support can be built into these.

Structure/sequence materials

As with *any* form of instruction, the material should be structured and organised to make its absorption by the learner as easy as possible. This means, for example, presenting the material in a logical sequence. This is particularly important if the content is dealing with sequential processes (such as in engineering, or construction, for example), or if the material requires that one body of skills/knowledge is necessary as a precursor to learning another. Sometimes the nature of this structure may be presented by the subject matter itself. At other times, some thought and planning may be required. Figure 6.3 shows an example of what Holmberg (1977) calls a concentric approach.

In Figure 6.3, material (1) is presented and consolidated in various ways; then secondary material is brought in to support it. The skill/knowledge of the student is then checked. At this point (2), another part of the subject is introduced and treated in a similar way. Then attention is again given to the first topic to consolidate and widen the student's knowledge. Thus an issue or problem can be dealt with in several different but supporting study units, with the result that the learning whole is greater than the sum of the parts.

Develop content

Having decided on the structure and flow of material, the detailed content can be added. If you are producing a large-scale programme, and you are co-operating with other colleagues in writing it, you will need to set out and agree a system of specifications for writing the course. These will include the tone to be adopted (formal/informal), the style of writing (for example, average length of sentences, use of abbreviations, etc.), and how readings and activities are to be used.

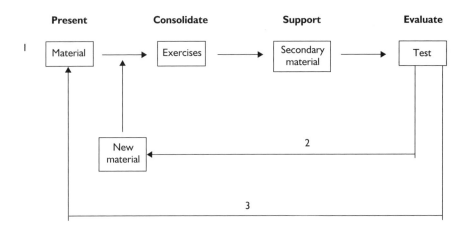

Figure 6.3 *The concentric approach to material presentation*

Stage 2: Design

Design activities/readings/case studies

These are crucial to the success of any set of resource-based learning materials because they add to the 'colour' of the materials, providing interest and stimulation, as well as providing the student with a greater depth of understanding. Activities should be relevant and should not be included merely to break up the textual discourse. Lockwood (1992) suggests that the design of activities should be:

- dispersed at regular intervals in the instructional materials
- focused on each key element of the content
- easy to identify typographically, for example, by being placed in a box
- expressed in a language that is fairly informal and that stimulates an 'implied' dialogue.

Above all, given the objectives of any programme, they should be pitched at the appropriate cognitive level. For readings, given the complexities of copyright law, it is usually prudent to avoid using photocopies of articles and instead to direct the students to a carefully selected textbook (but check, first, that the book will be in print for a number of years!). Case studies, particularly if they are topical, can help the materials to 'come alive', but need to be kept concise, otherwise they will dominate the text.

Design assessment

Assessment activities can be designed with many different objectives in mind. Assessment is described in more detail on page 147.

Design illustrations/graphics

The use of graphics can add essential support to the instructional message carried by the text. Lowe (1993) suggests that diagrams can have two functions:

- They can *parallel the text* to reinforce the material.
- They can provide *additional information* such as representing spatial relationships.

Avoid making graphics gratuitous (using them for their own sake), but always consider ways of making your text more interesting. If you cannot think of an illustration, look at commercial clipart packages (available on CD-ROM or on the web) for some ideas. Using graphics, however, does not mean just using illustrations and photographs. As Rowntree (1994) points out, even lists and tables are examples of using the graphics approach, and can add interest and clarity to the text.

Stage 3: Production/formative evaluation

Produce first draft

This is where the hard work begins! Since most of the production will be text-based, try to adopt approaches that allow you the maximum control over your materials. It is an advantage if you can type the materials yourself (new ideas may spring to mind as you do this). Above all, make use of the automatic document-producing facilities (such as numbering and paragraph layout) that come supplied with your word processing application.

Pilot

Piloting is the process of getting a small group of either colleagues or, more usefully, end-users, to try out a sample of the materials. It is often referred to as formative evaluation, and is used to elicit views on the quality of the materials while they are being developed. This is the moment of truth. You can pilot informally: 'What do you think of this?' Or decide on a more formal approach using, say, a questionnaire for users to complete. What kinds of question is it sensible to ask? Well, that, in part, depends on the nature of the RBL materials you have produced. Clearly, you may need feedback on the content itself and its sequence and structuring. You may want to know about whether users like the presentation of illustrations and graphics. Don't forget to ask at least one open-ended, 'catch all' question such as 'What other problems did you find?', so that nothing is left to chance.

Whichever you adopt, you should not attempt to influence the decision and should prepare yourself for some frank responses. Far better to take the criticism at this stage than when the materials are launched to a large audience.

Produce second draft

Build the feedback from piloting into the second draft of the materials. Of course, if the evaluation is quite negative, you may have to revisit some of the previous stages of course design, including the aims and objectives of the programme and the structure and sequence of the materials, to make adjustments. As Figure 6.2 (page 137) shows, there are remedial loops built into the design process, allowing, if necessary, for a cycle of step-wise improvement.

Test

While piloting is getting the views of users on the quality of the materials, testing (often called development testing or field trials) is seeing whether the materials actually work in practice. This is sometimes referred to as summative evaluation. If the objective is to, say, teach nursery nurses some of the principles of First Aid, can they put a splint on a broken limb after studying the course? If not, you will need to analyse why. Are there errors in the content? Is the material poorly sequenced? Are there vital, but missing illustrations? Is the use of language suited to the audience? Both piloting and testing may address similar issues, but the latter approach will also enquire about the impact the materials have had on learning itself. You now must enter a remedial loop (see Figure 6.2) to discover and correct the problem. You must eventually return again to the piloting stage to ascertain if the materials now work.

Case Study: *Evaluating and improving handouts*

We had a lecturer on my teacher-training course who was always going on about evaluation. He obviously thought he was some kind of expert on it. We all noticed, though, that he never evaluated his own sessions, so none of us took it very seriously. One day, though, my supervisor at my placement suggested I should construct an evaluation form and evaluate some of my lessons using it. He said it would be useful for my learning log and give me something good to discuss. I delayed for a while, but then decided it would be a good idea. I constructed a form and asked questions about my own delivery style, use of visual aids and use of handouts. I got positive feedback from most of the students on all these things, except the handouts – which surprised me. I'm not an expert with computers, but I always word processed handouts, so I thought the students would think they were okay. In fact, they thought they were boring. I've since then got together with some of my peers and introduced better font style and made more use of graphics.

(Student teacher, Greybourne College of FE)

ACTIVITY

Design a simple evaluation form that you can use for either the pilot or testing stage of course development. You might want to include issues such as:

- the nature and level of the content
- its sequencing and organisation
- the tone and complexity of language used (was it 'fit for purpose'?)
- the use of tables, figures and illustrations
- the general layout and design
- whether the materials were interesting
- whether the materials actually taught anything.

Elicit feedback on the quality of the form (for example, have you asked too many/not enough questions, was each question correctly phrased?) by asking a group of students to use the form in evaluating some materials you have produced.

Stage 4: Implementation/summative evaluation

Launch

If you have spent time and effort (often in conjunction with a team of developers) producing a programme, you may want to launch the course with a bit a 'splash'. This might include a special 'event' in the college's Learning Resource Centre, or publicity in the college's weekly newsletter.

Continuous monitoring

As Rowntree (1994) points out, it is important to collect information about the materials during the life of the programme. Subject matter, for example, changes so the materials may need regular revision. Groups of learners change so what was appropriate for one group may not be liked or work with another. Indeed, if the materials are to be used with several different, and diverse groups, it may be necessary to produce different versions of the programme.

What we have dealt with here is an ideal situation. The volume of RBL materials you intend to produce may not warrant such a rigorous approach. Nevertheless, be aware that the more you adhere to a methodical system such as this, the less chance there is of errors being made.

INSTRUCTIONAL DESIGN FOR RBL

We have looked at a systematic process for the production of RBL materials. What we now need is a set of principles that can help us in designing materials that can actually *teach*.

The events of instruction

One approach is Gagné, Briggs and Wager's (1992) nine events of instruction. These are important, because they encourage the designer to consider issues that will assist the learner in understanding the materials and applying their new knowledge.

Gaining attention

When designing resource-based learning materials, attention can be gained by various methods such as the use of graphics, or by the judicious use of typefaces or text layout (see page 150). Colour can also be effective in attracting attention.

Informing the learner of objectives

Objectives can be stated formally at the beginning of materials, or the general skills that learners should acquire can be indicated. As we saw in Chapter 4 clearly stated and measurable objectives are important for any course of instruction. They are particularly vital for resource-based learning because of the absence of regular face-to-face support. Hence, objectives can give learners a clear idea of the type and level of content that is to come. This is important if they need to know if the material is suited to their knowledge, abilities and perhaps reading level. Objectives might also act as motivators, setting out the skills or information that the learner is about to acquire. They also act as *advance organisers*, allowing the learner to make sense of the new material (in relation to what they already know) because the objectives indicate where they are going.

Stimulating recall of prerequisite learning

Stimulating the recall of learning can be achieved in a number of ways. This can be done, for example, through a pre-test, or by simply asking learners to think back to an earlier unit or module. Recalling previous learning allows learners to prepare themselves cognitively for the assimilation of new material.

Presenting the stimulus material

Presentation of the material will be largely dependent on your own skills and imagination, and will require the implementation of many of the ideas suggested in this chapter.

Providing learning guidance

A resource-based learning course, then, has to support and assist the learner as effectively as a tutor would. It must therefore be effective at 'hand-holding' and guiding. Methods of achieving this include the use of maps laying out the structure of the course, introductory 'handshakes' to greet the learner, navigational signposts (such as special symbols) to show the learner which way to go, and summaries. Guiding the learner might also mean pointing out what it is essential to learn, and asking questions of the student to stimulate thought and reflection. The learner should also be encouraged to draw correct and useful conclusions. One of the original commentators on distance learning, Holmberg (1977) argues that it is also more effective if guides to studying are built into the course itself rather than being provided separately. Clearly, the original development of key skills follows this advice. Supporting the learner also involves giving complete and clear explanations with relevant examples. Essentially, the material must be clear, lucid and sufficiently intuitive to stand alone (especially in the case of manuals where tutor support is absent). Guidance can be achieved through, for example, the use of activities or readings, or in the case of independent learning materials, eliciting feedback from the tutor.

Eliciting the performance

If the learning materials aim to teach higher-level intellectual skills such as rule-learning and problem-solving, then it is important that the learner is given an opportunity to practise the skill and to receive feedback on how well they have done. Usually, it is better if the first performances to be requested follow the path of examples given in the materials. Thus, having explained how a spreadsheet can be used to present data as a pie chart, get the students to key in some data and produce both pie and bar charts (the latter designed to extend the learner's skill).

Providing feedback about performance

Gagné, Briggs and Wager (1992) argue that there must be feedback on the degree of correctness in the performance. Self-assessment tests may allow the learner to establish for themselves whether they have understood a particular topic – especially where answers are provided somewhere in the text. Note, however, that the level of performance must match that set in the original learning objectives. It is possible to set self-assessment questions at a verbal information, concept-learning and rule-learning level. It is less likely that closed questions will assess problem-solving, so here there may be a need to involve a teacher in checking answers. Questions and tests may assist in the last event of instruction, retention and transfer. It is surprising, then, that, as Ellington and Race (1994) warn, in most RBL materials feedback is provided almost as an afterthought rather than being planned into the design of the materials well in advance.

Another essential feature of feedback is timing. If learners have produced an answer, they need to know whether they have got it right. Providing the answer within the resource-based materials can, obviously, facilitate this. If the materials involve independent learning, it may be the role of the tutor to provide this feedback within the class itself. In cases where a lengthy piece of coursework has been produced, it should be returned as soon as possible. A commitment to 'turn around' written work within a specific time is sometimes a feature of a college's student charter.

Assessing performance

A performance can be elicited and the results noted, but even now, can you be sure that the student has understood the material? You can only be sure that your assessment is reliable by providing more than one opportunity for this knowledge and understanding to be tested. Using the example of the production of pie and bar charts, you need to find out whether the student achieved the production of these graphs using an element of guesswork. Also important is validity. Did the performance reflect the original learning objectives set? You might like to review some assessment issues in Chapter 3.

Enhancing retention and transfer

For knowledge and new skills to be retained, it is vital that there is ample opportunity for practising their retrieval. This will happen more effectively if these are practised during the weeks or months of the programme rather than when, say, a new skill is just being taught. So you will need to include regular opportunities for practice and review, for example by using activities or case studies, throughout the materials.

Transfer can be aided by getting the learner to perform the results of learning in a *variety* of settings. Say, for example, that a student is studying A-level Economics, and has learnt some of the principles of supply and demand; at a later date, they could be asked to apply these principles to explain why some currencies fluctuate against each other in the international currency markets.

Teaching approaches

As with face-to-face teaching, there are a number of approaches or strategies that one can use when devising resource-based learning experiences, depending on the objectives. Some of these will take more care to successfully execute than others, and all require the developer to be aware of the characteristics of the target audience. In practice, a given set of materials may employ more than one of the following approaches.

Reading/viewing text or video images

This approach is ideal for those who do not require high levels of student–tutor interaction as part of their learning. Video can be effective when the learning objective requires the teaching of concepts where the demonstration of animation is essential, or in the teaching of attitudes or behaviours.

Tutorial

This is where learners are introduced to facts and concepts, the latter by providing examples and near non-examples, to enhance their ability to recognise them. Sometimes this may involve taking the learner through a set of stepwise procedures.

Drill and practice

These are practice exercises with either a self-check against provided answers, or where the responses are checked by the teacher/trainer. Such an approach can be used to assist in the learning of concepts and combinations of concepts as applied to routine problems. For young adult learners, however, care must be taken not to make the process of learning too repetitive and monotonous.

Guided discovery

Some concepts are most meaningfully learned through discovery by the learner. This approach requires the learner to carry out a step-by-step process and to record findings, after which deductions or generalisations are made.

Inquiry

This approach, often used in science and history teaching, involves providing the learner with discrepant events and 'what if . . .?' questions.

Learner–learner interaction

This is where small groups of learners come together when ready to engage in evaluative and/or design activities. Some higher-level skills would be very difficult to learn independently, without some human interaction.

Projects

While individuals should on some occasions be encouraged to engage in independent project work, this approach needs to ensure that adequate physical and intellectual tools (prerequisite skills) are available.

Readability

The readability of text-based materials is largely determined by the style in which they are written. Formal textbooks and manuals, for example, may contain long, complex sentences and a specialised vocabulary. As such, they are only understandable to a particular audience. In writing resource-based learning materials, therefore, you must write with the reader clearly in mind so that your materials are accessible. In determining the readability of any resource-based learning materials you have designed, it is advisable to use one of the various formulae that have been designed for this purpose. One of the most widely used is the Flesch Reading Ease formula. In calculating a figure, the formula uses two characteristics:

- the number of syllables per hundred words
- the number of words per sentence in a hundred-word sample.

The first takes into account the difficulty of words and the second the complexity of sentences. Fortunately, most word processing applications packages have built-in facilities for automatically calculating a Flesch Reading Ease figure.

> ### ACTIVITY
>
> Take an example of resource-based learning materials (it could be as small as a handout) that you have word processed. Using your word processing software application, perform a readability assessment of your materials. Keep a note of the score.

Calculating a Flesch Reading Ease score, then, is relatively simple, but what does it mean? The maximum figure is 100 with higher figures indicating simplicity of language. Table 6.1 provides an interpretation that should assist you in determining whether the text is appropriate for your learners.

Rowntree (1990) suggests a number of ways for making text more readable, including:

Table 6.1 *Suggested corresponding materials for various ranges of Flesch Reading Ease scores*

Reading Ease Score	Style	Average reading age	Suggested typical reading
90–100	Very easy	9–10	Children's book, Key Stages 4–5
80–89	Easy	10–11	Mills & Boon, *The Daily Star*
70–79	Fairly easy	11–12	*The Daily Telegraph*
60–69	Standard	12–14	Terry Pratchett stories
50–59	Fairly difficult	14–16+	Secondary school textbooks
30–49	Difficult	17–19	A-level texts/college textbooks
0–29	Very difficult	22+	Academic journals

- using the first person
- using contractions (don't, didn't, etc.)
- talking directly to the reader ('you may consider . . .')
- using active verbs and subjects ('use', 'demonstrate')
- using short sentences
- using rhetorical questions ('How shall we phrase questions, then?').

The extent to which you use any of these devices will depend on how formal or informal you want to make your materials.

Case Study: *Considering readability levels of learning materials*

I think that when you are already teaching, but studying for a teaching qualification part-time, you are under extra pressure to 'perform'. It is worse when your supervisor is one of your teaching colleagues, as was my case. This was probably why I got rather carried away once in producing a handout, and ended up spending hours producing an eight-page document. I was rather proud of myself. The next time I took that class, my supervisor decided she would observe me. As part of the lesson, the students read through some of the sections in the handout. I noticed that some of them stumbled over some of the longer words, and that there was a general restlessness in the class. My supervisor saw me afterwards and told me that many of the words and phrases I had used were just too complicated for these kinds of student. I felt really deflated, given the hard work I had put in, but it was a useful lesson to learn.

(Student teacher, Greybourne College of FE)

ACTIVITY

Take a short section of distance learning materials (say, 500 words in length). It could be something you have written yourself. Amend the materials in the light of Rowntree's recommendations by underlining problem areas and adding your alternatives. Are the materials now more 'readable'?

Setting activities

Activities are an essential aspect of a resource-based learning course. While *this* textbook is not an example of resource-based learning in the strictest sense, it too contains activities that, it is hoped, you have found useful, and that may provide you with an example of how they can be designed.

Most learning outcomes require that the learner is able to do more than just recite verbal information – the learner may be asked to *do* something (for example, analyse data, perform an experiment). Activities provide opportunities for such practice. By requiring the learner to apply their new knowledge or skill they must first fully understand it, so activities can also *reinforce* learning by getting the learner to review and assimilate what they have read. Particularly where higher levels of learning outcomes are sought (for example, problem-solving), activities may require the learner to *transfer* what they have learnt to a different or unique situation. Achieving transfer is important since it not only tests learners' understanding but allows them to use their new abilities across a potentially infinite number of new situations.

Assessment

Assessment should be a core component of resource-based learning materials because only through assessment can both you and the learner come to a clear understanding of what has been learnt. It can therefore also identify gaps in knowledge and misconceptions. Assessment, then, is not just a matter of marks and grades, it is an essential aspect of learning itself. Within the text, questions can help interaction by establishing a kind of 'dialogue' between tutor and learner. They can also require the learner to pause and check on their own progress. Assessment was examined in more depth in Chapter 3.

Assessment may take many different forms, including short answers, objective tests (multiple-choice, true–false, matching items), assignments and practical exercises. Usually, with applied vocational qualifications, the effectiveness of training will be assessed by how efficiently people perform their job in the working environment. A common and valid form of question in RBL materials is the use of self-assessment questions. Clearly, these only work if you provide the student with a set of 'answers' against which they can check their knowledge and understanding. When designing self-assessment activities, it is best to use closed questions because the number of potential answers is more limited and easier to handle.

Self-assessment questions (SAQs) assist in the promotion of *active learning* by participants. Well-written SAQs must:

- relate to the course objectives
- motivate the student by being realistic and varied
- be clearly written and in the appropriate tone.

The answers to SAQs must be accessible without being easily seen before the question is attempted. Obvious places to locate them would be after the learner has turned the page, or at the end of the materials. Whatever policy is adopted, the system for finding answers should be explained and practised the first time it is used.

Course organisation

This is as much a part of instructional design as any of the other aspects discussed so far. It includes, for example, planning how students are to be supported and tutored on the programme. As Chapter 9 shows, guiding and supporting students is of paramount importance in 14–19 education, but this chapter is mainly concerned with the pastoral welfare of students. For instructional design, we need to plan student support to match their learning needs.

Students using independent learning materials may receive some classroom support from the tutor, but for many distance learning students one of the major difficulties is isolation. Not only are they separated from the close attentions of a tutor, they are also isolated from fellow learners. Distance learning students often comprise part-time learners, which means competing priorities can get in the way of study. They may also be adults whose study skills need updating.

In the past, traditional methods of communication between tutor and students working at a distance would be by post or telephone. Today, the medium is usually electronic mail, which can include messages within the main body of the e-mail itself, or the sending of documents (such as drafts or completed assignments) as attachments to the e-mail. Another element of two-way communication is when students seek advice on how to tackle assignments or other practical exercises. Learning via resource-based methods means that the student may feel isolated from other learners and this may increase their anxiety.

PUBLICATION AND PRESENTATION OF MATERIALS

The quality of layout and presentation of the materials is important since poor quality study guides or workbooks can seriously hinder the impact of the instructional message, both distorting the message and demotivating the learner. At the most extreme level, this may be because they are just impossible to read. Another, more realistic, possibility is that, although readable, they are so badly set out that reading is a chore. On the other hand, well-planned and produced materials can enhance the impact of instruction.

Certainly, the spread of computer technology and the art of desktop publishing (DTP) has meant that even organisations of modest means can now afford to produce high-quality materials. The laser-printed document has now become the norm rather than the exception and an organisation's work will therefore pale by comparison if it is not up to a generally accepted standard.

Layout and instructional design

Human perception, that is, our sensory awareness of our surroundings, is *selective* because our basic perpetual capacities are severely limited. The designer should take this into account in the layout and presentation of materials. This means that the reader should not be expected to assimilate a large number of messages at the same time. For example, it is better to limit the highlighting of key words or graphics, as too much emphasis will tend to confuse the eye.

The design process should also ensure that information is presented at a *pace* (i.e. the amount per page) and in *quantities* (chunks) that are comfortable to the learner so that assimilation is made easier. You should therefore avoid the temptation to save printing costs by cramming as much information as possible on to one page. Recognition is another key issue. If it is desirable that the learner pays particular attention to a certain piece of text or graphic then this should be presented in a way that makes it stand out from the main body of the material.

Like perception, our cognitive capacities are also limited in terms of the way we get new information into memory, and how we retain it and retrieve it when necessary. This process can be helped by presenting information in a number of ways (text, diagrams, pictures, etc.) that repeat the information. Graphical representations also generally make information easier to recognise, process and to recall.

Attention to layout can also influence student motivation, another key influence on learning. The use of dense volumes of text, with few white spaces, pictures or diagrams, would be completely demotivating for many learners, particularly the young or those with low reading abilities.

Knowing your audience

We have seen that understanding the needs of learners is one of the central elements to good design. In some circumstances the key factor is getting your material noticed, as it is vital to catch the eye (such as in advertising). Here, words may be printed white on black or even upside down with little notice paid to legibility. But in general, for instructional materials, legibility is the key. Unfortunately, legibility itself is quite an ambiguous term. If you say that a block of text is legible what you mean is that *you* can read it, not necessarily that someone else can. McLean (1980) describes legibility as being a situation where 'the people we want to read it can read it in the conditions in which we think they will see it'.

To make something legible, the designer must know *what* is to be read, *why* it is to be read, *who* will read it, and *when* and *where* it will be read. Thus, the text you are reading on this page may be legible for you (sitting down and concentrating on it), but would, of course, be totally illegible if used on, say, a road-side advertising hoarding. Novels, for instance, are set as continuous blocks of text, it being assumed that the reader is likely to read at leisure and hence have the ability (and motivation) to cope with text presented in this uncompromising fashion. Resource-based learning materials, however, may have to deal with readers who are less well motivated or have lower reading age levels. The designer, then, may break the text up with sub-headings and diagrams to make it easier to read. Also, sections with headings are easier to relocate, a point to consider in learning materials that focus on intellectual skills. These are usually *not* learned through a single reading and the textual material may need to be referred to later as the skill is practised. The look of a page, then, will be determined by the nature of your material and who it is aimed at.

Desktop publishing

A personal computer (PC) and word processing package, or even a more sophisticated desktop publishing program, are necessary but not sufficient tools to produce high-quality DTP materials. Whatever your tools you will also need the design concepts to use them effectively. Some of the more important concepts are introduced in this section.

Quality of print

Recent developments in hardware and software present the designer with many choices, the first of which is that type (printed text) can come in a variety of resolutions, sizes and typefaces (fonts).

Resolution

The resolution of a piece of type that affects the apparent clarity and sharpness is determined by the number of dots or pixels that go to make it. A resolution of 600 dpi (dots per inch) is relatively low resolution compared to professional standards (such as you would find in a glossy magazine), but is more than adequate for most needs.

Type measurement

One of the great advantages of desktop publishing is that you have access to a variety of type sizes. Type size (height) is usually measured in terms of points: an inch is divided into 72 points. Thus a 12-point font takes up a maximum of 12/72 = 1/6 inch high space. Most resource-based learning materials should be produced in a 10 or 12 point font.

Type groups and type families

The typeface chosen can greatly affect the appearance of a document and there are hundreds to choose from. In practice, however, your choice will probably be limited by the typefaces available on your computer and those supported by your printer. Table 6.2 presents some examples.

ACTIVITY

Check which typefaces you have available on your own computer. Print out and examine an example of each typeface in its different weights (normal, **bold**, *italic* and ***bold italic***). Produce a handout using two contrasting fonts and ask a class of students which they prefer and why.

Table 6.2 *Typefaces and common uses*

Typeface	Common uses
Times Roman	Instructional materials such as study guides, handouts, etc.
Arial	Overheads and presentational materials
Courier	Letters and legal documents
Impact	**Newsletters and publicity materials**

Typesetting

Word processors produce typeset output whilst typewriters produced typescript. Typescript characters are 'fixed pitch', that is, they take the same width no matter how wide they look. Thus the 'm' is artificially compressed and the 'i' made wider with extra space on either side to make both letters the same size. This makes the spaces between characters uneven and the whole effect more difficult to read.

In contrast, typeset characters vary in width in proportion to the size of the characters. Thus an 'm' will be wider than a 'z'. In the language of desktop printers, these are referred to as 'proportional' fonts. Typesetting offers greater flexibility, takes up less space, offers more typefaces, weights and sizes, and adds authority to a document.

Since the type presented on the computer screen is also fixed-space, what you see on the screen should be the same as what you get as a printed copy in typescript only. Word processing applications now have a 'preview' page in graphics mode to accurately show how proportional fonts will appear in the final document.

Leading

This is the spacing between lines and is an important factor in typesetting. In the days of typesetting in the printing industry, strips of lead were physically placed between the rows of type (hence the name). Today, word processing applications use a default setting that provides an automatic size for leading.

Page layout

As we have seen, you must decide on the objectives of your document and the audience you are writing for. If it is of a 'serious' nature, then large, relatively unbroken blocks of text may be appropriate. If it is less formal, say a newsletter, or for learners with relatively low interest levels, then the information could be presented in two or three columns; pictures or diagrams could also be added. Note that it is not always necessary to fill every part of a page.

Use of space

Space is particularly important for resource-based learning materials since it affects the look or 'colour' of the text. It is important that the text does not look too dark or dense since, as we have commented, this can be intimidating and demotivating to the reader. The use of space may entail extra costs in terms of paper used, but will present a more friendly image that will be of benefit for instruction.

Headings

Headings and subheadings break up the text and act as signposts to help readers find their way round a document. Headings look better if they have a hierarchical structure. So use larger, bolder or upper case headings (or combinations of these) for important headings that come at the top of the hierarchy (for example, chapter or main section titles). Use non-bold, lower case for headings at the bottom of the headings hierarchy. Table 6.3 shows a way of indicating the hierarchy of headings (i.e. the structure) of a typical document.

You can use any headings structure you like, but above all be consistent. If you are numbering the headings and all those headings below the section headings start off

Table 6.3 *A headings hierarchy*

Title	Lower case, bold, 16 point type
UNIT 7	Upper case, bold, 14 point type
SECTION HEADINGS	Upper case, bold, 12 point type
Subheadings	Lower case, bold, 12 point type
Sub-subheadings	Lower case, italics, 12 point type

numbered as 1.1, 1.2, etc., they should be numbered in this way throughout the document. A useful hint is to always start at as high a level of numbering as possible. If you start with 1.1 and use 1.1.1, 1.1.2, etc., as the next level you will soon find yourself down to using, say, Roman numerals for subsequent levels. What do you use if you need a level below this? The problem usually does not arise for small documents or handouts, but for larger ones it can quickly become an issue. If you do find you need a hierarchy involving several levels of sub-subheadings, consider whether the structure of the document is becoming too complex and look for ways to simplify it.

Emphasis

It is relatively easy to add emphasis to key words or phrases by using capitals, bold and italics. If over-used, however, the effect is lost. Take care, then, to use emphasis sparingly. Also, be consistent. If you use italics for emphasis do not suddenly choose to use bold later in the same document. Finally, avoid using capitals for emphasis except in headings (they are ugly and unbalance a document) and try not to use underlining (a throwback to the days of the typewriter).

Footnotes

The use of footnotes will largely depend on the academic tone of materials you are producing. In scholarly works the use of footnotes might be quite extensive, for example, to quote references. In general, however, resource-based learning materials are meant to present a more friendly face and are therefore not usually presented in this kind of formal way. That is not to say that references are irrelevant, but that they will usually be placed either at the end of a chapter or at the end of the book or materials.

Lines and boxes

Lines, or 'rules', and boxes can add to the look of materials but should be used with care. Boxes can be used in a different thickness or with shading, but note that heavy lines or thick shading may unbalance the look of a page. As with most of the issues discussed in this chapter, if in doubt, experiment and ask for the comments of your colleagues or students.

Illustrations

As we have stressed, the use of illustrations such as graphs, drawings, pictures or photographs can add considerable interest to your materials and may be a central part of the instructional message. Today, there are numerous graphics packages available for producing high-quality graphs, while images, drawings and cartoons can be imported from clip art software held on a CD-ROM, DVD or on web sites (for example Google images). Such packages are usually inexpensive and some can offer you many thousands of images. Always remember that images are not always self-explanatory to the learner. Therefore sufficient information should be provided to make all figures, pictures or images self-standing and meaningful. Clarity is also assisted if titles for figures and tables are presented in bold or italics so that they stand out from the main text. On graphs all lines and axes should be labelled.

Cover design

The cover will probably be the first thing a learner notices about a resource-based learning package, which is why you want to create a good impression. Of course, the lengths you go to in designing and printing a cover will be largely determined by your budget since this can be a costly process. Another influence will be your kind of audience. If it is necessary to attract and motivate, then a stimulating cover may help, but if your reader is already committed to the course, then your budget might be better employed on other features.

Main text

As we have seen, the style of a typical page will depend on the nature of the audience and subject matter.

Captions

Typically, these are needed for illustrations, such as pictures, drawings or graphics, and they are normally set in different sizes or weights or kind of type from the text to avoid confusion. They should also be separated from the text by plenty of space or a thin ruled line.

Appendices

These are supplementary materials that the author does not wish to include in the main body of the book. In resource-based learning these may comprise readings, a glossary of terms, or lists of organisations for reference. Normally, the first appendix should appear on a right-hand page, and each new one on a new page, and they should follow the typographical style of the main text (although they may be set in smaller size).

Bibliography

In a scholarly book, this will appear at the back, with the name of the author, book title, and place and date of publication. In resource-based learning materials such a formal bibliography may not be necessary. A compromise is to list references at the end of each chapter or unit. As usual, whether references are needed depends on the audience you are writing for.

Index

An index is an important element in any 'serious' book and is usually set in two sizes smaller than the main text. To differentiate a subject from its sub-sections use can be made of bold and italics, or a different face and indenting, while each new letter of the alphabet should be indicated by a space and a capital letter. In the final analysis, you will make your decision on whether to use an index according to your budget, timescales and design specifications.

ACTIVITY

Take a small 'poor-quality' document that you have produced in the past. This may be a set of notes for students, study guide or short article. Use a highlight pen to indicate typographical problems and errors. Then reproduce the document in desktop published form.

Review Questions

1 What are the three broad categories of RBL materials, and which gives the greatest direct tutor support to the learner?
2 What learner characteristics must be considered when designing RBL materials?
3 Identify the four stages in the systematic design of RBL materials.
4 If your college was to launch a major distance learning programme, make a list of the organisational and administrative issues that would need addressing for its success.
5 Give four reasons why RBL materials should use illustrations and graphics where relevant.

SUMMARY

- Resource-based learning materials are best utilised when learners possess degrees of perseverance and good study habits; this is particularly so when the amount of tutor support is minimal, such as in the case of distance learning.
- If resource-based learning materials are used to support a programme of any size, care should be taken to produce these materials according to a system incorporating: planning, design, production and implementation/evaluation.
- In designing materials, care needs to be taken to ensure that readability levels are appropriate to the target audience.
- Make the materials lively, engaging and interactive by the use of questions and activities; make use of graphics and illustrations and the principles of typography to enhance the professional 'look' of the materials.

Suggested Further Reading

Lockwood, F. (1998) *The Design and Production of Self-Instructional Materials*, London: Kogan Page

Another practical resource, including sections on addressing the needs of the target audience, producing a course proposal and writing student learning activities. Clear and well written.

Rowntree, D. (1997) *Making Materials-Based Learning Work*, London: Kogan Page

A useful and practical guide from an author who has written more on this subject than virtually anyone else.

Rumble, G. (1997) *The Costs and Economics of Open and Distance Learning*, London: Kogan Page

A useful guide to calculating the cost of resource-based programmes. It's more than you think!

7 INFORMATION AND COMMUNICATIONS TECHNOLOGY AND RESOURCE-BASED LEARNING

Objectives

After reading this chapter, you should be able to:

- describe the range of information and communications technology (ICT) media available to teachers
- use the internet to search for educational materials
- select media appropriate to individual learning needs
- use a range of technical media for teaching and learning.

Information and communications technology (ICT) covers a wide array of media, including the use of computer-assisted learning incorporating multimedia (such as CD-ROM and DVD), the internet and world wide web, video and video conferencing, and a relatively new arrival, the interactive whiteboard. Sometimes all or some of these media may be integrated into a college's learning resource centre. What is significant is that the range, and often the functional sophistication, of some of these media is changing, often, it seems, at a rapid pace. Furthermore, all teachers in the 14–19 sector are going to have to develop their skills and knowledge in using these media. This is partly because ICT potentially offers tremendous opportunities in terms of the richness of learning experiences, but also because 14–19 education is moving towards student-centred models of learning. The Government is quite specific on the significance of ICT for the future, seeing it as a core element in the strategic planning process for every college.

THE SIGNIFICANCE OF ICT FOR LEARNING IN 14–19 EDUCATION

The lives of an ever-increasing number of people in the world are being touched by the inexorable march of information technology. Whether we like it or not, it is difficult to avoid the impact of IT on our lives. Many people are excited by these developments, some seeing them as liberating and democratising the world we live in. Others, though, remain sceptical of these changes, refusing to recognise their significance and avoiding, where possible, any contact with them. The ostrich approach, however, may be difficult to sustain, especially in the world of education (and particularly the 14–19 sector), where ICT is making a significant impact.

Integrating ICT into the vocational qualifications

One reason why ICT is becoming increasingly important in the world of post-compulsory education is the far-ranging changes that have taken place in assessment and accreditation systems. Vocational qualifications, for example, are linked to a more student-centred mode of delivery, which, potentially, ICT in learning can deliver. This is because, with a vocational qualification, the students' workplace environments will invariably require the use of ICT in some form or other. As noted by the National Council for Educational Technology (NCET, 1996), ICT can be used in a wide variety of ways, for example getting students to use:

• word processors to produce neat documents or to amend and revise reports, or to use spell-checkers or a thesaurus
• spreadsheets to perform common mathematical calculations
• CD-ROMs to access information
• the internet to communicate on a world-wide basis
• multimedia authoring software to develop interactive computer programs.

We shall examine some of these applications in this chapter. The point that needs to be made, however, is that some of these elements of ICT now need to be *integrated* into the student's mainstream work.

It is also worth noting that ICT does not always have to be used just as a teaching and learning tool. NVQs/SVQs require considerable monitoring of student progress, since college funding is now linked to individual student progress and achievement. Most colleges have computerised management information systems (MIS) into which the tutor may be required to input data, and from which she or he may seek to extract information. Sometimes, however, the MIS may be so inflexible or lack robustness, that tutors devise their own information system using a spreadsheet or database. As noted by the Higginson Report (FEFC, 1996e), ICT may become an essential tool of course management.

The computer as teacher

The use of the computer in teaching has many different descriptions: computer-assisted learning (CAL), computer-based learning (CBL), computer-assisted instruction (CAI), and integrated learning systems (ILS), to name but four. Today, it is often referred to as information and communications technology (ICT) and the platform used to deliver it a virtual learning environment (VLE).

Whatever it is called, a well-designed computer program can:

• deliver factual information
• present simulation and animation that can be controlled by the student
• test mastery and understanding
• record student progress.

Tutors seem to be fairly divided as to the value of using computers in teaching. Enthusiasts often make exaggerated claims for the power of the medium, others see it as an expensive diversion of resources. Yet, as we shall see, the use of VLEs, e-mail and the web (to name but three elements of ICT) are all now enhancing learning opportunities for students (and teachers!).

ICT and the new management systems

Many FE managers have also welcomed the introduction of ICT into the college curriculum, partly as a means of saving on expensive staff teaching costs. This hope, however, is almost certainly either erroneous or wildly optimistic. The use of ICT for learning involves the initial outlay of quite considerable amounts of money. Forgetting, for the moment, some of the more state-of-the-art elements, such as video conferencing, even the cost of basic computers can take a significant chunk out of the annual college budget; then there is the cost of maintenance and depreciation. When ICT is introduced into a college, this must be done as part of coherent, and well-conceived long-term strategy.

Virtual learning environments

Virtual learning environments (VLEs) can offer a range of provision, from acting as an additional resource to conventional classroom learning, through to the provision of completely stand-alone on-line delivery of distance learning programmes. The functions required of a VLE will be somewhat different in each case, but whatever the target student group, most VLEs will provide registration details, basic facilities for the delivery of on-line courseware materials, and a description of the course and its objectives. Mason (in JISC, 2002) presents three alternative models of on-line delivery, namely:

- The *content and support model*, comprising courseware materials supplemented by some tutorial support. The overall level of interaction is low, with the course being quite similar to a traditional teaching programme.
- The *wrap-around model*, where course materials are supported by activities and on-line discussions.
- The *integrated model*, based on collaborative activities, discussions and joint assignments. Course materials are dynamic and based upon individual needs and on group activities, with resources being contributed by both students and tutors as the course evolves. In terms of pedagogical principles, this is very much in the constructivist tradition.

At the current time, it is probably the case that most FE colleges are closer to the content and support model than the integrated.

The Joint Information Systems Committee (JISC, 2002), a body that provides strategic guidance on ICT to further and higher education institutions, suggests that a typical VLE should consist of the following elements:

- the creation of on-line materials that have been 'chunked' into discrete elements
- the tracking of student activity and achievement against these elements
- access to learning resources, assessment and guidance
- on-line tutor support
- peer group support
- interactive communications, including e-mail, group discussion and web access.

Most VLEs will deliver all of these elements, so any FE institution deciding on whether to invest in a VLE system will have to make some strategic decisions based upon:

- cost
- the number of students who will be using the system
- staff training
- how to integrate the VLE with the college's management information system.

One of the most common VLEs on the market is Blackboard. The following description is offered, not to suggest that Blackboard is the best VLE system (although it is used by many FE colleges) but to demonstrate in more detail what a typical VLE can do. Blackboard, essentially, comprises a core content 'repository' with four functional areas, namely:

- *Learning content management.* This allows content to be placed within a specific course or programme, or shared (as, say, core content) across a number of programmes. Imagine the time saved if the content of such a core course has to be updated. It also becomes possible to specify which content or 'learning objects' are seen by which students. Hence, permissions to view a section of a course can be granted to individuals, a specific class or the entire college. Learning objects can comprise text-based files, PowerPoint presentations, or individual images.
- *E-Portfolios.* E-portfolios are becoming increasingly important vehicles for demonstrating achievement and personal development. The e-portfolio facility allows students to offer evidence of their achievements, skills and qualifications. The system also contains templates and a 'creation Wizard' to guide students through the process of e-portfolio development. Once created, e-portfolios can be made available on-line to individuals, groups of users by course, or across the college, or to users outside the college.
- *Virtual hard drives.* Before this system, students often had difficulty sending large files to each other or to a programme tutor, particularly when sending the file across the internet from a home computer. With the Virtual Hard Drive this is not necessary, as all students' files can be stored, managed and shared from the same Blackboard-based system. Within the Virtual Hard Drive section of Blackboard, each student will have a series of pages that include:
  - My Content, a personal storage area;
  - Course Content, comprising only the courses the student is taking;
  - Institution Content, for general information about the college, such as the names of departments, vacation dates, etc.;
  - Library Content, where librarians can add subject-specific content.
- *Library digital asset management.* This allows tutors to search, access and incorporate digital library resources into the course they are designing within Blackboard.

Note, however, that a VLE can be just one (but important) element in a large management learning environment (MLE) – see Figure 7.1. Within this environment, the VLE is linked to library resources (including catalogues and on-line materials) and to the college's Administration and Management system. The latter includes student registration and enrolment, student records and the college's course catalogue. In principle, then, the MLE provides a holistic system through which students can be registered, their names uploaded into the VLE against specific on-line courses and eventually assessments downloaded back to the central administrative system.

As far as course content is concerned, these descriptions of a VLE largely assume that a teacher is creating 'chunks' of material within the VLE. Sometimes, however, these materials may contain not only the course content itself, but links to pages on the web, often as a means of supplementing the core content, or as a means of illustration. Take, for example, teaching about the weather. Not only might we place

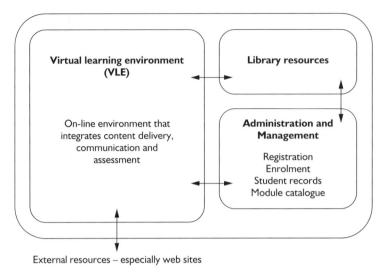

Figure 7.1 *Representation of management learning environment including virtual learning environment*

some descriptions of weather patterns in the relevant VLE learning content repository, we might provide web links to real time weather forecasts all over the world, as well as interesting illustrations of extreme weather conditions. In addition to using the web via a VLE, students may also be encouraged to use the web as a learning resource in undertaking their own research on a specified subject. So it is to the web that we now turn.

THE INTERNET AND WEB IN TEACHING AND LEARNING

What is the internet?

The internet is a collection of thousands of computer networks in many countries spread across the world, which links together individuals, groups and organisations. It embodies many elements, but primarily it is a communications network (for example, electronic mail) and a store of vast amounts of information, much of it now disseminated through one of the most popular features of the internet, the world wide web (www). Another important feature of the internet is the fact that files (say, a word processed document) can be sent as an attached file with an e-mail, or by using software designed for this purpose.

It is impossible to gauge how many people are now linked to the internet, but it is probably over 800 million people in over 200 different countries. Some people gain access to the internet via their educational institutions, in which case the facility is likely to be free of charge. Others go on-line at home, accessing the internet through an internet service provider. The following case study describes internet use at Greybourne Sixth Form College.

Case Study: *Using the internet at Greybourne Sixth Form College*

Students have had access to the network for about ten years. The network consists currently of two servers with 44 terminals for both staff and students. There is a terminal in each of the four staffrooms, 20 in the library, another 10 in the Learning Resource Centre, and 40 in the IT room, which is used for applied vocational courses in IT.

Who uses the net?

The Learning Resource Centre is a drop-in facility and is open 9 a.m.–9 p.m. It is staffed by two full-time and two part-time facilitators. They provide help and advice and their permanent presence in the Centre tends to discourage any access to unsuitable sites. The Centre is nearly always busy and it is often difficult for students to find a seat.

What has it been used for?

Students use their personal logins to access the college's VLE. They can then augment their assignments using net resources. For example:

- *Business Studies* Students have used corporate sites like CocaCola and Tesco as part of marketing assignments, and have been required to collect business statistics.
- *Business/Economics* Students have been using the sites of the main banks.
- *Politics* Use has been made of the web pages of the main UK political parties, on-line newspapers, the Yahoo politics section, and sites such as the White House.
- *Leisure and Tourism* Students have accessed the sites of many towns and district councils, various tourist boards and tourist attractions across the world as part of their assignment work.

Conclusion

We have found that students quickly pick up www techniques after only a little instruction from facilitators. They often seem to be more confident than the staff.

(Head of Information Systems, Greybourne Sixth Form College)

ACTIVITY

Locate a computer room at your teaching or training institution. Identify all programs that are available (application programs such as word processing, and spreadsheets, etc., as well as VLEs and teaching packages) and what they do. Consider how each of these programs can be used by you, the teacher, and by your students.

The world wide web

The world wide web was developed by CERN (European Laboratory for Particle Physics, based in Geneva, Switzerland) for distributing documents from one part of the organisation to another. The web was developed as a *distributed hypertext system* that could be easily accessed through any desktop computer. Hypertext means that words, phrases or objects within a document on one computer can be linked to each other within a document, or to documents on a different computer, even if this machine is on a widely separated network. Take a look at Figure 7.2; words such as 'Teaching and Learning' and 'Policies and Strategies' contain hypertext links to other web pages that deal with these subjects.

The web now comprises many millions of pages, placed on-line by thousands of business organisations, educational institutions and individuals. Many governments, too, have not been slow to appreciate the potential of the technology. To look at web pages you need a web browser, such as Internet Explorer or Netscape. Figure 7.2 is viewed through Internet Explorer. In using a web browser, it helps to understand some of the basic concepts of web design.

Hypertext markup language

All web pages are created through a coding system using hypertext markup language (HTML). This assigns features called tags to, for example, the headings and body text of documents, so that a web browser knows how and where to display these features (although, just to make life complicated, different browsers may display tags in different ways!). For example, a bold heading is created by the tags:

<b> words of heading </b>

Figure 7.2 *Home page of Further Education Resources for Learning*

Tags are also used to define a hypertext link to another part of a document or a different document. Web documents can be created in ordinary text files (using, for example, Microsoft Word). HTML documents (which are often called 'pages') can also include colour graphics and clips of digitised video or audio.

Uniform resource locator

Another feature of the web is the uniform resource locators (URLs). These are standard ways of specifying the location of internet files – in other words, they are web addresses. Take the following URL:

http://www.campus.ac.uk/

The first part of a URL identifies the protocol necessary to retrieve the file. In this case, 'http' (hypertext transfer protocol) means that this is a web page. Http allows a networked computer to look out for and respond to incoming requests for files ('hits'). For a list of typical ways of using a URL to identify an internet protocol see Table 7.1.

Table 7.1   *Using URL names to identify file protocols*

URL	File protocol
http://	Web page
Gopher://	A gopher server
news://	A Usenet group
ftp://	A file that can be downloaded from an FTP server

The second part of the URL (www.campus) specifies the domain name of the machine on which the file is located. In this case the computer is at a fictitious organisation called 'campus'.

The next part of the URL (ac) identifies what type of organisation this is. In this case the 'ac' stands for 'academic', in other words a school, college of further education or university, or perhaps an organisation with some connection with the academic world such as a research agency. If the educational site is in the USA, it is likely to end with 'edu'. Other domain names are specified in Table 7.2.

Not surprisingly, the final part of the URL, (uk), tells us that this academic institution is based in Britain. Other examples of addresses include 'us' for the USA, 'au' for Australia and 'de' for Germany (Deutschland).

Directories, search engines and portals

The web contains such a vast amount of information (currently about 1,000 million pages) that it is a daunting task finding one's way around it. Understanding the concepts behind URLs helps, because it may allow you to find a site by making an educated guess as to its location. For example, if you know that an organisation is likely to have a web site and that it is, say, a university in the UK, then the following might do the trick:

http://www.<name of university>.ac.uk

Table 7.2 *Domain names and their meanings*

Domain name	Meaning
com	commercial companies or corporations
co.uk	UK company
gov	Government agencies, e.g. the Teacher Training Agency
org	not-for-profit organisations
net	companies involved in Internet infrastructure
biz	business
info	information
mil	military sites
ac	academic (UK)
edu	academic (USA)

If, however, you want to find information on a specific subject or concept, then you will have to use a directory or search engine.

Directories

For a directory, people from the directory organisation comb the web for relevant sites, and then make a link to those sites. Yahoo (www.yahoo.co.uk) is an example of a useful and powerful directory. This contains a list of subjects (such as Arts and Humanities, Education, News and Media). You choose a category that you think is most likely to contain the information you are seeking. By clicking on this category you are then taken to another page of more focused categories; here, you can click on what seems interesting, or input one or more keywords into a search facility (the box near the top of the screen with a 'search' button to the right of it).

ACTIVITY

Using your browser, input the URL for Yahoo:

  http://www.yahoo.co.uk

From the Yahoo home page, select 'Education' (this will help narrow the search, and will improve your chances of success). Then input a subject for the directory to locate. Print out the first page of search results.

Search engines

With search engines, or robots, a computer program automatically searches the web for new material, and then makes links to it. An example of a popular search engine is Google (www.google.co.uk). Again, the facility exists for inputting key words or short phrases that the engine will use to attempt to locate information for you. After each search, a list of possible sites will be listed, and you can choose to see a descriptive summary of each site, as in Figure 7.3. Note that Google also provides you with images (which can be useful for cutting and pasting into a presentation) and access to thousands of discussion groups.

It is important to note that you can input the same query to different directories or engines and get a different set of possible sites presented to you. So if a search does not come up with what you are seeking, use a different directory or engine; alternatively, input a different term or expression.

Portals

A more recent development has been the creation of portals – sites that incorporate the functionality of both search engines and directories.

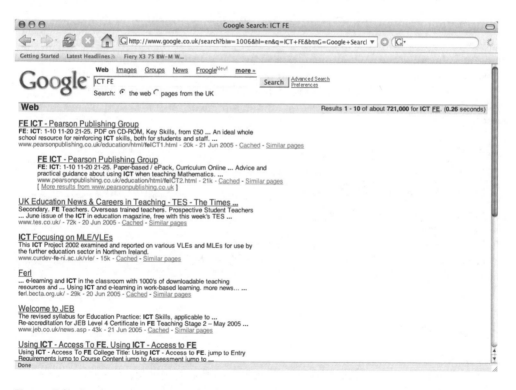

Figure 7.3 *Search results on 'ICT in FE' using the Google search engine*

> **ACTIVITY**
>
> Using your browser, input the URL for Ask Jeeves:
>
> http://www.askjeeves.com/
>
> Put in the same subject for a search as in the previous activity. Note that Ask Jeeves lists the 'hits' from several search engines, many of which give you different alternative web sites.

The internet as an educational resource

The internet offers teachers a number of excellent educational facilities, some of which have enormous potential. With the kinds of student-centred learning required by the applied vocational courses, students are being asked to search for information themselves. This is increasingly going to take place through some of the new electronic information sources and mailing services.

Information systems: ERIC (Educational Resource Information Center)

This is the largest educational database in the world (containing around a million bibliographic references), and includes abstracts of documents and journal articles, plus papers, conference proceedings, literature reviews and curriculum materials. ERIC provides information in subject areas such as adult and vocational education, assessment and evaluation, and reading and comprehension skills.

> **ACTIVITY**
>
> Locate ERIC at Syracuse University:
>
> http://www.eric.ed.gov/
>
> In Search the Database, type in 'VLEs' and look at the Search Results.

Electronic mailing services

Usenet
Usenet is a *distributed bulletin board*, which means that Usenet conferences or newsgroups involve users 'dropping into' or out of discussions. Unlike Listservs (see next section), where users receive all messages (and therefore may suffer from e-mail overload), with Usenet, users access only those messages they want to receive.

ACTIVITY

Take a look at the UK Usenet web site at:

http://www.usenet.org.uk/

Click on Index to Newsgroups then find the UK education section.

Listservs
Listserv is an example of an e-mail handling system that allows users to subscribe to, contribute to, or unsubscribe to a mailing list. An example of a Listserv is Mailbase, which is a mailing list designed to make group communications between researchers and academics easier across JANET (the UK's Joint Academic Network), the system that links most of the UK's institutions of higher education. Mailbase allows groups of academics or research staff with common interests to e-mail each other with news of meetings or to distribute reports and papers. Users can send a message to all other members of a particular group.

ACTIVITY

Locate the Mailbase home page, which also contains an A–Z of discussion lists:

http://www.mailbase.ac.uk/

Next, search for your own choice of names and descriptions of open lists:

http://www.mailbase.ac.uk/search.html

Educational journals and materials
An increasing number of academic journals are now being presented on the internet, many of them by United States universities. You might consider using a search engine to locate an electronic journal for a subject that interests you.

Using the internet in teaching and learning

Hopefully, by carrying out some of the activities in this section, you will have noted some of the advantages of using the web with your own learners. Provided they receive sufficient guidance on how to access, store and synthesise information, students may be able to use the web as a highly versatile and vast resource for their studies.

Clearly, the internet provides many facilities for the support of distance learners, including e-mail, computer conferencing, gopher servers and, of course, the world wide web. Rather than discuss distance education on the web here, carry out the next activity.

ACTIVITY

Look at some of the web sites in Table 7.3, most of which deal with FE or contain pages related to FE. Make a note of those that you think might be useful to you.

Some notes of caution

It is, perhaps, worth adding just a few notes of caution about the uses of the web in education.

- Not all learners may like or benefit from using information sources such as the web; their self-regulatory skills, for example, may not be sufficiently developed and the sheer scale of information facing them may be too daunting.
- The information contained on the web varies considerably in quality, and its accuracy and authenticity may sometimes be open to doubt. It is wise to inject such notes of caution into your students.
- Do not become too reliant on a particular web site always being available for student research. Sites come and go. Check on its availability before sending students off to use a site as a resource.

ACTIVITY

Think of strategies for guiding learners to evaluate the data they find. What part can/should tutors play in identifying sources? How do these skills differ from those needed to search more conventional media such as libraries?

USING VIDEO AND AUDIO

Video is a very powerful medium that is often used when words are unable to describe a situation or a process. Its motion captures people's imagination and, with added sound, colour, special effects and drama, different aspects of teaching or learning objectives can be explored.

Video can bring the world to the classroom by illustrating a vast variety of subjects – the wonders of nature, the intrinsic behaviour of the animal kingdom, amazing human potential and relationships, the variety of cultures, races and nations, and all sorts of technological processes and operations. This medium has many advantages including:

- provision of full-screen motion pictures together with audio
- consistency of teaching
- consistent quality
- bringing experts and 'authorities' into the classroom
- opportunities for distance learning
- availability in the students' own time

Table 7.3 *Useful organisations and their web sites*

Organisation	Web site	Contents include
Learning and Skills Council (LSC)	http://www.lsc.gov.uk	Information about funding, government policy and initiatives
Learning and Skills Development Agency (LSDA)	http://www.lsda.org.uk	LSDA programmes, events, publications and research reports
Office for Standards in Education (Ofsted)	http://www.ofsted.gov.uk	Inspection reports by institution and by subject
Further Education Resources for Learning (Ferl)	http://ferl.becta.org.uk/	Ferl events, case studies, resources and subject links including web sites
Higher Education and Research Opportunities in the United Kingdom (Hero)	http://www.hero.ac.uk	Directories of HE and FE institution, government departments, professional bodies and special needs associations
British Educational Communications and Technology Agency (Becta)	http://www.becta.org.uk	On-line bookshop, Becta projects, and links to organisations concerned with ICT
National Grid for Learning	http://www.ngfl.gov.uk/	Further education 'hub', SEN centre and resources for FE tutors and learners
Further Education National Consortium (FENC)	http://www.fenc.org.uk/	The FENC catalogue of resources and contacts for specific enquiries
The Guardian	http://education.guardian.co.uk/	Click on Talk to engage in on-line discussions on many subjects

- a safe learning environment
- enjoyment and therefore motivation of students.

Against these, a number of potential drawbacks should also be kept in mind:

- content may not always be as directly relevant as the teacher would wish
- the video may be regarded by the students as entertainment rather than education
- technical problems if the video does not work or breaks down.

In contrast to video, audio is a cheap and, like video, a relatively easy medium to use both in a group and in individual situations. The result is that today, thanks to advances in technology, it is possible either partly to replace the instructor with an audio recording of his or her voice, or to enhance the instructor's ability to teach by including other audio sources.

Applications of audio and video

One of the first applications of audio has been in the area of language training. Obviously, learning a language (which is principally an oral process) employs the ability to utilise this medium to its full potential. Considering the resources that are usually available in educational institutions, it is relatively easy to produce audio tapes for use both to enhance lectures or for private student study.

Like audio, video can be used either in a lecture situation or for independent study by students. In a lecture environment, television or a video camera can be used as a demonstration aid to display to a classroom of students those things that the eye could see in a chosen situation – the view out of a window, down a microscope, inside the stomach, etc. Although the image produced is on a two-dimensional screen, movement of the camera or the object being viewed can demonstrate three-dimensional aspects.

It is possible to record pictures, and indeed sound, from a video demonstration and use the recording again at a later date. Alternatively, ready-made video programmes can be used to supplement lectures. However, care must be taken as there are not many off-the-shelf programmes suitable for the lecture environment. Lecture theatres equipped with video display facilities can be used either by providing a number of television sets around the theatre or by a powerful video projector, such as a Barco, which will display the image on to a white screen similar to film or slide projection. In the latter case the room needs to be darkened.

Video can also play a major part in independent study by the student. There are many excellent ready-made educational videos produced for this purpose. Some come supplied with workbooks to which the student is referred during a number of pre-determined pauses inserted in the video. The student is usually requested to watch a short sequence of the video and then to stop the play-back and refer to the workbook. Sometimes the student will also be requested to carry out some exercises before continuing with the rest of the video.

One of the drawbacks of video production is that it can be expensive and very time-consuming. Even so, you may decide that a production of your own is a better solution but make sure that you do not re-invent the wheel; somebody else may already have produced what you intend to record.

Integrating video into the classroom

To integrate video into teaching:

- preview the video and make a list of its main points; if necessary, use the video counter to identify those parts of the programme that will be used
- book the necessary equipment and make sure you know in advance how to use it
- before the teaching session, go to the room you will be using and check the equipment is there and in working order
- arrange furniture in the room and blinds/curtains so that all students can view the screen without dazzle.

Video and audio must never be used as a cheap substitute for the teacher. Care must be taken to ensure that the content of the medium is relevant to the target audience. Due to the limited channel capacity of audio (obviously, it addresses only the person's aural senses) its impact is limited and may induce boredom if used for more than a brief period. Care must also be taken to ensure that use of the medium is essential to the chosen learning objectives.

ACTIVITY

Locate a number of educational video catalogues. You may find these in a college library, or learning resource centre, or by inputting the phrase 'educational videos' into a web search engine. List those programmes that might be relevant to any subjects you teach. Find out whether any of these are already owned by the college, and whether tapes can be ordered on approval. Take steps to view as many of these tapes as possible, noting which ones you may be able to use in the future.

USING COMPUTER-MEDIATED CONFERENCING AND ELECTRONIC MAIL

We have seen that self-directed learning is an integral part of studying for some of the applied vocational qualifications, and that we are moving away from teaching-by-telling to more collaborative forms of communication. Forms of computer conferencing, such as video and audio conferencing, computer forums and electronic mail (often provided through a VLE), all provide considerable potential for this kind of interactive dialogue between learners, especially distance learners, and potentially on an international basis.

Video and audio conferencing

Video conferencing is not one technology, but a function that can be delivered by a number of different formats. It ranges, for example, from live video lectures to large audiences, to a point-to-point, individual-to-individual desktop PC communication.

In general, large-scale set-ups are delivered via satellite links, involving one-way video and two-way audio, i.e. 'interactive television'. The advantage of this kind of system, apart from the fact that video is full-motion and high quality, is that its costs are not independent of distance (unlike, for example, cable). It tends to be used, therefore, where large distances and many sites are involved. Clearly, the drawback of such a system is the lack of visuals from the receiving site. Equipment costs are also high.

Small-scale delivery (often in the form of Desk Top Video Conferencing [DTVC]) involves conferencing between relatively few points, and usually relies on compressed video. Compression relates to one of the central difficulties of small-scale video conferencing. All data (whether text, sound or video) are usually transmitted down telephone lines, but the problem with video is that it demands such enormous amounts of bandwidth (the amount of information that can be transmitted along a carrier every second). For example, telephone lines are designed to carry the human voice at roughly 2,400 bits per second; video requires 234,375,000 bits of information every second. The solution to this problem is to convert the analogue video signal into a digital format and to compress the image and to transmit information only on those parts of the video image that are actually moving. The more movement there is in a video clip, the greater the compression needed, and the greater the loss of clarity, colour and continuity of motion. The introduction of broadband is, however, helping the speed of data delivery.

This kind of video conferencing platform is most effective for those situations where full-motion exposition is not essential, but where participants need to collectively examine, say, documents, equipment or still visual images.

Advantages of using video conferencing

Video conferencing in its present form offers a number of distinct advantages for users in that it:

- allows genuine dialogue between participants
- permits full two-way communication of content, including verbal and graphical presentation of objects
- eliminates the costs of travel.

Drawbacks of the medium

These include:

- delays in transmission signals, meaning video and audio are often out of synchronicity
- for telephone transmission, the video output is slow and not full-screen
- two-way video conferencing is still no substitute for real face-to-face interaction since important non-verbal communication signals may be filtered out.

Given some of these disadvantages, it is possible that video conferencing is more suited to non-interactive lecturing to large groups of dispersed students, especially when detailed visual material has to be presented.

Using computer conferencing and electronic mail

Computer conferencing (or computer forum) is a system of electronic communications that takes place between two or more people. Typically, a computer conference will take place between a tutor, say, operating from home or from work in an FE college, and a group of students, and between the students themselves. All will be linked together by the internet; so the students will connect to the college via their own computers, sending and receiving data through telephone lines via a modem. A computer conference takes place through the relaying of text messages from one participant to another, these messages either arriving on everyone's screens simultaneously (a synchronous conference) or at different times, as and when participants log on to their systems (asynchronous).

Clearly, computer conferencing has a number of advantages for both tutors and distance learners, including:

- flexibility and speed of communication
- interactions can take place between students without them having to be present in one place or at the same time
- discussions are structured and purposeful.

Against this must be set some of the disadvantages:

- it lacks the spontaneity and social warmth of face-to-face communication (including video and audio conferencing)
- not all members of conferencing groups actually participate (so-called 'lurkers')
- problems may occur with hardware and software.

Nevertheless, despite these drawbacks, when students are widely dispersed, the interactivity of computer conferencing, albeit through textual messages, is often found by distance learning students to be quite valuable.

In using computer conferencing, Kimball (1995) identifies a number of ways in which a conference moderator can help to make a conference work. These include:

- define the role of participants; is the moderator expected to provide expert knowledge, support, or encouragement, or all of these?
- create an ambience by setting the tone of the conference; show how members should respond to comments
- nourish the conversation; keep adding new material, not only in terms of content, but also in terms of new kinds of message, for example, questions, statements and case studies.

USING MULTIMEDIA

What is multimedia?

Multimedia comprises the seamless integration of text, sound and graphics within a single computer environment. For example, a multimedia program could deal with the subject of European birds – the program would offer vast amounts of textual information, audio clips on some birds (probably the most melodious), video clips of the most spectacular fliers, all sewn together by an audio commentary. The structure of the program will probably be hypermedia, allowing the user to click on individual words, or images, to access new information.

Multimedia vastly exceeds the kind of functionality offered by what used to be known as computer-based training (CBT), a software format that often suffered from text-overload and a tendency to use the sequential presentation of information through a learning strategy too often limited to drill and practice. Modern multimedia is usually delivered through CD-ROM (compact disc read only memory), a format offering software for the games market, as well as business training and education; this has produced a mass market for the medium and therefore falling costs of both hardware and software.

Multimedia myths

Let us first of all dispel some common myths about the use of computers in learning. One of the most common myths is that the computer can replace the classroom teacher. This is simply untrue. Multimedia programs can play an important part in, say, introducing a subject, preparing students to study it, or as reinforcement and follow-up, but they should not usually be expected to carry the main burden of the teaching effort. As we shall see in the next section, computers will also often constitute a useful resource as part of a college's learning resource facilities, and provide a platform for students' self-directed study.

Another, and no less insidious myth, is that the computer, as a teacher, is more effective than the classroom tutor. While there has been plentiful research over the years to 'prove' this to be the case (often for specific groups of learners or subjects), most of these studies have been methodologically flawed. Those studies that have followed some of the essential ground-rules of research have found that, when compared to tuition from a teacher, at best, some students do no worse in terms of what they learn. So why use computers and expensive multimedia software at all? The answer is probably that:

- most students tend to like it
- students tend to find most multimedia programs interesting
- multimedia can play an important role in student self-directed learning
- used with large numbers of students, the costs of teaching delivery can be reduced.

It is important, however, that multimedia is selected as a teaching tool when it can fulfil actual learning objectives. There is a real danger that, because of its general

---

ACTIVITY

Take a look at the very large range of CD-ROM titles presented at the Virtual Teachers Centre within the National Grid for Learning web site. Access the site at:

http://vtc.ngfl.gov.uk/docserver.php

In the Search field type in 'CD-ROMs' and choose your subject from the drop-down box. While some of these resources are aimed at school pupils, many are of value to the 14–19 sector.

appeal, it can be used more for its entertainment than educational value. Also, because most commercial multimedia programs are made for a mass market, they can often be rather generalised and not sufficiently detailed or demanding for an academic student audience.

Here, as we saw with video programmes, your first step will be to evaluate thoroughly the program and satisfy yourself that the learning it delivers fully meets the learning objectives you have set for your students. If the multimedia program is merely exciting to watch and entertaining, its use with your students may be entirely gratuitous (and of little educational value). But how do you tell if the program is worth using? One approach is to evaluate it using a set of standard criteria, such as those presented in Table 7.4.

Table 7.4   *Criteria for evaluating a multimedia program*

Objectives
1   Are learning objectives defined?
2   Are learning objectives relevant to your own learners?
3   Are learning objectives met by the end of the program?

Content
4   Is information presented in appropriate 'chunks'?
5   Is the sequencing of material logical?
6   Is the material pitched at the appropriate level?
7   Is the material relevant/accurate/up-to-date?
8   Are appropriate instructional methods used for the content (e.g. tutorials, questions, simulations)?
9   Are opportunities offered for active learner participation?
10   Is assessment valid for the content?
11   Is assessment valid for your own learners?
12   Does the content avoid cultural bias or stereotyping?
13   Is the language accessible for your own learners?

Presentation
14   Is the screen design logical
15   Is effective use made of graphics?
16   Is effective use made of video and audio?
17   Is effective use made of colour (e.g. avoidance of 'clashing' or saturated colours)?

Ease of use
18   Is the program easy to load and launch?
19   Is navigation logical and easy?
20   Are directions on using the program consistent and clear?
21   Is there access to on-line help when required?
22   Is off-line material provided to support the program?

> **ACTIVITY**
>
> Take the checklist in Table 7.4 and use it to evaluate a multimedia program. If neces-
> sary, type up the checklist and add your own questions. You now have a tool for eval-
> uating multimedia programs for your teaching.

Integrating generic courseware

Having evaluated a multimedia program and satisfied yourself that all, or at least
some, of its content is of relevance to your students, you then have to consider ways
of integrating its use into your teaching strategy. Since the very essence of using
multimedia is that it facilitates student-centred learning, you will expect students to
study the program independently. This might be during periods that are timetabled for
individual study, or, perhaps, during the period designated for your subject, during
which all students will work at their own computer workstations (say, in a learning
resource centre).

For this to work successfully, it is essential that the students understand what the
learning objectives of the program are. These may, or may not, be stated by the
program itself. If stated, they may not necessarily be what *you* are hoping the students
will learn from the program. It may be necessary, then, for you to produce a *front-end*
to the program, such as a paper-based handout that states your learning objectives
clearly, and specifies what sections of the multimedia program you want your students
to study. One problem, of course, is that, if the program is visually attractive and
interesting, students might quickly become absorbed in looking at all parts of it, not
only those related to their studies. A way around this is to focus their attention by
setting assessment tasks, such as collecting evidence (if this is an applied vocational
course), or researching material for an assignment (if the subject is being studied for
GCSE or A-level). Again, assessment tasks may be specified as part of the 'front-end'
document.

Designing multimedia programs

If you find that there are insufficient multimedia programs in your subject area, you
may be tempted to produce one of your own. Before you do this, however, you need
to be aware that this is not necessarily an easy step. Table 7.5 provides a brief
checklist of the sorts of steps you will need to take.

Why list this rather long litany of tasks, when most trainee teachers have absolutely
no intention of getting involved in a project of this type? The answer is that
multimedia is now so popular in many FE colleges, that, at some time in your
academic career, there is every chance you will be approached to initiate a project, or
to become involved in some capacity.

Yet the history of computer-assisted learning is littered with disastrous projects,
initiated by enthusiastic amateurs who think that producing effective interactive
computer courseware is no different to writing a manual or study guide. It is hoped

Table 7.5 *Checklist for designing multimedia programs*

1   Scope the project (produce learning objectives, statements of general content, profile of the target audience, time for development, computer platform and budget).
2   Produce a proposal providing details gathered as part of scoping.
3   Choose the platform (screen resolution, sound parameters, speed of CD-ROM drive, etc.).
4   Select the media and techniques: the treatment (when video, audio and text are to be used).
5   Design the interface (colour, icons, sound, etc.).
6   Select the project team (programmers, video and sound personnel, secretarial support, technical support, script writers, instructional/interactive designers, subject matter experts, presenters).
7   Manage the production of the audio track.
8   Manage the shooting of the video.
9   Supervise the generation of graphics.
10 Supervise the fusion of media through authoring/programming.
11 Test the program.
12 Document the program, including all specifications and program coding.

that Table 7.5 gives you a clear indication of some of the complexities involved in multimedia production.

In considering whether to produce multimedia courseware in-house, it is useful if you consider (and pass on to other interested parties) the following:

• Visually appealing and instructionally effective courseware is difficult to produce by the inexperienced.
• The time taken to produce courseware is invariably much longer than anticipated at the outset (approximately 400–800 hours of development time per hour of student courseware).
• Good quality courseware requires a multiplicity of skills (instructional design, graphic design, programming), which means that a team approach is highly desirable, if not essential.
• Authoring systems that are both easy to use (i.e. do not need computing skills) and yet are functionally powerful exist only in the minds of software salespeople. If you need high levels of interactivity or complexity in your program, then the skills of a programmer are vital.

In sum, an hour of student learning using multimedia courseware could cost anything from £10,000 to even £100,000 to develop, depending on the degree of complexity of the program and the amount of video and graphics used. It is not the intention here to dissuade colleges from producing in-house multimedia courseware. It is suggested, however, that such projects need very careful planning and budgeting. Given the costs involved, it is likely that these projects are better tackled on a collaborative basis between a consortium of colleges. Indeed, the Higginson Report (FEFC, 1996e) recommends that commercial software developers should also be involved.

Using interactive whiteboards

While not in the same league as an 'all singing, all dancing' multimedia program, interactive whiteboards in the classroom are proving invaluable in enhancing students' active learning experiences. The interactive whiteboard (IWB) is, essentially, three pieces of equipment – a computer, data projector and the whiteboard itself. In essence, this turns the whiteboard into a large computer screen that can be used to project images from a computer (replicating exactly what is on the computer screen), or into a space on which the teacher and students can write. Hence, the technology is ideal for whole-class teaching, with the screen being used to display PowerPoint presentations, web pages, DVD programs or CD-ROMs. This flexible technology also allows what has been written on the whiteboard (by the teacher or students) to be saved and downloaded onto a computer disk and sent to a printer. It even allows the teacher to annotate comments on top of presentation slides or web sites that can later be removed or printed.

An example of how IWBs can be used to generate whole-class collaboration is through mind mapping. Students can be asked to develop ideas that explain or illustrate a concept. Mind mapping software can be used to capture and expand on their ideas in the form of a mind map diagram, which is captured into the software program and presented through the interactive whiteboard screen. Once the exercise is finished, the screen is then saved to disk and printed and the diagrams distributed to the class.

USING LEARNING RESOURCE CENTRES

As we saw in Chapter 5, there is no, single, widely accepted definition of what constitutes a learning resource centre. Broadly, however, they could be said to be rooms or locations providing a selection of packages and materials dealing with a range of subjects, linked to some type of student support mechanism. Yet, due to the diversity of materials held in such centres, and the systems for student support, the actual term allotted may differ from college to college. Hence, you may notice titles such as Open Learning Centre, or Independent Learning Centre. This designation of title may be rather arbitrary or accidental; on the other hand, it may reflect a coherent and planned philosophy towards such centres.

'Open', for example, may be alluding to a commitment to greater student access to packages and materials; 'independent' may suggest an emphasis on just that – encouraging students to study on their own and in their own time. Indeed, as we saw in Chapter 3, changes in the curriculum, particularly with the introduction of applied vocational qualifications, now require a much more student-centred approach to teaching and learning, although this has not affected all subjects equally. The student-centred approach has also, as we have seen, been encouraged to a significant extent by the opportunities for independent study offered by technological changes such as the spread of PCs, CD-ROMs, DVDs etc. Clearly, learning resource centres can play a significant role in such learning – one reason for the growth of the number of colleges that have built learning resource centres, *and* the greater importance of such centres to the teaching and learning process. Armsby (1994) suggests that this is, in part, due to government pressure to move in this direction.

What are learning resource centres?

Typically, a learning resource centre will contain a variety of structured materials, sometimes referred to as learning packages. Few are entirely self-contained, that is, they will require some input from a tutor, but they will usually embody:

- teaching texts that explain the content
- a guide through the learning tasks
- some informal self-assessment and progress check
- formal assignment(s) for marking by a tutor
- attainment tests for external marking.

In terms of management and organisation, learning resource centres can comprise:

- *decentralised networks* in which control, the service offered, and its co-ordination may be diffused across the organisation
- *fully centralised organisation*, in which the services and its organisation are brought together both organisationally and physically.

The latter is the result of 'convergence', a strong trend emerging in many FE colleges, in part the result of college incorporation. Convergence can create significant economies of scale, integrating library services, information technology centres, open access centres, language laboratories, curriculum workshops, reprographics, materials production, media services and learning support units. The result is that academic and support staff can combine to offer students 'a total learning environment' (Armsby, 1994: 83). But the downside of integrating resources in this manner is the danger of inflexibility.

Getting students to use learning resource centres

The extent to which you will make use of learning resource centres will probably depend, largely, on the nature and organisation of its provision within your teaching institution. Some colleges, for example, place a central focus on these centres, converting taught courses into modular ones, with an emphasis on individualised work. Others, in contrast, may only use learning resource centres as an adjunct or backup to their traditional teacher-led sessions. Essentially, the functions of learning resource centres can be deemed to be:

- remedial
- supplementary (to existing courses)
- replacement (of existing courses)
- creation (of new courses).

It is essential that an institution has a policy on this – that it has decided how its learning resource centres should be integrated into the teaching process.

In encouraging your students to make use of learning resource centres, two factors are important. One is the physical layout and resources offered by the centre, and the other is the way in which you guide your students in using them. Clearly, there is a connectivity between the two. In terms of the facilities offered by the centre, they should be *planned* for their purpose, not set up as an afterthought in some college annexe. They should be well decorated, bright and welcoming, and students should have space in which to relax or socialise, since they cannot be expected to work incessantly. This may also be helped by the establishment of a quiet study atmosphere in the actual work areas. Above all, space should be provided for single subject workshops, when tutors can give their vital input to small groups of students. Next, a generalised learning room should be established, probably in the library – although opinion is divided here; some welcome the library's client-centred ethos, whilst others argue that the learning room requires a different ethos, organisation and staffing pattern.

When it comes to planning the use of learning resource centres for your own learners, one essential decision that needs taking at an early stage is whether to use those materials offered by the centre or to develop your own. To make this decision, it might be helpful to carry out the following activity.

ACTIVITY

For a subject you intend to teach, define your learning objectives. Evaluate existing materials held in your college's learning resource centre to establish whether they meet all or some of these objectives. If they meet a sufficient number of your objectives, use the materials. After the lesson, evaluate the result:

- Were your objectives met?
- Were the materials sufficiently flexible to suit your purpose?
- In future, would you use these materials again, or would you modify them or develop your own?

If you need to develop materials of your own keep a careful note of the time it takes you and any problems that arise. After using the materials in a lesson, get your students to evaluate the materials for their quality. This might include clarity of explanation and professional presentation.

As you may have noted in the above activity, a problem arises when you locate learning materials that meet some of your criteria, but not others. In this case, you might find it necessary to develop (probably in paper-based format) a 'front-end', performing the same purpose as the multimedia front-end discussed earlier in this chapter. This will comprise the learning objectives you wish to set your students, and a map for locating the resources you want the students to use, including the resources you have designed yourself such as worksheets, tutorials, audio tapes, etc. In this way, you may successfully integrate your own in-house materials with external, commercial packages. Alternatively, you may decide that the results look rather amateurish, and it is more satisfactory for the learner to be offered a complete, integrated package. In making this decision, Table 7.6 may offer some assistance.

In evaluating a commercial package, ensure that it:

- sets out its objectives (learning outcomes) clearly and that these are valid (for *your* purposes) and flexible

Table 7.6   *Criteria for deciding between using in-house and commercial packages*

	In-house packages	Commercial packages
Advantages	Flexible and designed for a specific audience Can be amended and updated	Professional layout and presentation Lower average costs of production when produced for mass audience
Disadvantages	Costs of development (materials and staff time) Often specific to needs of teacher/ designer and not to other teachers Difficult to produce if ICT involved, e.g. CBT or web	Inflexible Sometimes highly priced if ICT component

- explains how it works and how the various parts (if there are any, for example worksheets, videos, audio-tapes) are integrated
- describes the type and quality of support required
- provides re-usable elements (such as workbooks or worksheets)
- provides internal assessment
- is sufficiently modular to allow student access to specific, relevant parts (avoiding redundant learning).

Avoiding problems

The potential problems with using learning resource centres should also be borne in mind so that they can be avoided. Firstly, these centres are not a replacement for the teacher. Unless learning materials have been designed to be used by distance learners (and, even here, some support is necessary), they will always require some tutorial input, often more than the original designers of the packages expected. The level of live input will also depend upon the profile of the target audience; not all learners possess high levels of self-organisation and motivation to learn on their own. Others may have developed a dependency culture as far as their learning is concerned, so the very thought of learning independently fills them with fear and dread. The managers of learning resource centres, and teachers who make use of them, will have to consider how *all* students can be helped and supported.

Another important consideration is the way in which centres are staffed, organised and resourced. Staff must be knowledgeable and trained to support the varied groups of learners who come through their doors. The time periods allocated to student study in the centres must be sufficiently long to allow them to complete a particular module or task. It may also be useful if staff have a working knowledge of the type of accreditation system the student is studying towards, particularly if this involves competence-based learning, since they may, on occasions, have to act as assessors.

The following case study is based on an interview with the resource centre manager at Greybourne College of FE, and shows the college's philosophy towards resource-based learning.

Case Study: *Resource-based learning at Greybourne College of FE*

In terms of structure, we have a central resources centre, based in the library, which has computers, DVDs, CD-ROMs, books, journals, audio and a classroom and seminar room within it; I also have two cross-college workshops, an IT workshop and a Communications workshop.

Resource-based learning has allowed us to deliver more flexible teaching across the curriculum. This has worked well when students have been supported by a tutor, but did not work well when students were required to work on their own. FE students come to us often with low qualifications, short attention spans and a need for a range of activities within a lesson period to retain their interest. If a tutor is not present, then students need to be older and more academically able. Resource-based learning has worked particularly well with applied vocational qualifications because they are very practically based.

In the open access IT workshop students are supported by facilitators who help students with their IT skills, and they might do some assessment if it's observation for, say, NVQ. But the point is, the workshop is looked after. Empty workshops that are just full of resources are dire for FE. They might work with more mature students, but even they like somebody around.

In terms of implementing resource-based learning there has been some fear and suspicion on lecturers' part. Perhaps a fear that you would take their jobs away, which, of course, you're not. There is perhaps also a misguided notion that you can sit anybody down in front of a learning pack and they will learn it. You have to use it carefully and know your students. If the student is young, it needs to be a very specific resource-based task with a deadline on it, and you need to tell them exactly where to go to do it, and you need to check that they've done it. Or make it so attractive that they want to do it. For some of them IT and the internet are attractive. The library did a project on supporting the tutors and finding nice web sites for their students. If a tutor wants their students to use the web, and they say what assignments their students are going to be doing, the librarians will pinpoint web sites and help to guide students. We are also using an intranet through which we can share information and resources.

(Head of Learning Resources, Greybourne College of FE)

ACTIVITY

Go to your college's learning resource centre and evaluate a random sample of resources in those subject areas you teach. Discuss with those running the centre how they support learners, and how they can help you.

Review Questions

1 Suggest five reasons why ICT may become more significant in 14–19 education.
2 State two reasons why an FE college might set up a video conferencing facility and two reasons against such an activity.
3 You have to advise the colleges' principal on whether the number of the institution's workstations that deliver the internet should be increased. Suggest six internet functions that you think could have educational value to your students.
4 Both multimedia and the internet offer ideal self-directed learning capabilities. How self-directed should this be? List ways in which learners can be supported.
5 Make a short list of reasons why your college's learning resource centre should be expanded.

SUMMARY

- The spread of information and communications technology into 14–19 education is now an integral part of official government policy.
- With the advent of strong trends towards student self-directed and independent learning, ICT is now being seen as a significant tool in delivering such learning.
- One of the major challenges facing teachers is developing in students the skills to make full use of the technology and to learn independently.
- The internet and world wide web provide a major opportunity for both independent and collaborative learning, as well as a huge source of information.
- Teachers need to explore ways of supporting learners in making effective use of the new technology, and to integrate ICT into their curriculum planning, where appropriate.

Suggested Further Reading

Ellington, H., Percival, F. and Race, P. (1993) *Handbook of Educational Technology*, 3rd edition, London: Kogan Page
This is a useful, general introduction to various educational resources, including a chapter on resource centres.

Hall, B. (1997) *Web-Based Training Cookbook*, New York: John Wiley & Sons, Inc.
A guide to building your own web pages, and includes numerous examples of 'good practice' web sites, some of them on a CD-ROM disc.

Hussein, S. (2005) *Developing E-learning Material: Applying User-Centred Design (E-Guidelines)*, Leicester: NIACE
A short, user-friendly introduction to designing e-learning materials, written for non-technical practitioners.

Joliffe, A., Rilter, J. and Stevens, D. (2001) *The Online Handbook: Developing and Using Web-based Learning*, London: RoutledgeFalmer
Provides advice, tools and techniques on developing learning systems and operating and managing on-line learning.

Maier, P., Barnett, L., Warren, A. and Brunner, D. (1998) *Using Technology in Teaching and Learning*, 2nd edition, London: Kogan Page
Addressing a higher education audience, nevertheless this book contains some valid advice on integrating technology into learning. It includes numerous activities and also useful web addresses.

8 PREPARING FOR AND DEVELOPING THROUGH TEACHING PRACTICE

Objectives

After reading this chapter, you should be able to:
- identify the skills and aptitudes you need to develop on teaching practice
- devise personal strategies for getting the best out of teaching practice
- cope with, and learn from, lessons that do not go to plan
- deal confidently and effectively with the 'politics' of your placement institution.

For those undertaking pre-service training, teaching practice is likely to be one of the most unforgettable experiences of your life. Yet there will be far more to teaching practice than merely teaching. Lesson preparation will probably take up most of your time. You will probably have to battle to acquire a more complete knowledge of your subject matter, whilst at the same time puzzling how to structure the material into a lesson. In addition to teaching, you will be building personal working relationships with teaching staff (including your supervisor) and with your students.

For those training in-service, much of the above may still apply. Your course will not include teaching practice as such, but will, in a sense, constitute one extended period of teaching practice. Added to this is the fact that a proportion of your teaching sessions will be observed and assessed, some by an assessor from your accrediting institution and some by a nominated supervisor from your own institution. This chapter, then, will still provide valuable advice, pertinent to your own situation.

PREPARATION FOR TEACHING: THE CREATIVE USE OF MICRO-TEACHING

During pre-service training, you should have a number of opportunities to gain some experience of teaching. This is sometimes known as *micro-teaching* and will often take the form of a simulated 'class' with your fellow trainees as the audience. This is an ideal way to start, particularly for those who have no experience of standing up and speaking in front of people. Those who have been teaching for some years (which may include those who are now training in-service) forget just how traumatic this is for those who are doing it for the first time. This latter group may feel that, since they teach as part of their everyday job, this section is irrelevant to them; it is suggested, however, that there may be some ideas here that may be useful to you.

In your first micro-teaching session you may be tempted to provide yourself with a number of 'props', such as extensive notes to read from. Whilst a natural reaction, this is not the best approach. In adopting this strategy, you will soon find yourself merely reading from your notes, losing all eye contact with the audience, and any semblance of spontaneity or interaction. This is not teaching. You need to plan for the micro-teaching session in just the way you would organise yourself for a normal class on teaching practice. You start, then, with a lesson plan. Decide on your aims and objectives; then decide on the content of the session, how the various elements of the subject matter will be delivered, and the activities of all participants (you and the students). Plan which resources you will use, including handouts and visual aids (see Chapter 6).

From the outset, it is important to recognise that teaching does not necessarily involve you, the teacher, talking at all times. Such a lesson would quickly demotivate your students. As we saw in Chapter 2, if students are to learn, then they must be *active* participants in the classroom. Far from being the dominant figure in the class, you may be a guide or facilitator of learning, assisting students on an individual basis. Of course, this does not mean to say that there is no place for a teacher-led presentation, say, to introduce or summarise a topic. This is a skill that you must develop. But the point here is that the lecture is not necessarily the chief focus of the teacher's activities.

Acknowledging, however, that you will probably need to present *some* material as part of the micro-teaching session, you need to ensure that the material is:

- logically structured
- succinct
- stimulating to the audience
- reinforced by relevant visual aids.

Review Chapter 6 and look at the advice provided by Ellington and Race (1994) on designing materials. Well-structured visual aids, such as overhead transparencies, can help you in a number of ways:

- They give the audience a clear indication of the structure of the material.
- They can provide for some visual interest and excitement.
- They provide useful prompts for you to frame your presentation around. Far from having to stare down at a set of detailed notes, the overheads allow you the physical freedom to walk around and to make eye contact with your audience; they also allow for a more spontaneous delivery.

For more on preparing and delivering presentations review *Lectures* in Chapter 5, page 104.

ACTIVITY

Prepare material for a short presentation (say, about five minutes). Produce a set of overhead transparencies. Deliver the mini-lecture and obtain feedback either by recording the session on video or by getting a colleague to observe you.

PREPARATION FOR THE PLACEMENT

Identifying your learning needs

Teaching practice is a unique opportunity for every student teacher. It is a discreet allocation of time in which you are permitted (with some support from experienced teachers) to put into practice what you have learned as part of your professional training, and to experiment with a variety of different approaches to teaching. You will get the most out of such an experience, however, if you decide at the outset what you, as an individual, want to get out of it. This may be clear only in a very general sense at the beginning of the practice period (or periods). But you should soon be thinking about and identifying a number of key areas you want to work on and to develop. For example, not all student teachers feel comfortable at the outset, standing up and talking in front of a 'large' audience (20–30 people might be construed as large to an inexperienced student teacher). Opportunities could be sought to gain practice (and feedback on performance) in this area. Another example would be to improve the use of overheads, making them readable and more interesting to the viewer. In this case, guidance could be sought from an experienced teacher (mentor) acknowledged to be rather good in this area, or from someone involved in the audio-visual services of the college.

There are a number of sources that can be used to help in the identification of your learning needs:

- Some issues will probably emerge during micro-teaching.
- Your tutors on the Cert. Ed. or PGCE course may have mentioned some areas for improvement.
- Supervised teaching practice sessions at your placement will, almost inevitably, throw up some issues that demand attention.

ACTIVITY

Using a word processing package, make a three-column list. In the first (left-hand) column, think of areas that could benefit from development. In the second column, produce an action plan for each learning area, and, in the third column, how its achievement is to be assessed.

Visiting the institution

This section is written particularly with the interests of pre-service teachers in mind. Those of you in-service presumably will be relatively familiar with your own institution and may prefer to move on to page 188. At this point, however, it is perhaps useful to make clear the nature of the relationship between the institution training you, and where you will be gaining your teaching experience. For those of you in-service, this may be the same institution. But whatever your situation, it is likely that you will have someone assisting you as a student (who we will refer to as your tutor) and someone responsible for assisting you as a teacher on your placement (who we will call your supervisor).

Reconnaissance

It was Napoleon who said: 'Time spent on reconnaissance is rarely, if ever, wasted'. This would certainly apply to teaching practice. You are going to spend several weeks in a new institution in which a multiplicity of activities take place. Teaching, of course, is one of them, but also of importance are:

- student guidance
- course development
- marketing
- assessment
- validation.

There will be planning meetings and meetings to discuss student progress. In order to make yourself familiar with all these activities, you need to develop a sound understanding of what takes place in your teaching placement institution, so that you can plan to observe and take part in as much as possible. Hence, make sure that you visit your placement well before you are expected to teach there. It is likely that your professional training course will have planned this for you as part of your course. Plan what you want to discover on the visit and use the experience as a fact-finding mission.

Negotiating a timetable

From your own perspective, you will want a timetable that reflects some of the learning needs you identified in the last activity. It is likely, for example, that you will want to teach a range of subjects (within limits) and at a number of academic levels. The broader your experience on teaching practice, the more you will learn. This breadth of experience will also stand you in better stead for attaining paid employment once you have qualified.

Clearly, however, a highly eclectic timetable will make greater challenges on your time (particularly for preparation), and may, in some circumstances, be unfeasible. You may need to seek advice both from your training institution and your supervisor on teaching practice about how you can broaden your experience without over-stretching yourself.

Meeting your students

One of the worst aspects of any new situation is fear of the unknown. One of the most significant unknown factors is the students themselves. How friendly are they? Are they keen to learn or are they disruptive? Do they ask easy or difficult questions? It is important that the time spent before teaching practice is devoted to preparing yourself rather than worrying. Any visit to your teaching institution, then, should ideally involve an opportunity to meet with some or most of the students you will be teaching. This could be informally, outside the classroom. It should also, however, include the chance to observe them in a classroom environment. This is an opportunity to gauge the general ability level of different accredited courses and, therefore, how you will 'pitch' the complexity of your teaching materials and methods.

This is also an ideal opportunity to view a broad spectrum of subjects being taught by a variety of teaching methods. Make sure that you observe more than just your own subjects being taught. If you are a sociologist, see someone teaching engineering or motor vehicle maintenance. If you are an A Level English language specialist, also observe someone teaching special needs. In making your observations, it helps if you decide in advance *what* it is that you are expecting to see (so preparing an observation schedule, as in the following activity, can help). When making your observations of students and teachers it is also important that, whatever you feel about what is happening in the classroom, you keep your views to yourself, that is, you observe confidentiality.

ACTIVITY

The observation schedule should include the subject and level of the class, number of students, location, etc. Then add a number of observation categories; you may find a simplified version of a category system discussed by Wragg (1994) useful, keeping a tally of each time a behaviour occurs. Table 8.1 illustrates this.

Watch out for and note down student reactions to: different teaching methods, the style/tone of the teacher, student interactions with each other. Note in particular any subjects or activities they like/dislike and hypothesise why. If you are going to teach a class, learn as many students' names as you can.

Table 8.1   *Observation categories in the classroom (after Wragg, 1994)*

Practical knowledge	Types of learning	Types of course
Teacher asks questions	//////////	10
Teacher gives command	///	3
Teacher gives praise	////////	8
Teacher gives criticism	/	1

GETTING THE BEST OUT OF TEACHING PRACTICE

Negotiating with supervisors

Whether you are a pre-service teacher or in-service, your supervisor is one of the keys to a successful teaching practice. For those pre-service, the role of the supervisor will probably include:

- finalising your timetable
- arranging with other staff to allow you to take over their classes

- sitting in some of your classes and providing feedback at the end of the session
- helping you with any problems that arise either with students, staff or administrators
- formally assessing some of your sessions.

For those in-service, the supervisor will probably:

- discuss your development needs with you
- arrange to assess some of your teaching sessions
- agree to complete the necessary documentation that charts your progress.

Whilst all supervisors inevitably have their own objectives for you, it is essential that you communicate *your* needs to them (refer back to the activity on page 186). As already noted, you will need, for example, to negotiate a varied timetable, to gain experience of teaching as broad a range of student abilities, subjects and qualifications as is feasible. This will enrich your experience and give you a better grounding in how it is to teach different groups. You will also have to negotiate how often your supervisor, or a teacher nominated by them, supervises you while you are teaching. It is important that you accept the presence of professional teachers in the classroom, as this is an invaluable way of getting feedback. Yet it is also the case that, with some experience, there will be times when you want the responsibility to take the class with no on-lookers. In the final analysis, you will have to accept whatever frequency of visits your supervisor decides. Regard this less as an imposition than as a professional teacher willing to give up their precious free time to help your development.

It is important to recognise and acknowledge the fact that supervisors receive very little reward for the task – apart from the personal satisfaction of assisting the transition of someone into the profession. The following case study looks at the experiences of some supervisors (gleaned from a series of interviews), including why they volunteered for the job, and the difficulties they have faced. This, hopefully, will provide you with some insights and understanding of your supervisor's role.

Case Study: *The role of the supervisor*

Supervisor, Greybourne Sixth Form College
I became a supervisor because I'm a college mentor, and that means that I'm responsible for helping to improve the quality of teaching throughout the college. My particular role is focused on new members of staff and helping them into teaching. In terms of difficulties, the biggest one is when you know that what the trainee is saying is factually incorrect. I suggest to them afterwards that it was not the full story! Another difficulty is not allowing myself to step in when things go wrong – that's a big temptation.

Supervisor, Greybourne College of FE
I was first approached by the college authorities after another student had been successfully supervised by my predecessor. My main frustration with the job is, given all my other activities, not being able to spend as much time helping the student teacher as I would like. Also completing all the paperwork efficiently and on time has not been easy. But I have very much enjoyed being a supervisor.

ACTIVITY

Talk to your own supervisor about their motives for accepting the role. Discuss with them what they think they gain from being a supervisor and any of the frustrations they face.

Getting to know your colleagues

For those of you training pre-service, you will gain little from going into your teaching institution only to teach and then rushing off home. By spending some time in the college's staffrooms you will get to know some of the staff and, more importantly, they will get to know you. Building professional relationships with colleagues is not just a matter of protocol or convenience. It is a means of establishing professional bonds and informal networks that can, in the long term, be of considerable help to *you*. As Cooper and Rousseau (1996) acknowledge, these social networks can often appear subtle and informal, especially to any newcomer to the organisation. Those training in-service will be better positioned to identify these social networks, but perhaps agree that building such professional relationships within them is never easy.

Firstly, by getting to know staff, you will be able to listen to people whose experience of teaching and 14–19 education exceeds your own. This is not to say that all their comments will be valid, but you will learn a lot about the 'folklore' of the staffroom (see the following activity), and about teachers' strengths (and prejudices). Secondly, you may gain new subject knowledge or information about college procedures or resources, any of which might be very useful to you.

Getting to know your students

Each student is, of course, an individual with their own learning and developmental needs. A class, however, is also a group, which means that you have to be aware that group dynamics may play a part in the interactions between you and the group and within the group itself. In the UK, the development of theories of small group behaviour largely began with the so-called 'Northfield Experiment' in a military hospital during the Second World War. Here, experiments found three main patterns of behaviour when groups were given problems to solve:

- a *dependency culture* where an attempt was made to make a leader take all responsibility for decisions
- *fight-flight* – an attempt to find a solution through escape or conflict
- *pairing* – the establishment of relationships between pairs of group members whom the rest of the group rely on to find a solution.

Since then, research into the functioning of groups has mainly come from two sources: one is psychotherapists working in clinical practice, seeking answers for clients with various kinds of psychological problems or disorders. The second has largely involved training managers in large organisations, and has revolved around an attempt to understand how and why their employees behave in the ways they do.

ACTIVITY

Examine some of Wragg's (1994) ideas that he suggests form part of the folklore of the staffroom. These and similar ideas may emerge from getting to know staff better. Select four that you think are the most valid for yourself.

- Start by being firm with students: you can relax later.
- Get silence before you start speaking to the class.
- Control the students' entry to the classroom.
- Know and use the students' names.
- Prepare lessons thoroughly and structure them firmly.
- Arrive at the classroom before students.
- Prepare furniture and apparatus before the students arrive.
- Know how to use apparatus, and be familiar with experiments before you use them in class.
- Be mobile; walk around the class.
- Start the lesson with a 'bang' and sustain interest and curiosity.
- Give clear instructions.
- Learn voice control.
- Have additional material prepared to cope with bright and slow students' needs.
- Look at the class when speaking and learn how to scan.
- Make written work appropriate (for example, to the age, ability, cultural background of students).
- Develop an effective questioning technique.
- Develop the art of timing in your lesson to fit the available period.
- Vary your teaching techniques.
- Anticipate discipline problems and act quickly.
- Avoid confrontation.
- Clarify and insist on your standards.
- Show yourself as a helper or facilitator to the students.
- Do not patronise students, treat them as responsible beings.
- Use humour constructively.

One of the first attempts to categorise the behaviour of groups was by Bales (1950). By observing the interactions within groups, he determined that there are broad categories of group behaviour (see Table 8.2).

Bales (1950) suggests that the interaction process for problem-solving within groups usually consists of asking questions (categories 7–9, above), followed by attempted answers (4–6), followed by either positive (1–3) or negative (10–12) reactions. As far as teachers are concerned, they need to create a balance between task role behaviour (categories 4–9), group growth roles, and the behaviour of individuals whose behaviour is non-productive for the group. Group growth behaviour can be seen, for example, in the behaviour of:

- the *encourager* – the person who gives warmth and support and facilitates the sharing of ideas to other members of the group.

Table 8.2   *Categories of group behaviour (adapted from Bales, 1950: 9)*

Category	Category	Action	Description of behaviour
Positive: Social socio-emotional area	1	Shows solidarity	Raises others' status, gives help, reward
	2	Shows tension release	Jokes, laughs, shows satisfaction
	3	Agrees	Shows passive acceptance, understands, concurs, complies
Neutral: Task area	4	Gives suggestions	Direction, implying autonomy of others
	5	Gives opinion	Evaluation, analysis, expresses feeling, wish
	6	Gives orientation	Information repeats, clarifies, confirms
	7	Asks for orientation	Information, repetition, confirmation
	8	Asks for opinion	Evaluation, analysis, expression of feeling
	9	Asks for suggestion	Direction, possible ways of action
Negative: Social or socio-emotional area	10	Disagrees	Shows passive rejection, formality, withholds help
	11	Shows tension	Asks for help, withdraws out of field
	12	Shows antagonism	Deflates other's status, defends or asserts self

Negative examples of group behaviour can be seen in:

- the *blocker*, who contradicts or refuses to accept the ideas of others (without giving any reasons)
- the *recognition seeker*, who constantly looks for praise or attention
- the *dominator*, who 'puts down' other students' contributions, and who tries to control the direction of the discussion
- the *avoider*, the person who withdraws from discussion and avoids contact with other members of the group.

Getting to know your students will entail also getting to know which of them, if any, adopt positive or negative roles towards the group, particularly if these roles manifest themselves over a number of classes. As a manager of the group, as well as a teacher, you will need to think of strategies for addressing these behaviours.

Handling your supervisor

Achieving a productive relationship between you and your supervisor will depend, at least in part, on the extent to which you both understand each other's objectives. You might find it instructive, therefore, to have an insight into the typical traits that supervisors wish to see in their trainees. The following list is a compilation of views gleaned from a number of college supervisors about the traits they like to see in student teachers:

- conveying a sense of self-confidence
- preparing and structuring materials thoroughly
- gauging what students already know at the start of the lesson, and drawing on their own knowledge and experience
- getting the students engaged, committed and enthused
- using the role of analogy so that material connects with what the students know and are thinking
- delivering spontaneously and in engaging manner
- using constructive student activities (for example, discussing, demonstrating, simulating)
- conveying the subject matter with conviction
- demonstrating good classroom management techniques
- being a self-starter (knowing what to do – and getting on with it!)
- demonstrating a good grasp of theory
- demonstrating a knowledge of the 14–19 context, for example the difference between modes of assessment of applied vocational qualifications and A-level.

Handling visits by assessors and external examiners

Visits from assessors

All courses leading to accredited teaching qualifications, whether they are part-time or full-time, are formally assessed. Written assessment may take a number of different forms (for example, ranging in formality from closed book examinations to coursework assignments, or a mixture of the two). It is also likely that all, or a sample of, student examination scripts or written assignments will be sent for scrutiny to the course's external examiners, who are independent and experienced practitioners, usually of respectable academic standing, appointed to ensure the objectivity and veracity of the assessment process.

An important task for your assessors and the external examiners is also to visit a sample of students on teaching practice. These teaching practice visits fulfil a number of purposes. Firstly, there is a sense in which the visits are designed to assist you by providing you with help, advice and guidance as part of your professional development. Assessors and examiners come with a wealth of experience and can provide you with valuable feedback. Secondly, the visits are designed to promote the reliability and validity of the assessment process. *Reliability* in assessment is defined by Mehrens and Lehmann (1984) as 'the degree of consistency between two measures of the same thing'. In other words, if you were to weigh yourself on the same set of scales now and then in ten minutes' time, you would expect the scales to give you a similar reading. In educational terms, if two assessors were measuring a student's achievement on a piece of written work, you would hope that, working independently, they came to a similar score or mark. On teaching practice your teaching abilities will be measured by one or more supervisor or teacher. As in a doctor's surgery, the more 'second opinions' (or even third or fourth opinions) there are, the more likely it is that the judgement will be a fair and accurate one. Clearly, the views of an assessor or external examiner can help here because not only are they an additional contribution to the assessment process, they also have an overview of standards required.

Validity is also central to the assessment process. This means that the sorts of assessment questions asked are firmly linked to the purpose of the assessment process itself. So, for example, in assessing your teaching performance, a question, say, about why you selected one teaching method as opposed to another would be valid; conversely, a query about your opinions on how the college was managed would not be! Still on the theme of validity, the examiners may also be interested in the extent to which the whole experience of teaching practice is a valid test of your abilities. For example, an examiner might find that the student received only grudging support from a supervisor, was given only the most demanding classes to teach and an overloaded timetable (including unfamiliar subjects to teach). This would not constitute a valid assessment of the teaching process. Examiners would comment on this in their reports to the accrediting institution. This institution would, in turn, be required to take action as part of its quality assurance processes.

Visits from external examiners

It should be borne in mind, then, that any assessed sessions by your training institution's assessor or any visit from an external examiner will include discussions between that examiner and supervisors and other teachers involved in supervision duties. The second purpose of an external examiner's visit, then, is to assess the quality, or otherwise, of the teaching placement. Questions may be asked about resources and facilities available to student teachers, and how the supervision process is handled. In other words, the visit is as much about assessing the quality (validity) and environment of the teaching institution as it is about assessing student teachers. And when student teachers *are* visited by the examiner, it is the extent to which the student teacher has been prepared for teaching practice by their training course that is

ACTIVITY

Imagine that you are to receive a visit from an external examiner. Make a list of things you would do to prepare yourself for the visit to ensure its success (from *your* standpoint). Consider factors such as:

- ensuring you know exactly which date/time/class the examiner will be visiting (and that this class will be in college, not on a field trip!)
- what areas of your teaching need development so you can show you are addressing them in your preparation and delivery
- establishing how and when the examiner will feed back the results of the visit to you.

also under scrutiny. For example, a group of examiners, visiting different institutions, might find that most student teachers from the same teaching institution use only didactic teaching methods. Questions would then be asked at the post-course examination board meeting (attended by academic staff of the training institution as well as the examiners), about training in the use of teaching methods.

Being assessed when 'in trouble'

It is also the case (and you may have anticipated this already) that visits by external examiners may be because a student teacher is 'in trouble'. If a student teacher is, say, not progressing at an acceptable speed, and is even in danger of being failed on teaching practice, course managers will want a number of opinions of the student's progress (the issue of reliability again). If you hear that you are to be visited, there may be no way of telling whether you fall into this category. It would be wise, however, to *reflect* for a moment about your overall performance, and obtain the views expressed by supervisors about the standard of your teaching. If you are aware of some of the difficulties you have faced, and feel that you have been chosen for an examiner's visit because of these, then clearly you will need to perform to the best of your capabilities during the visit.

One of the greatest enemies of any sort of cognitive activity is acute nervousness. Knowing that you may fail teaching practice is unlikely to instil a feeling of composure. Nevertheless, it is important that you remain as calm as possible and that you:

- examine those aspects of your teaching that have already been highlighted as requiring development
- in planning the lesson, ensure that these issues are addressed (see the activity on page 194).

After observing you teach, the external examiner will, just like your supervisor, provide you with verbal feedback on your teaching session. You may agree with some of the things that he or she says and disagree with others. What is important is that you do not become defensive and, as a result, argue and reject the feedback you are given. Not all examiners (or supervisors, for that matter) are always right. You may feel that there are elements of subjectivity in some of the things they say. Nevertheless, as detached observers in your classroom they are better positioned than you to observe and note many of the interactions that are taking place. It will also almost always be the case that they have many more years of teaching experience than yourself. In most cases, therefore, it is wisest to listen and to learn. If there are any issues you do not understand, ask for clarification, and thank them for their feedback.

Personal presentation

Our perceptions of a person are strongly influenced by their appearance, including the way they dress and present themselves. As Handy (1993) points out, these role signs such as dress have been used to suggest the degree of formality or informality of social gatherings, and, to an extent, the social standing of individuals. In perceiving people, especially their status and roles, we first collect data on them. Personal presentation often forms the core of this data, so we need to be aware of the messages our personal presentation emits.

Colleges do not tend to have an official 'dress' policy, but you will notice while you are on teaching practice that many staff present themselves quite smartly. Social anthropologists may note that dress codes tend to vary between departments; business studies staff, for example, usually dress quite formally (business suits are the norm) as though they were actually working in business or industry (perhaps because they want to imbue their students with a business 'ethos'). Conversely, some staff in, say, the arts and humanities are usually less formal. The best policy is to dress comfortably and smartly, especially at the beginning of teaching practice. It is easier, then, to relax this formality if it is not the norm.

Preparing for the jobs market

While on teaching practice, it might seem rather premature to be considering how to get a job or to change jobs. Whether you are training pre-service or in-service this is, in fact, an ideal time to start making preparations. To obtain paid employment you must develop the skills, competencies (and attitudes) that are attractive to a potential employer. Whilst on teaching practice, there are a number of ways in which you can help yourself. Some of these are addressed in the next activity.

ACTIVITY

Find out if the college is recruiting for any posts in, or close to, your own subject interests; try to obtain a job specification and examine it carefully to see what types of skill and expertise are demanded. If there are subjects you need to gain experience teaching and you manage to obtain this information early on in the teaching practice, then there may still be time to negotiate with your supervisor some teaching in this area. It might also be useful talking to those who wrote the job description and who take part in interview panels for their views. So, in summary:

- look at some of the college's job specifications
- examine what subject areas are expanding or contracting
- gain feedback from course managers or personnel on your own suitability.

SURVIVING THE 'DISASTROUS LESSON'

You may emerge from one or more lesson feeling depressed, frustrated or inadequate because you felt the session, for whatever reason, was a shambles. It is important to note that this may be only *your* evaluation of the lesson, whereas others, the students or a supervisor, present at the session, may take an entirely different view. The first task after a session like this, then, is to check whether your perception is accurate. There are several ways of doing this. You could, for example, ask the students themselves (but be prepared either for vociferous feedback, or, just as likely, polite silence). Alternatively, you could (and should), seek the advice of your supervisor, particularly if they were present, or of another professional teacher, to whom you could describe the session. In all the problem cases discussed in this section, if the disaster is caused by a 'problem' student, discover whether this student displays the same behaviour in other teachers' classes. Often you will find that this is the case. This suggests that the problem is one faced by the student and is independent of your style or quality of classroom management and teaching.

If it emerges that the problem is at your own door, and that the students dislike an aspect of your teaching, you should keep the event in perspective. You are not the first teacher in history to experience something go wrong! This has happened to all teachers at one time or another. Indeed, in a sense, the risks of this occurrence should be continuous for all professional teachers, since we should always try out new approaches and ideas. What is important is that you should *reflect* on why the lesson did not go to plan, learn from the event, and take action to ensure it is not repeated.

As we saw in Chapter 2, reflection is included in Kolb and Fry's (1975) model of the learning cycle. In principle, the learning could begin at any point in the cycle, but in practice, one would often expect to commence with concrete experience (in this case the disastrous lesson). Implicit in this cycle is the assumption that, through reflection, the formulation of new concepts and generalisations and their testing in new situations, learning takes place. Hence, after a disastrous lesson, one would expect a reflective practitioner to:

- collect data (for example, own observations, student or peer evaluations)
- conceptualise the issues and problems that arise
- generate new ideas for action.

Jarvis (1995) warns that reflection is not necessarily innovative and that not all reflection inevitably leads to learning.

Some practitioners (not only in teaching but in other professions such as health care) now choose to keep a learning log that describes a record of their experiences and their reactions and learn from them.

ACTIVITY

Boud (1992) suggests that we can assist ourselves to reflect. He recognises that it is difficult to be part of an event and to distance ourselves and reflect on it at the same time. Therefore reflection is aided if we can utilise natural breaks in the flow of events, and take time out from activities. He suggests that, in interacting with events, we can develop our reflective powers if we develop:

- 'noticing', that is, the act of becoming aware of what is happening in and around the learning milieu
- 'intervening', or taking action within the event.

In a learning activity of your choice, 'notice' what is occurring by noting your thoughts on paper (for example, in your learning log); in this, or another event, intervene by becoming actively engaged with the people or objectives involved, and then 'notice' the impact of your intervention (so completing the cycle of reflection-in-action).

Having looked at reflection, in the next section we will look at some of the typical events that can occur on teaching practice and suggest possible remedial action.

Disruptive students

This is probably the greatest fear of most trainee teachers. Disruption can take many forms and can, of course, vary in scale, ranging from mildly irritating behaviour (for example, the persistent, deliberate cougher) to full scale revolt! Your ability to cope with disruption will be largely determined by the extent to which you can:

- anticipate events
- interpret these events
- formulate speedy remedial action.

You may often, for example, be aware that disruption is about to occur, long before it does (so allowing remedial planning well in advance). If a particular student was noisy and lacking concentration in your class during the previous week, you may be expecting this to happen again. Be careful, however, not to allow previous events to 'colour' your attitude towards individual students. In what is now quite a venerable study, Rosenthal and Jacobson (1968) found a strong link between teachers' expectations and the performance of their students. So, if you believe that a student is disruptive (and you somehow transmit these feelings, say, through non-verbal communication), you may actually trigger the very disruption you fear.

Wheldall and Merrett (1989) recommend a 'positive teaching' approach to handling disruption. Firstly, it is important to identify precisely the nature of the student's activity. Human behaviour is often open to alternative interpretations, so there must be no room for ambiguity. It might help, for example, to count the number of instances of a behaviour. Secondly, try to identify those items or events that the student finds rewarding, and structure your teaching so as to make access to these rewards dependent upon behaviour. In behaviourist terms (see Chapter 2) this means using positive reinforcers such as praise and encouragement when a desired feature of behaviour occurs. If, as increasingly likely with the growth of inclusive strategies, your class contains students with special needs, then you may want to consider some of the strategies outlined in Chapter 5.

ACTIVITY

Look up the college's student charter. What are the procedures for dealing with disruptive students? Check with your supervisor that you fully understand them and know how to implement them.

Attention-seeking students

There can sometimes be a fine line between a student who is an enthusiastic contributor to class discussions and someone whose behaviour can be construed as attention-seeking. A student crosses that line when the frequency of their contributions becomes intrusive to the rest of the class. The behaviour of these students is also disruptive because they make the majority of verbal contributions in the class, to the point where even students with valid contributions to make are interrupted and feel marginalised by the attention-seeker.

Like the disruptive student, the attention-seeker is doing this for a reason. Often, such a person is suffering from a deep sense of intellectual or emotional insecurity (or both). In terms of group dynamics, this person may also be someone who is fighting for leadership of the group. Alternatively, in Erikson's (1965) classic model of human development, many college students are in the throes of identity formation, meaning that self-esteem and trust of others may both be in doubt. Of course, the reasons for the student's behaviour may go far deeper. Look back at Chapter 5 for the discussion on students with special needs.

Yet whatever the reason for the behaviour, it is up to the teacher to ensure that the rest of the class does not suffer. As Wheldall and Merrett (1989) point out, admonishing the student provides the attention being sought and merely acts as positive reinforcement. A better approach is to reduce the number of attention-seeking interventions by giving less eye-contact to the perpetrator. In addition, give more eye-contact and non-verbal communication (for example, hand gestures, smiling, etc.) to others most likely to contribute. Also, ask specific students by name for their views on a topic. If all else fails (and with the persistent attention-seeker it may), you will need to uncover the underlying reasons for the behaviour. This may mean asking to see the student outside timetabled hours so that you can raise the issue. This, of course, must be done with sensitivity, since you may be alerting the student to issues that she or he is unaware of. Their initial reaction may be one of hurt and surprise, so you need to ensure that the student is aware of *your* motives – the need to manage the class for the benefit of all. You also must make it clear that your intention is *not* to silence the student, but to ensure that everyone contributes. You need to prepare yourself for counselling the student and may, in some circumstances (for example, if the student seems emotionally upset by your questions or comments), advise the student to contact the college's counselling services. If you begin to suspect that the student has undiagnosed special needs, then you may need to talk to the college's special needs co-ordinator about bringing in professional help.

Uninterested students

The opposite of the attention-seeker is the uninterested student, again a problem, but obviously for different reasons. Lack of interest can take many forms: a generally bored expression (but take care here, this may be a natural facial expression for some students!); lack of attention and an inclination to be easily distracted; yawning, fidgeting, etc. Some students may be uninterested one day, and valuable contributors the next. In general, though, the uninterested student will often display this characteristic with predictable and depressing regularity. (In considering why some students adopt such attitudes, you might like to review the section in Chapter 2 on motivation.)

In practical terms, if this lack of interest only occurs in *your* class, then this may mean the student dislikes either the subject you teach, yourself, or both. In these circumstances, try to organise an informal 'chat' with the student, say, at the end of a lesson, to uncover what the real problems are. You might find, for example, that the student is having difficulties understanding the subject, with the result they have fallen behind and have mentally 'switched off'. Your task here would be to assist the student by, say, offering remedial tuition so that they can acquire more entry knowledge back into the subject. It is remarkable how a teacher's interest in a student can generate reciprocal interest by the student in a subject. Alternatively, the lack of interest may stem from the fact that they have lost interest in your course. Here you will have to make use of the college's student support system and consider re-timetabling if there is still time to switch courses.

Emotional students

The sight of a student displaying emotional symptoms, such as weeping, is not that uncommon. As we saw in the Introduction, the majority of students in further education are in the 16–19 age group. Most students, then, are at a stage in their lives when they are experiencing considerable physical, emotional and intellectual changes. New bonds (both working and personal) are being forged (and lost). Students feel themselves pressured by the demands of their peer group. It is hardly surprising, then, that occasionally life becomes difficult and emotional crises ensue.

As a teacher you have a responsibility to the students who want to learn and to the student who is exhibiting emotional symptoms – but not necessarily to both at the same time. In other words, you cannot simultaneously teach and comfort effectively. To minimise the disruption caused, it is often best to extricate the student from the class with the minimum of fuss. A quiet and tactful word such as: 'If you're not feeling well perhaps you'd like to leave us for a few minutes' can often achieve the desired results. Set the students some work and get to see the 'problem' student as soon as possible. If he or she has disappeared off to the toilets, it might be advisable to get another student to check if they are physically well; it might be the case, for example, that the student is in need of medical attention.

Diagnose the seriousness of the problem as quickly as you can. This, though, will depend on the extent to which the student is willing to divulge his or her problems to you. Essentially, you have three courses of action, depending on the scale of the difficulty:

- invite the student back into the classroom when they have recovered their composure
- allow the student to take the remainder of the lesson off (but ask to see them later so that you can satisfy yourself that they have recovered – and so that you can set them work to catch up on what they missed)
- refer the student to the college's counselling or medical service, whichever is appropriate.

Supporting students who are presenting emotional difficulties requires a sympathetic approach. It is essential, however, to pass the student on to professional counselling help if you believe the underlying causes of the problem remain.

Late students

Some students are never late, many occasionally late and a hardened minority persistently late. It is the latter whose behaviour is usually a manifestation of other problems, often associated with disinterest or discontent. Just occasionally persistent lateness will be a symptom of more hardened anti-college attitudes. Whatever the causes, lateness should never be tolerated – it is harmful to the education of the student involved, disruptive to the class (late entry will often cause the teacher or a student to pause in their contribution) and disrespectful to all.

You should always make it clear to the late student, and the class, that the late entry has been noted ('Late again John', or a meaningful glance at your watch and a scowl in the general direction of the student). Make sure that disruption is minimised by, if you are discussing an issue, continuing with as little break in the flow as possible. If the class has embarked on a task, walk over to the late entrant and give them the task to start immediately. Be busy and business-like. If the late entrant is very persistent in this behaviour, ask to see them at the end of the session and ensure that the rest of the class has heard this request. You are not just a classroom teacher but a manager, and you are establishing behaviour parameters you expect all to adhere to. Since, as a student teacher, you are in charge of another teacher's class, it would be as well to inform her or him of the problem and what action you have taken. As usual, check that your supervisor agrees with your action and take advice, if necessary.

'We've done this before!'

On teaching practice you will be taking over the classes of someone who has taught the students, probably, for several or many months. As part of planning your contribution, you will, hopefully, have examined the scheme of work and discussed what issues have been covered with the class teacher so that you do not repeat them. Sometimes, though, this will not prevent the inevitable cry from the students of 'We've done this before!'. Having spent several hours preparing a lesson and, possibly, even looking forward to participating in it, you will reflect that you may have had better days! In terms of reacting to the situation you have, essentially, three options:

- change the lesson and do something else
- plough on with what you have prepared
- abandon the lesson completely.

We can discount the last option immediately, because you have a commitment to teaching this class that must be fulfilled. As far as the other options are concerned, both have their advantages and dangers. One of the skills of a teacher is flexibility, and it is certainly possible, given sufficient subject knowledge, to change the focus of a lesson. But you will recall in Chapter 4 how much care is demanded in planning the aims and objectives of a lesson, even before the issues of teaching methods and resources are addressed. It is unlikely that these can be invented 'on the hoof', and to attempt to do so might only result in chaos. If the students are to know what they are doing, teachers have to be doubly sure of their own role and material. Careful and thorough planning and preparation can never, therefore, be abandoned.

In deciding to continue with your original lesson plan, there are two reasons why this is probably the most sensible course. Firstly, it is certainly feasible that, in making their assertion, the students believe they are right, but in fact they are mistaken in their opinion. Secondly, you can use the lesson as a revision session and to consolidate what the students say they have learnt. The amount of material that students often 'unlearn' is a salutary lesson for all. In a classic study in 1885, Ebbinghaus (Myers, 1998), for example, found that, in learning a list of nonsense syllables, retention rates dropped rapidly in the first few days, after which the amount of memory loss levelled out (see Figure 8.1).

Using the session for revision, and being taught by a different person, probably using different teaching methods, may also allow the students to 'see' the subject from a different perspective. When faced with a chorus of 'We've done this before', then, do not be defensive. Acknowledge the students' statement, be positive, and set the focus of the lesson as 'Seeing how much you really know'. Provided all view the session in this positive light, it can be constructive and informative.

The technical breakdown

Just as actors are forewarned against working with animals or children, so the greatest fear of many teachers is the breakdown of equipment. Without being too fatalistic, this is most likely to happen at those moments when the lesson hinges particularly on the efficient functioning of the technology. For example, a video recorder for playing a key programme fails to even start, or the bulb 'blows' in the overhead projector. Such events are a hindrance to teachers whatever their experience. However, the more experienced teacher will have a number of strategies at their disposal for ensuring that the technical breakdown does not sink the entire lesson.

Firstly, there are ways of minimising the chances of the technical breakdown occurring. The obvious one is to always check that the equipment is working well before the lesson commences. Set up the overhead projector before the students arrive and ensure that it works. It is far more likely that a bulb is 'dead' before you start than to have one blow in the middle of a lesson. Even if this happens, most modern overhead projectors have double bulbs, so you should be able to switch immediately to the spare. Check your options with the AVA technician well in advance. In the case of VCRs or DVDs, try out the equipment the day before you wish to use it, and, if you can, in the presence of the audio-visual technician. Not only observe how they operate the equipment, but ask to copy their actions yourself. A common error, for example, is not to know the location or number of the video channel on the television. Many students, for reasons that will remain a mystery, do know this information and will take pleasure in telling you when you get, say, the VCR running

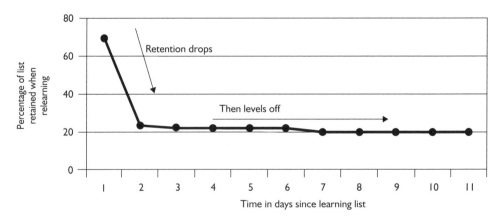

Figure 8.1 *A curve of forgetting (after Ebbinghaus, 1985, adapted from Myers, 1998)*

but cannot obtain a picture. Knowing the video channel in advance will save you this common embarrassment.

The double-booking

As we saw in the Introduction, student numbers in the 14–19 sector are expanding, in part as a response to government initiatives. This, inevitably, will put pressure on limited resources such as teaching rooms and other college accommodation. A typical disaster on teaching practice is to turn up to your allotted teaching room, only to find a classroom full of busy occupants. To anticipate such an occurrence, it is wise to get to know who in the college is responsible for room allocations. Write down their telephone number and carry it with you at all times. In the event of your room being occupied, one quick phone call could tell you that *you* have 'ownership' of the room, in which case you are on firm ground for politely evicting the current occupants. If you are second in the queue for this room, this same telephone number may give you access to any alternative rooms on campus.

In the worst possible scenario you will be roomless. The flexible teacher always has alternative strategies at their disposal. One, for example, might be taking the students to the library, or a learning resource centre, and setting them a project that requires independent study.

We have seen that disasters can present themselves from a variety of sources. In the following case study we provide an actual example from a student's own experiences of teaching practice.

Case Study: *Negotiating timetables with supervisors*

I had arranged with a teacher to take one of his sessions on a research course delivered to qualified nurses. It was about qualitative research. We discussed the content of the session and he wrote down what it should contain. I asked him what they had previously studied about qualitative research and he said: 'This is level one – assume they know nothing'.

This was to be my first teaching session, and as such I was keen, enthusiastic and painfully slow. It took me four days to prepare it. Anyway, there I was – OHTs, reading lists, handouts. It was to be a fabulous session, interesting and entertaining, containing the regulatory group work and feedback activities.

The session was on Monday, but I arranged to meet the teacher on Friday morning to go through my lesson plan. He was late for the meeting. After one hour of discussing the lesson with him, I asked him whether the students had any experience of quantitative research, as I had planned to do a comparison. He went to get details and returned to tell me the session was, in fact, focused on a particular aspect of qualitative theory: phenomenology, grounded theory and ethnography – all of which I had planned only to touch on. Everything else I had planned to teach had already been covered in the course, and the students were at level two not level one, so would already have a good grounding in the content I was intending to cover. My first reaction was disappointment. My second reaction (and the strongest) was blind rage.

(Student teacher, Greybourne College of FE)

> **ACTIVITY**
>
> Discuss this case study with a colleague on your Cert. Ed or PGCE programme. Each of you write down three questions this student should have asked his or her supervisor before agreeing to take the session. Compare your three questions.

In the light of the problems highlighted in this section and the 'horror story' in the case study, Figure 8.2 looks at a brief summary of how it is possible to cope with the unexpected.

Remember, the kinds of disasters outlined here are not inevitable and happen relatively infrequently. But forewarned is forearmed. Whatever the problem, note it as part of your learning log and discuss it with your supervisor and peers.

THE POLITICS OF THE PLACEMENT: DOS AND DON'TS

The experience of your teacher training course will already have suggested that teaching is a multi-skilled occupation performed, whilst on teaching practice or training in-service, initially at least, in front of strangers (both students and your supervisor). You are developing your skills in an institution where everyone else appears more experienced than yourself. Finally, the hours of toil required to prepare yourself well for each teaching session may leave you feeling physically and mentally tired, even exhausted. It is small wonder that, amidst the stress of teaching practice, some students may also find the 'politics' of their placement institution difficult to understand and to cope with. In these circumstances some students make 'political' mistakes that impact on their general performance and on their chances of success.

What do we mean by 'politics'? Clearly, this is not alluding to formal party politics of any kind. By politics is meant the system of status and power negotiations that take

---

Avoiding
- Negotiate a timetable that meets your needs as well as those of the teaching institution.
- Ensure that you have seen schemes of work for programmes so that you do not duplicate other teachers' sessions.
- Anticipate student disruptive behaviour by careful observation.
- Check technical equipment thoroughly prior to use.
- Develop a range of flexible classroom management techniques including controlling the 'geography' of the classroom (seating arrangements) to encourage/discourage levels of interaction.

Coping
- Have alternative materials and strategies available for when things go wrong.
- Check your own perceptions/interpretations of events with experienced others, e.g. your supervisor or experienced teachers, so that you build up a bank of knowledge.
- Ensure that you know the college's policy for handling disruptive behaviour and student sickness or problems during teaching sessions.

Figure 8.2 *Checklist of key strategies for coping with (and avoiding) disasters*

place at a formal, semi-formal or informal level within the institution. Handy (1993) suggests that individuals will always have their own values, objectives and interests that they would like their organisation to adopt. Furthermore, there will be pressure groups and blocking groups, as well as groups pursuing joint interests and other groups protecting theirs. At a college level, for example, political relationships might include collective bargaining between trade unions and management. Whilst most negotiations take place behind closed doors, it is more than likely that issues from these discussions will spill over into corridors and staff rooms, impacting on the interests of various groups and individuals. When on teaching practice, the extent to which you might wish to involve yourself in the politics of the organisation may be, partly, determined by your status. If, for example, you are training in-service, your position will be more secure and long-term than if you are training pre-service and attending a college only for the duration of your teaching practice. Those who attend a college purely for a short-term placement would do well to *observe* and *learn* from the politics, but not to get directly involved themselves. This particularly includes discussions held in the public gaze of staff rooms or other areas where people congregate.

ACTIVITY

Make a list of the various interest groups you have observed at work in your teaching institution. Give examples of pressure groups and blocking groups.

Review Questions

1 Describe at least five elements that a typical lesson plan should contain.
2 List four ways in which you can prepare more effectively for your teaching practice.
3 Give four examples of negative group behaviour. Which appears most commonly in your classes?
4 Suggest ways in which you should prepare yourself for the visit of an external examiner.
5 Imagine two scenarios from teaching practice that could be construed as 'political', and explain how you would handle them.

SUMMARY

- Put as much effort in terms of systematic preparation into your micro-teaching sessions as you would on teaching practice itself.
- Prepare by visiting your placement institution (if you are pre-service). Try to meet your supervisor to start early negotiations on your timetable, and try to meet as many prospective students as possible. If training in-service, establish a clear working relationship with your supervisor as soon as possible.
- On teaching practice get to know your colleagues, students and your supervisor as closely as possible. Recognise that there is more to teaching than standing in front of the class.

- Get to understand and utilise the dynamics of group behaviour.
- Develop personal strategies for reflection and active experimentation. Be 'open' to feedback on your performance from both students, staff who observe you and your supervisor.

Suggested Further Reading

Kyriacou, C. (1998) *Essential Teaching Skills*, 2nd edition, Cheltenham: Stanley Thornes
Written with school teachers in mind, but provides easy to read and practical advice, useful to all entering the teaching profession.

Petty, G. (2004) *Teaching Today*, 3rd edition, Cheltenham: Stanley Thornes
See particularly Chapter 8: Classroom Management and Chapter 9: Discipline and Problem-solving.

Wallace, C. (2002) *Managing Behaviour and Motivating Students in FE*, Exeter: Learning Matters
Provides advice, practical ideas and case studies on managing and motivating students.

9 RECRUITING, GUIDING AND SUPPORTING STUDENTS

Objectives

After reading this chapter, you should:

- be aware of the diverse needs of students in post-compulsory education
- be familiar with the characteristics of 'good practice' in student guidance at the three stages of entry, on-programme and exit
- appreciate the contribution of specialists, such as careers advisers and counsellors
- have started developing skills as a personal tutor.

Effective student guidance is integral to successful learning and achievement. Teachers in post-compulsory education are generally appointed because of their occupational background and subject knowledge. Skills in advising, tutoring and counselling students often have to be learnt 'on the job'. Providing guidance in post-16 education is a particularly challenging task because of the diversity of students. The needs of adults returning to study are quite distinct from those of full-time students in the 14–19 age group. The fact that funding is often linked to student retention and achievement has raised awareness of the importance of good guidance. A range of teaching and support staff are involved in this activity. Many are professionally trained in specialist functions such as careers and counselling. In this chapter, this area is analysed by examining how student guidance is provided at the three stages of:

- *entry* – guidance into the institution
- *on-programme* – guidance through the institution
- *exit* – guidance for progression to higher education and employment.

GUIDANCE IN

The historic role of FE is to provide a second chance for school leavers and adults, and in so doing to restore their self-esteem. A significant proportion of students coming into further and adult education bring with them a legacy of perceived failure. Many school leavers and adults enter FE with few formal qualifications. It is therefore vital to ensure that they receive appropriate advice and counselling so that they select a learning programme that meets their needs. Since 1993 colleges have also been under intense pressure to increase enrolments as successive governments have sought to increase levels of participation in post-compulsory education. The Kennedy Report (FEFC, 1997b) emphasised the importance of widening participation to include individuals who do not at present enter any form of formal education and training. Rising to this challenge will require skilled and professional guidance. Typically guidance at entry will involve the following:

- liaison with schools, employer and community groups
- marketing and promotion of courses
- impartial recruitment and selection.

These aspects are treated in more depth in the sections below.

Liaison with schools, employers and other community groups

Students in FE and adult education come from a wide range of backgrounds. In general FE colleges, the majority are usually adult students, studying on a part-time basis. In sixth form and tertiary colleges, the majority are school leavers who have chosen the college environment in preference to continuing at school. Colleges have been keen on responding to the national imperative to enhance access and create a culture of lifelong learning. Many colleges place great importance on 'outreach', that is networking with other groups in the community, the LLSC, adult education, schools, employers and the voluntary sector to draw people into learning.

Working with local schools

Full-time students in the 16–18 age range form a significant cohort for most colleges. Some of the larger sixth form and FE colleges have over 2,000 full-time students enrolled on one- and two-year full-time courses. Successful liaison with local secondary schools therefore is crucial to recruiting school leavers. Across the country, relationships between schools and colleges vary considerably. Between 1979 and 1997, the Conservative Government encouraged market disciplines in education and there was often intense competition between schools and colleges for students. Since 1997, the Labour Government has placed great emphasis upon collaboration. Many colleges, schools and adult education providers work in partnership for the benefit of learners. The following case study, based upon Greybourne Sixth Form College, is an example of secondary schools and local colleges working closely together.

Case Study: *Greybourne Sixth Form College and its partner schools*

Greybourne Sixth Form College works closely with eight partner secondary schools in the borough of Greybourne. Each year it recruits about 850 students, mainly for its GCE AS-level, A-level and advanced vocational courses. Roughly two-thirds of these come from the eight partner schools. Each school has a single point of contact at the college, that is a member of staff who acts as their liaison tutor.

There is a detailed programme of pre-course induction for Year 10 and Year 11 pupils to familiarise them with the options available at the Sixth Form College. The liaison tutors work closely with pastoral staff from the schools. Year 11 pupils attend a series of open days at which they are able to sample different courses at the college and to get a 'feel' for life in the very different environment of a specialist 16–18 institution. This is followed by application to the college and a personal interview for each pupil.

Relationships with the two other secondary schools in the borough are less relaxed. These schools re-established their sixth forms during the 1990s and are in direct competition with the college. They are keen to hold on to their own Year 11 pupils, as well as to attract leavers from other schools. Both have small sixth forms, with fewer than 150 students, and are only able to offer a choice of 15 GCE A-level subjects, in contrast to the 47 subjects offered by the college. Tutors from the college have great difficulty in building good contacts with staff from these schools and are only given limited access to Year 11 pupils.

ACTIVITY

As the case study above suggests, competition between school sixth forms and colleges can have a marked effect on the quality of guidance that students are given. In Greybourne the collaborative relationship between partner schools and the Sixth Form College appears to aid progression to further education.

Investigate the links between your college, or one familiar to you, and local schools. What evidence is there in your college of effective liaison with local schools?

Liaison with employers and community groups

In one sense, liaison with schools is the simple part of the equation. Adult students are a far more diverse group than school leavers and a much less 'captive' market. Much research (FEDA, 1995a) on part-time adult learners has drawn national attention to the fact that, for many mature students, learning is still an unfamiliar habit and effective advice and guidance is critical to success. The Kennedy Report reinforces the importance of good pre-entry guidance:

> *Every would be learner needs access to good quality information, advice and guidance to help them through the maze of learning opportunities. Advice and guidance has an important role to play in getting the 'best fit' between learners and the opportunities available.*

> FEFC (1997b)

Liaison with large and medium-sized employers is a well-established aspect of the FE system. Colleges have traditionally recruited many day-release and evening students from local industry, who look to FE to provide vocational education and training. Many courses, for example National Vocational Qualifications (NVQs), are focused upon occupational areas and staff from colleges and industry have to work closely together to assess students' progress (see Chapter 3). Employers expect regular progress reports on the students they are supporting. There is a considerable problem with liaising with smaller businesses, which often regard training as an expensive luxury. Colleges usually have great difficulty in drawing students from small enterprises into training. Some innovative colleges have managed to get round this obstacle by delivering education and training in the work setting, at times that meet the requirements of the workers and managers of the organisations.

The majority of adults who enter further education are not supported by employers. Some 60 per cent pay their own fees and are motivated to learn by a wide range of personal factors. It is this group of adults that the Kennedy Report was particularly concerned with. For many of these adult returners, even walking through the doors of a large college is a formidable challenge. Basic factors, for example the manner in which they are welcomed by staff at reception, can make a huge difference to their perception of whether the college is an 'adult-friendly environment'. For this reason many colleges have located drop-in access centres in town-centre locations with staff on hand to guide adults 'through the maze of courses and qualifications'. Many adult students return to learning through enrolling on adult education courses held in community venues, such as local schools. Such centres provide a vital route for adults wishing to return to learning. Entering a centre that is a familiar part of the local community is far less formidable for those lacking the confidence to negotiate with large organisations.

ACTIVITY

Spend three half-hour periods in the reception area of your college or adult education centre. Make a sketch of the location of reception and other guidance services available for adult students. Observe carefully how adults are 'received' into the college. Ask the receptionists and other staff who deal with initial enquiries what procedures exist for providing initial guidance to potential part-time students. Write-up your findings as a short report and then compare them with those of colleagues on your Cert. Ed. or PGCE course, who have undertaken an identical exercise.

Marketing and promoting courses

The last decade has been an intensely competitive period for most colleges. The imperative has been to expand student numbers in order to survive. Given this imperative, it is not surprising that much effort has gone into marketing and promotion. Many large FE colleges have a senior manager in charge of this area. The quality of promotional materials, for example the web site, the prospectus and course leaflets, is often very high. Students, like other consumers, have become used to a high standard of publicity. Colleges normally present their publicity materials in both written and electronic forms and include:

- clear information on courses, entry requirements, modes of delivery, fees, assessment, prospects and destinations of successful students
- publicity on enrolment procedures and payment methods
- information on finance, accommodation and childcare services
- details of interview and selection procedures
- equal opportunities policies and practice
- procedures for awarding credit and recognising prior achievement.

Of course, the marketing process involves more than publicising courses and other services. It is also concerned with investigating how effectively the organisation is meeting the needs of its existing customers and researching the extent of unmet needs in the local community. Many colleges devote considerable energy to these forms of investigation and research. It is very common for the marketing unit to make use of SPOC (Student Perception of Provision) and EPOC (Employer Perception of Provision) surveys. SPOC surveys are usually carried out on at least two occasions per year:

- after enrolment and induction to assess what students thought about their entry into the college
- at a mid-year point to assess students' perceptions of teaching and guidance.

Some colleges also make use of exit surveys to determine what those who have left the college, either with a qualification or not, think of the various aspects of the service.

ACTIVITY

Locate and visit three web sites – ideally one each from a sixth form college, a general FE college and an LEA adult education centre. What information do they provide about the advice and guidance services available at each provider? Which do you think is most helpful and why?

Impartial recruitment and selection

The most fundamental principle of good guidance is that it should be impartial and objective. Many professionally trained staff, such as 'Connexions' and careers advisers, are committed to this principle. There are of course, difficulties in practice with ensuring impartial guidance, particularly where colleges and schools are competing fiercely for students. In very large colleges, there is sometimes competition between departments to attract the best students. This internal completion can also militate against objective guidance.

Student services

Since incorporation many large FE colleges have developed central admissions and guidance units under the control of a single manager. Staff in such units tend to specialise in providing student guidance and often do not have a teaching commitment. Several specialists often work closely together, for example careers advisers, student counsellors, accommodation officers and staff with expertise in student finance. This collection of student services is often located close to reception, so that it is highly visible. There will often be a standard admissions procedure, at least for applicants to full-time courses. Central guidance staff will try to work closely with course leaders and tutors to ensure a smooth entry into the college. Typically such units will also work closely with external agencies, such as the local connexions service and local universities. Careers information, in documentary and electronic form, will often be maintained centrally. For example, there will often be a careers room with a collection of materials on different careers and HE institutions.

In smaller colleges, guidance is often organised in a less centralised and more informal way. In these it is common for all staff, including senior management, to be involved in the recruitment and admissions process. For example, in many small sixth form and agricultural colleges, informal contacts between staff and students are very good and there is a strong tradition of pastoral care and student support. However, there can be disadvantages to an over-reliance on informality. Often resources are not available to employ specialist staff, such as student counsellors, and little emphasis is placed upon critically reviewing the pattern of provision.

Case Study: *GAS at Greybourne College of FE*

Admissions and specialist student services are the responsibility of a central unit – GAS (Guidance and Access Services) at Greybourne College. GAS has 11 staff who devote the majority of their time to guidance. There is a manager, three staff who co-ordinate the admissions system, two HE and careers advisers, two student counsellors, a finance and accommodation officer and two general administrators.

There is a centralised admissions process for all full-time courses. Students apply for courses using a standard college form. Where students are clear about their choice of course, the applications are logged centrally and then sent to the appropriate schools. Where the admissions staff judge that students need more detailed initial counselling, they invite students into the college for a careers interview. GAS liaises closely with tutors in each college school. There are explicit standards and procedures governing how interviews are to be conducted and the overall admissions process from receipt of application to course offer. Each year GAS is subject to a critical review that contributes to the college self-assessment report (see Chapter 10).

Although GAS plays a particularly critical role in providing advice to students at the pre-entry stages, it is also involved in offering guidance to students during the whole year. The finance and accommodation officer provides advice to students experiencing financial hardship. She is an expert on sources of student financial support. The HE and careers advisers work closely with tutors in the schools to assist students with applying for university or jobs. The student counsellors offer a confidential service to all students. GAS also works closely with other units in the college, such as the learning support unit and marketing. The aim is for students to experience an integrated set of services that meet all of their needs.

ACTIVITY

The fictitious GAS unit at Greybourne is fairly typical of how specialist student services are organised in large general FE colleges. Compare and contrast its operation with the organisation of specialist student services at a college you know. Can you identify any problems with concentrating student services into a large central unit?

GUIDANCE THROUGH

Guidance through, or as it is often described 'on-programme' support, refers to all the advice and guidance that students receive during their time at college. It encompasses induction at the start of the course, the accreditation of prior achievement, the provision of learning support and procedures for monitoring and recording progress. The effectiveness of the college's tutorial programme is central to the success of much of the above. Most new teachers in FE and adult education will quickly find themselves in the role of personal tutor. Much of the section below therefore focuses upon the skills and capabilities needed to discharge this crucial role.

The support that students need

According to one commentator (SCED, 1992), some 15 per cent of students are likely to present psychological problems of one sort or another. Some of these problems can be solved by skilled personal tutoring. Others require skilled student counselling or other forms of specialist help. Consider the following case study.

Case Study: *A tale of two students*

Colin

Colin is a student on the GNVQ Foundation course in Business at Greybourne College of Further Education. He has a physical disability and uses a wheelchair. He is 18 and has spent the last three years in a residential college. He enrolled at the college following a decision to move back to his home town and live with his parents. Having been in a college where all students had a disability, he has found it difficult to adapt to the experience of being in a minority of students with a disability in Greybourne College.

He approached the college well before the start of the academic year and was initially interested in undertaking the full-time GCSE programme. Following an interview with the careers adviser at the college, he decided to undertake the GNVQ programme. He felt that he would prefer a course based on continuous assessment. He has made a very good start to the course. He has handed all the required assignments in on time and received pass or merit grades in his assessments so far.

The college's equal opportunities policy is displayed in the reception area and occupies a prominent place in the college prospectus. It claims to welcome people with disabilities. Colin has mixed feelings about its success. Whilst physical access for non-ambulant students is good, the corridors do tend to get extremely busy in between classes and he is often late in arriving for lessons. A more significant issue is the attitude of many of his teachers. The majority do not seem to understand how to provide for the needs of a disabled student. They are willing and helpful, but seem to lack training. Colin has two tutors, the GNVQ co-ordinator who manages assessment on his course and a 'special needs' tutor who is based in the learner support section of the college. His special needs tutor has a good understanding of his specific disability, but there often seems little communication between her and his course co-ordinator.

Nadine

Nadine is a mature student in her mid-thirties. She has two children under ten and has recently separated from her husband. She is keen to 'pick up the pieces' and plans to go to university to take a degree in English Literature. Unfortunately she lacks the required entry qualifications. She did not stay on at school to complete her GCE A-levels. Instead, she trained and worked as a personal secretary in the insurance industry. She left work shortly before the birth of her first child.

She heard, from a friend, about the college's Access to Higher Education course, which is especially designed for adult returners and leads on to degree programmes at the local university. She applied to the college in good time and was accepted immediately on to the programme. Although she is highly able, she lacks confidence. The pressures caused by the break-up of her marriage have taken a heavy toll.

Each student on the Access to HE course is allocated a personal tutor who they meet weekly. Nadine is very pleased with her tutor. She built up a rapport with her very quickly and soon felt able to explain her personal situation. She is gradually building up her self-esteem. She finds that working with other mature students on the Access programme has been brilliant. Many have a similar background to herself and the teachers encourage the students to support each other. Nadine is heavily in debt and has applied for a grant, from the college's access fund. She found the staff in GAS enormously helpful and is hopeful of gaining some financial support.

ACTIVITY

Think back to your own experience of further and higher education. Make a list of the types of problems that you experienced and the people who helped you. Do you think that the problems that younger students experience are totally different from those experienced by mature students?

Problems affecting younger students

For students in the 14–19 age range, the experience of studying in a large college is often quite different from the more protected atmosphere of school. The following are typical of the problems that they may encounter.

Learning to be self-reliant and independent

At college, teachers will expect students to be self-motivated and to organise their own time. Most full-time students will have between 15 to 17 contact hours per week, so that there will be long periods when students will be expected to undertake private study. This is quite a challenge for young students, especially when they have come from the more structured and disciplined environment of school.

Making the transition from youth to adulthood
The period of later adolescence is often one of conflicting emotions and changing demands. At college young people will experience much greater freedom in terms of their personal relationships. They may find love, sex and other personal issues quite difficult to cope with. Inevitably their personal happiness will influence their studies.

Conflicting demands of home, work and college
Generally students will have much greater flexibility and choice about how they manage their finances and time. Many will still be heavily dependent upon their parents. A lot will be dependent upon part-time earnings to keep themselves afloat. Balancing the conflicting pressures of study, home, part-time jobs and new personal relationships is difficult for anyone. Yet as evidence (Martinez, 1998) indicates, managing these conflicting pressures successfully is critical to students completing their qualifications.

Insecurity and peer group pressures
The norms and practices of the student's peer group are vitally important. Many students become extremely insecure about 'being different'. Stereotypes abound, for example most students will not want to be labelled as 'geeks or toffs', i.e. obsessed with study rather than having a 'good time'.

Problems experienced by adult students

Adult students make up over 70 per cent of the enrolments in further and adult education. Mature students have distinct needs and colleges that recognise this and adapt their provision accordingly are likely to be more successful in retaining them. The following are typical of the problems that they are likely to encounter.

Stereotypes of education
Often adults' last experience of education will be their school days. Some will therefore bring with them fears, insecurities and stereotypes dating back to their own experience of school. Managing study time and building up skills of independent learning is usually a formidable challenge.

Developing study skills
Whilst many adults will have a deep desire to learn, they will often need assistance with the practicalities of essay writing, note-taking and using a library or computer.

Developing assertiveness and self-esteem
Often mature students are surprisingly diffident and unsure of their own capabilities. It is difficult for them to appreciate that many of the life skills that they bring with them can be transferred to learning. Teachers and tutors need to pay much attention to praising them and building up their confidence.

Basic skills

The Basic Skills Agency (1994) has estimated that 1 in 5 adults experiences problems with basic literacy (for example, filling in an enrolment form) and basic numeracy (calculating change). Many adults in this category will even lack the confidence to approach a college. Yet it is precisely this group that the Kennedy Report (FEFC, 1997b) was addressing in its call to FE to widen participation. In Chapter 3, there is a full outline of how colleges make use of diagnostic screening to assess students' learning needs and to then make provision for remedial education.

Developing skills as a personal tutor

The above case study and summaries of typical problems experienced by 16–18 and adult students illustrate that the most critical skill needed by a personal tutor is to have empathy, in other words to be able to identify with the problems facing both younger and adult students. Empathy is not enough, however! It has to be combined with objectivity and detachment. Much evidence (Martinez, 1998) indicates that the role of personal tutors is absolutely central to being able to retain students and to enable them to achieve their target qualifications.

Developing effective skills as a personal tutor is an important aspect of working in colleges and universities. Jaques (SCED, 1992) identifies four key functions of the personal tutor:

- *to be a 'friendly parent' to students who feel lost in the comparative anonymity of FE and HE* Clearly, this role is more important with younger students than it is with adult students. In the first few weeks of term, many school leavers experience great difficulty in entering the 'bigger world' of FE and HE. Personal tutors need to be particularly sensitive during this difficult transition period. Colleges provide an important 'half-way house' between the more protected world of the family, community and local school and the less personal world of work and higher education.
- *to act as agent at the interface between the personal and the academic* In FE and HE students will be faced with teaching and assessment from different subject specialists. During their immersion into new forms of teaching and marking they will need a friendly guide and mentor. The personal tutor plays a key role in acting as interpreter and guide to the uninitiated. Academic cultures can be very frightening, especially to adult students who have not been in the educational system for many years.
- *to keep a watching brief on problems that students are likely to encounter* Anticipating problems is a critical skill for all personal tutors. The tutor will have pre-knowledge of what events occur during the academic year and when the pressure points normally arise. As in health, so in education prevention through anticipating problems is half the cure.
- *to support and facilitate the student in progressing through the stages of personal development* For both younger and older students, the period in education is a journey. Learning at its best is about growing self-awareness. There is an enormous difference between the diffident 16-year-old at the start of the course and the confident 18-year-old armed with appropriate qualifications and ready to move on to work or further education.

So what then are the critical skills to emerge from the above functions? The next case study, based on the training of tutors at Greybourne Adult Education Service, provides an indication of at least some of them.

Case Study: *Liam Patience comes to Greybourne*

In recognition of the critical importance of good tutoring, Greybourne LEA and the two colleges, Greybourne Sixth Form College and Greybourne College of FE are co-operating in a staff development programme for personal tutors. The three partners are jointly funding and running the four day course, which has already been labelled – 'Liam Patience'.

The acronym LIAM stands for listening, intervening, advocating and mentoring, which are seen as the four core skills needed to be a successful tutor. Patience, in dealing with students and other staff, is the over-riding virtue. Each day of the course involves tutors in engaging in role-play exercises to sharpen these skills.

Listening
Teachers are often much better at talking than listening. Yet lending a sympathetic ear to students is fundamental to good tutoring.

Intervening
Having objectively established the difficulties that students are experiencing, tutors have to make a judgement about how, if and when to intervene. On some occasions, no action is the best alternative – on others a timely intervention can make all the difference to keeping a student on the course.

Advocating
On many occasions, the tutor has to act as the student's advocate. Most commonly, this involves representing the student's problems to teaching staff. Occasionally, the tutor will have to contact other services within and outside the college. This may arise, for example, when advising the student about financial issues.

Mentoring

The objective of sound mentoring or coaching is to make the learner self-sufficient. If the tutor performs his or her role well students should become increasingly able to cope on their own. It requires skilled judgement to determine at what point to guide and at what point to stand back!

ACTIVITY

Do you agree that the four skills listed above are critical to good tutoring? Can you think of others that have not been mentioned? Look back at critical stages in your own educational development and consider how and when you were helped by skilled personal tutors.

The tutorial programme

Most full-time students, and some part-time students, will attend a weekly tutorial, often timetabled for an hour. Many colleges will have a written tutorial policy and will have a structured framework for the activities that take place during tutorial sessions. Some of the common components of such tutorial programmes are described below.

Student induction

At the start of the course, it is usual to have a carefully planned induction programme. Student induction will have several aims. Some of the most common are to:

- introduce students to the college, its staff and the services it provides
- familiarise students with their chosen course, its teaching methods and assessment
- assess students' needs for additional learning support
- inform students of their rights and obligations under the college charter
- provide a supportive environment in which the student can make contact with his or her peers.

The personal tutor is the key to successful induction. She or he is the student's first point of contact and their friendly face during the first few days in a new environment. Induction will involve many other people in the college. Examples of these include:

- senior staff responsible for key college services, for example the IT manager and the head of student services
- teaching staff who will have weekly contact with the student
- other specialists, for example the college nurse or chaplain.

A critical part of induction is making an accurate assessment of the personal factors affecting each student's learning and any needs for additional support. Many students come to FE with fundamental weaknesses in literacy and numeracy and undiagnosed problems such as dyslexia. Most colleges use diagnostic screening during the induction process to assess students' capabilities. Procedures for initial assessment are discussed fully in Chapter 3. Once diagnostic assessment has taken place, it is common for the tutor to receive advice on each tutee's capabilities and then to monitor the student's progress with basic skills by working with specialist tutors.

To provide evidence to LSC that students have received appropriate guidance at the start of their courses, colleges usually require each student to read and sign an individual learning contract. This document signifies that students are aware of the choices available to them and have committed themselves to a specific learning programme, following suitable advice at entry and induction. Colleges are also required by DfEE to publish a charter that describes students' rights, opportunities and responsibilities (DfEE, 1994).

Learning to learn

Successful learning and good guidance are not separate activities. They are two sides of the same coin. There is increasing evidence that many students coming out of the school system, especially those who have not been successful at Key Stage 4, have difficulty in applying themselves to study. One of the key roles of the tutor is to assist students with learning to learn.

There is now a great deal of interest in this area and many practical techniques have been developed for improving students' study skills and unlocking their learning potential. In 1974 Tony Buzan published his famous work, *Use Your Head*. His approach is centred around the technique of mind mapping. Mind maps are pictorial representations of knowledge that are quite different from linear patterns used in traditional reports and books. Figure 9.1 is an example of a mind map on the skills needed by a tutor. It presents the skills encapsulated by the acronym 'Liam Patience' in a different form. Mind maps are based upon the simple idea that 'a picture is worth a thousand words'. There is considerable evidence that we think visually and that, by using mind maps, we can organise our thoughts more effectively and increase our capacity for recall and analysis (North, 1996).

Individual action planning and records of achievement

The links between good guidance and successful learning discussed above are all based upon the simple premise that adult students learn most effectively when they are actively involved. That is why participative approaches to teaching (see Chapter 2), which engage interest and draw upon the learner's experience, are widely applied in further and adult education. Individual action planning is designed to achieve the active participation of the learner in setting realistic goals and monitoring success in achieving them. The use of action planning is common throughout sixth form, FE colleges and to a lesser extent in adult education. It takes many forms. The critical

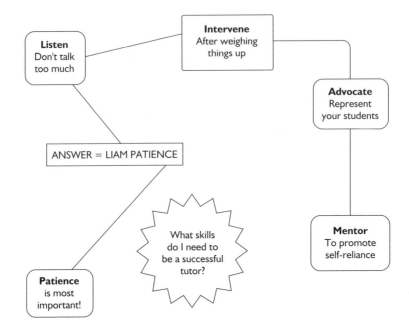

Figure 9.1 *An example of a mind map*

ingredient is the one-to-one relationship between the tutor and student. Green (FEU, 1994a) identifies four key questions that the tutor will help the student address through action planning:

- Where am I now?
- Where do I want to be?
- How am I going to get there?
- What are my next steps?

These questions are applicable at any stage of the learner's career through the educational system and can be used as part of guidance at entry, on-programme and at exit. Many school leavers will be used to some form of action planning in school. The record of achievement (ROA) and progress files are devices commonly used by schools and, to a lesser extent, in colleges for applying the principles of action planning. Many colleges make use of Individual Learning Plans (ILPs) for the same purposes.

At regular intervals, usually termly, students meet with their tutor to review their ILP or ROA and to consider the next stage in their development. In other words they return to the questions listed above: Where am I now? Where do I want to be? How am I going to get there? What are my next steps?

Monitoring attendance and achievement

Monitoring attendance, particularly for full-time 16–18 students, is an integral part of the pastoral system. Measuring pass and success rates is even more critical. These aspects of achievement are excellent indicators of the success of the course in fulfilling

ACTIVITY

Action planning is an integral part of students' work on most applied vocational courses. Each student is required to maintain a portfolio of evidence that shows clearly what work they have completed and how they have defined and are achieving their learning goals. Your task is to research how action planning is built into a particular vocational programme. To do this, you could talk to some students and tutors, look at the course specifications from the awarding bodies and obtain information from the Qualifications and Curriculum Authority (QCA).

its objectives. LSC publishes benchmarking data on retention, achievement and success rates and many colleges use these national data as an integral part of their quality assurance systems (see Chapter 10). The following case study compares the procedures used for monitoring attendance and measuring achievement at Greybourne Sixth Form College and Greybourne College of FE. You may wish to look at the activity that follows it before reading about these two fictitious examples.

Case Study: *Monitoring attendance and retention rates at the two Greybourne colleges*

Greybourne Sixth Form College
Greybourne Sixth Form College pays close attention to monitoring student attendance and retention rates. Teaching and support staff are fully aware that funding is dependent on the ability to retain students and enable them to attain their target qualification. Each teacher maintains a register of student attendance and reports more than two consecutive absences to the student's tutor. The tutor therefore gains an overview of student attendance over time and can detect any unusual patterns, for example regular absences from a particular lesson. There are four senior tutors who organise six-weekly case conferences of students identified as being at risk.

Each student receives a half-termly written progress report with details of attendance and marks received for assignments. The personal tutor arranges an individual appointment with each student to go through their attendance and achievement record and to discuss particular problems. Each student is required to identify an individual action plan for the next six-week period. Parents are informed about how the tutorial system operates at the start of the year. They are also invited to attend a parents' evening each year to discuss their son's or daughter's progress.

The system described above is highly effective. The average attendance rate on GCE A-level and advanced vocational programmes was 94 per cent during the last academic year. The average retention rate, over the same period, was 92 per cent. These are above the averages for the FE sector. Although the current monitoring system is working well, it is enormously time-consuming. The college is now considering moving to an electronic registration system whereby each student would carry a swipe card with a unique individual code. This would be used to record daily attendance and the data could be fed into the college management information system to allow analysis of attendance and retention patterns.

Greybourne College of FE

Greybourne College has adopted a tutorial policy that entitles all full-time students to a structured induction to the college, a personal tutor and access to specialist counselling, learning support and careers advice. All full-time students are also provided with a weekly tutorial period. The implementation of the policy is left to individual schools. Given that the college has 5,000 part-time and 2,000 full-time students on a wide range of courses, it was not thought appropriate to run a uniform system across the college.

The arrangements for student support at the college were recently inspected. Inspectors praised the tutorial policy and the wide range of specialist student services. They were however critical of the implementation of the tutorial system. They found wide variations in the quality of personal support provided across the schools and were particularly critical of the systems for monitoring attendance. In response to this criticism, the college has introduced a programme of staff development for personal tutors across the college. It has also strengthened its procedures for reviewing the quality of tutorials in the college.

ACTIVITY

You are part of the central guidance team at Greybourne College of FE. Following the issues raised by inspectors, you have been given the task of investigating the systems different colleges use for monitoring student attendance. You should present these findings in a brief background paper for the Head of Student Services.

GUIDANCE OUT

Guidance out has the aim of smoothing students' progression to higher education and employment. It is the third stage of the student support system and involves:

- careers advice on HE and employment
- assistance with applications and interviews
- post-results counselling
- monitoring and analysis of student destinations.

Careers advice on HE and employment

Most colleges will seek outside help from qualified careers advisers. In most colleges, it is common for external careers or Connexions advisers to be available on one or two days per week to provide personal interviews for students. It is also common for them to work with personal tutors and to make presentations on HE and employment as part of the normal cycle of tutorials.

In addition, most colleges have a careers room that contains a resource of both printed and electronic information on different careers. The DfEE and many universities provide students with detailed guidance materials, available on CD-ROM and the internet. For example, most colleges make use of the Education, Counselling and Credit Transfer Information System (ECTIS), which is a database on higher education. It will usually be the responsibility of a specialist student adviser to maintain this resource.

Assistance with applications and interviews

For students in the 16–18 age range, applying for higher education or employment is a new and challenging task. Completing a personal statement for the UCAS form or a curriculum vitae (CV) for a potential employer requires a wide range of abilities. Many sixth form and tertiary colleges have become very specialised in preparing students for these tasks. The next case study of a fictitious student at Greybourne Sixth Form College is an example of good practice.

Case Study: *Simon applies to university*

It is late in the autumn term and Simon has had offers from four different universities. He wishes to study history and anticipates that it will be difficult getting into his first choice university. He has attended one interview at a university that has a compact arrangement with Greybourne Sixth Form College. He found this really demanding, having never been exposed to a group of university academics at 'close quarters'. So far his most demanding conditional offer is for grades ABB at GCE A-level and his lowest offer is for grades BBC.

He feels that he has had excellent support from the college with all aspects of the UCAS applications process. Highlights have included an HE fair at the college, visits to university open days and advice from tutors on how to complete the UCAS form. It all started in the summer term of his first year when his tutor asked every student to complete a 'dummy' UCAS form. This really brought home to everyone how difficult it was going to be to project themselves on paper. The college insisted that all UCAS forms had to be completed by the end of October, well before the official UCAS closing date. After completing his form he was offered three one-to-one mock interview sessions. He took this offer up and feels the mock interviews have been really helpful in sharpening up his interviewing technique. Although Simon is only half-way through the process he has been extremely impressed with the professionalism of his tutors.

ACTIVITY

Investigate how guidance for students applying to higher education is organised at a college with which you are familiar. How does the quality of guidance compare with the case study above?

Post-course counselling

The availability of a post-course counselling service for students who have just received their results can be absolutely critical to their success. Students who have not achieved the qualifications required for progression to HE or employment will feel particularly vulnerable. They will need skilled and sympathetic advice. Many colleges offer a guidance service from mid- to late August to coincide with the publication of GCSE and GCE A-level results. For example, many sixth form colleges spend time helping students who have not achieved the GCE grades required from universities.

Another aspect of exit counselling is to follow up students who have withdrawn from their courses before completing their qualifications. This activity enables the college to learn about the factors that have influenced students' decisions. Research (Martinez, 1998) indicates that students leave before completing their qualifications for a variety of reasons. Some of these, for example personal and financial reasons, are beyond the control of the college. Others are directly linked to students' experiences at college, for example poor teaching and tutoring.

ACTIVITY

Many colleges devote considerable effort to identifying students at risk of withdrawing from their courses. For example, some colleges have introduced 'super tutors', that is staff who spend most of their time on the guidance function rather than teaching. By carefully analysing withdrawal rates and relating them to social factors, such as gender and neighbourhood, it is often possible to identify the probable characteristics of students at risk. Working with colleagues on your Cert. Ed. or PGCE course, make a list of the social factors that you think may influence non-completion. Then compare your list with that summarised in recent research. The 1998 FEDA report (Martinez, 1998) provides a good summary of this research.

Monitoring student destinations

The collection, analysis and use of destinations data is a critical ingredient in many colleges' quality assurance procedures. The review of data on student destinations, whether to HE, employment or other forms of training, enables course teams to assess how far the course has met its aims. For example, it would be surprising if only a minority of students on a GCE A-level course progressed on to university. This would cause the course team to question the success of the course.

Many colleges collect data on both the intended and actual destinations of their full-time students. During tutorials, students are usually required to indicate their intended destination to tutors. After course completion, many colleges make contact with students to determine the match between students' intended and actual destinations. Chasing students up after they have completed their qualifications is often a time-consuming task. Many colleges use a mixture of penalties and incentives to gain information on what students are doing after college. The following case study illustrates how Greybourne College of FE tackles the task of monitoring student destinations.

Case Study: *Monitoring student destinations at Greybourne College of FE*

Each year, the college publishes a report on students' achievements – one aspect of this is a summary of the destinations of full-time students. Students are subdivided into categories according to course type – GCE A-level, GCSE, GNVQ, BTEC National Diploma, etc. The data are aggregated from the records of course teams, who are required to report on both the intended and actual destinations of students.

The annual report on student achievements is presented to the corporation and academic board each autumn. The last report raised three significant issues for the college:

- Why did 40 per cent of full-time students on intermediate-level courses leave before completing the full qualifications, and what are they doing now?
- Why was there a 5 per cent decline in the proportion of GCE A-level students progressing to higher education?
- Why did only 40 per cent of students on Foundation level programmes continue on to FE programmes in the college?

Following a review of these issues by governors, the senior management team has been requested to check how the college compares with other general further education colleges and to report to the next meeting.

ACTIVITY

Find out how the system for collecting and analysing data on destinations operates at your college (or a college with which you are familiar). Investigate how information on student destinations is collected and what role personal tutors play in the process.

Review Questions ————————————————————

1   Make a list comparing the different needs for guidance of school leavers and adults.
2   Define the part played by personal tutors at the three stages of entry, on-programme and exit.
3   Identify the contribution to student support of specialists, such as careers advisers and counsellors.
4   Give reasons why good student guidance is important for retaining students.

SUMMARY

- This chapter has focused upon student guidance at the three stages of entry, on-programme and exit.
- Learning and guidance are not distinct activities, but the two sides of the same coin. The personal tutor plays a key role in helping students make the most of their individual learning styles and succeed in their chosen courses.
- Research has indicated that there is a close link between effective guidance, learning support and student retention.
- The personal tutor will work closely with other specialists, such as careers advisers and student counsellors.

Suggested Further Reading

North, V. with Buzan, T. (1996) *Get Ahead: Mind Map Your Way to Success*, Poole: Buzan Centres
An entertaining description of how mind maps can assist students to learn.

Walters, K. and Quilter, R. (2003) *Sink or Swim? Guidance and Support in Adult and Community Learning*, London: LSDA
A useful guide to supporting adults and the issues that face them in returning to learning.

10 QUALITY ASSURANCE

Objectives

After reading this chapter, you should be able to:
- describe how quality is commonly defined in post-compulsory education
- employ recognised criteria for assessing the quality of your own teaching
- take part in course monitoring, validation and review
- understand institution-wide systems for quality assurance and self-assessment
- make use of some common performance targets and measures.

Continuously striving to improve the quality of students' learning and achievement is integral to good professional practice. As a teacher, you will make use of quality assurance procedures at three levels:

- You will attempt to critically evaluate the effectiveness of your own performance by assessing the success of your own teaching and the achievements of your students.
- As a member of course and subject teams, you will be involved in a planned sequence of validation, monitoring and review activities, for example analysing student feedback about the quality of the course.
- At a college-wide level, you will encounter a range of formal processes for quality control, for example those relating to the self-assessment process. Many of these will have been developed in response to the requirements of inspection and the demands of the awarding and examining bodies.

At the heart of all quality assurance systems is a desire to improve the quality of student learning and achievement.

QUALITY AND QUALITY ASSURANCE

What is quality?

Here are some typical descriptions:

- 'Quality – we recognise it when we see it.'
- 'Quality is keeping the customer satisfied.'
- 'Quality is excellence.'
- 'Quality is high standards of teaching, learning and achievement.'
- 'Quality is conforming to external requirements, from inspectors, IiP assessors, etc.'
- 'Quality is about setting, monitoring and improving standards.'
- 'Quality consists of a set of procedures for checking that targets are set and met.'
- 'Quality is measuring achievement and value added.'

Quality and quality assurance

It will be apparent from the above list that there is no common and agreed definition of what constitutes quality. This is as true for further education and training as it is for other fields. At the outset, it is worth making a distinction between the concept of quality and that of quality assurance (QA). The first four of the above definitions relate more closely to the concept of quality than QA. They are about outcomes rather than processes – outcomes in terms of standards, excellence, reputation and the notion that there is something intrinsic about quality that makes us instantly recognise it when we see it. This distinction between quality as outcomes and quality assurance as process is a central point and will be developed further in this chapter.

There are problems of course when we start unpacking any one of these definitions. For example, it is not straightforward to define who the customers are in post-16 education. They could be students, employers or other community groups (Muller and Funnell, 1991). All of the above statements are somewhat subjective – we recognise quality when we see it! Quality is about excellence and satisfying the customer! Although the statements are somewhat vague and relate to people's perceptions, they represent an important strand in the quality debate. Perceptions about quality are often based on the first impressions of an organisation. These are important in arriving at a judgement. For example, the very first encounters that students have with the staff at a college will influence their perception of quality. These perceptions could be based upon how they are greeted at reception, whether the building looks shabby to whether the food in the college canteen is seen as appetising and reasonably priced. These perceptions are formed long before the student even encounters any teaching.

The last four definitions above are really about quality assurance – they all refer to procedures and measures for checking that quality is being maintained or improved. Setting standards and using performance indicators to measure whether they are being achieved is a more precise science than the more difficult business of defining desirable outcomes of learning. However, the ultimate purpose of all quality assurance procedures is to improve quality. Therefore, before we turn to a more detailed discussion of quality assurance, it is worth spending a little more time in analysing the concept of quality in education, to decide what exactly we are trying to assure and improve.

Four sets of criteria or alternative strands are commonly used to assess the quality of educational provision:

- accessibility
- teaching and learning
- students' achievements
- validity.

Accessibility

Accessibility raises questions about the groups in the local community from which a particular course recruits its students. The central mission of further education is commonly seen as providing access to lifelong learning and training, i.e. giving school leavers and adults a second or third chance that is often denied by other parts of the educational system (FEFC, 1997b). The central theme is *social inclusion*. To determine the accessibility of a course, managers will usually review procedures for marketing, recruitment, selection and equal opportunities. This will involve retrieving and analysing data on the composition of the student cohort in terms of age, gender, disability and ethnicity. Questions of accessibility inevitably lead to asking which groups are excluded from participation in learning.

ACTIVITY

Throughout the book you will have used the three case studies: Greybourne College of FE, Greybourne Sixth Form College and Greybourne Adult and Community Education Service. With reference to the list of courses in Appendices 1–3, attempt to assess the extent to which these different providers serve community needs. Carefully consider the types of school leavers and adults in the local community that they each recruit.

You might find it useful to reflect upon the following criteria when assessing the accessibility of each of these providers:

- their entry requirements
- the types of publicity materials they might use
- their recruitment and selection procedures
- data on student cohort – age, gender, ethnicity and disability
- their links with key community groups – employers, schools, etc.
- the flexibility of curriculum – entry, exit points, modularity, etc.
- what they charge for courses – fees, payments
- their systems of student support – tutorial and guidance systems.

Teaching and learning

For most students, the effectiveness of teaching and learning will be seen as central to quality. Much of the external quality assessment through inspection is concerned with evaluating and grading the quality of teaching and learning. In determining the effectiveness of teaching and learning, course teams will usually review the following:

- methods of teaching, learning and assessment
- course documentation, such as student handbooks and guides
- appropriateness of the teaching team
- accommodation and specialist equipment
- student feedback
- student performance.

Students' achievements

For the individual learner, success is often seen in terms of achievement, reaching a desired goal – usually a particular qualification and/or employment in a chosen career. The success of individual teachers and course teams can also be measured using data on attendance, retention and achievement. Schools and colleges are required by the Government and funding agencies, such as the LSC, to publish a range of performance data on students' achievements. Later in this chapter there is an analysis of some of the more common performance indicators. The following list gives an idea of the areas that are usually included in a review of students' achievements:

- attendance and student retention
- achievement of qualification aims
- pass rates for all or parts of qualifications
- success rates
- in-course assessment and examinations
- value-added measures
- student destination to HE, employment, etc.
- relationship between targets for course and actual performance.

Validity

The fourth dimension of quality, validity, is concerned with the relevance of a learning programme to its overall objective. In other words, it asks the question: Has the course achieved its aims? For a vocational course, such as a National Vocational Qualification (NVQ), this will involve reviewing the suitability of the structure and content in meeting the employment needs of the industry or occupational sector for which it has been designed. Employers and professional groups are likely to play a major part in this aspect of review. The following activity involves a consideration of the issue of validity.

ACTIVITY

In deciding whether a course meets its aims, teachers will often assess information on the following areas:

- employer needs and feedback
- analysis of course design and content
- arrangements for work experience
- student destinations and earnings data.

Select a vocational course with which you are familiar and try to assess critically the relationship between its aims, structure and content, using information on the four aspects listed above.

You will find that these four criteria are all important in assessing the quality of provision. In the next sections of this chapter, we will turn our attention to procedures for quality assurance and you will find that questions of accessibility, teaching and learning, students' achievements and validity will keep recurring. In the next section we will look in more detail at procedures for reviewing the quality of teaching, learning and achievement.

ASSESSING THE QUALITY OF TEACHING, LEARNING AND ACHIEVEMENT

At a very simplistic level, teaching can be described as an *input* in the educational process, whilst student learning and achievement can be described as *outcomes*. The quality of teaching is clearly not the only input that determines how much students learn and achieve. The individual teacher is limited by the resources available at the institution, for example the quality of teaching accommodation and equipment. Each individual student also brings to the learning situation a unique set of skills, knowledge and behaviour patterns. These reflect their previous experience of education and the other sociological factors discussed in Chapter 2.

Designing teaching and learning strategies that meet students' needs is absolutely vital in the post-compulsory sector because students, especially adults, spend a comparatively short length of time at college. Most courses will last for one or two years and some will last for only a term. The majority of students in further and adult education attend on a part-time basis often for two or three hours each week. As a reflective and self-critical professional, the FE teacher will try to take all these factors into account and manage the learning situation so as to maintain student motivation and promote student achievement.

Observing and evaluating the effectiveness of teaching

Observing teaching in order to make an objective assessment of its quality is a sophisticated process that is normally undertaken by experienced and trained professional colleagues. The observation of teaching has become quite routine in post-compulsory education and is normally related to one of the following processes:

- the assessment of teaching practice
- induction of a newly qualified teacher
- an evaluation of teaching performance for staff appraisal
- the college's self-assessment of its specialist provision
- external inspection.

Further details of these are provided in Table 10.1.

Whilst the reasons for observing teaching will vary, skilled observers will normally make use of explicit guidelines. You are likely to find details of these in internal college documents, such as the staff handbook and the college quality manual, and in the inspection frameworks published by the LSC, Ofsted and the Adult Learning Inspectorate (responsible for the inspection of adult and community and work-based learning). These frameworks provide details of the criteria used by inspectors for assessing the quality of teaching, training and learning. It is worth studying them carefully as they provide well-considered approaches based upon many years of experience.

Guidelines for evaluating the quality of teaching and learning

Many colleges and other providers have developed their own procedures for evaluating standards. Often there will be a system of regular lesson-observation managed by the

Table 10.1   *The observation and evaluation of teaching*

Reason for observation	Observation by?	Comment
Teaching practice	Teaching practice supervisor	Compulsory part of assessment for a teaching qualification
Induction of a new teacher	Head of department or subject leader	To monitor early performance and provide professional support
Staff appraisal	Usually immediate line manager	To collect evidence of performance as part of appraisal
College self-assessment procedure	Senior colleagues trained for this purpose	Linked to college's preparation for inspection
Inspection	External inspectors	External quality assessment

Quality Assurance Manager. So as a new teacher you will find that you are observed teaching regularly. In other words, this will be a routine part of the QA process of the organisation. Usually, colleges will have devised lesson-observation systems that draw upon the inspection frameworks devised by Ofsted and the Adult Learning Inspectorate (ALI) and most particularly the 'Common Inspection Framework' (Ofsted and ALI, 2001), as the case-study below illustrates.

Case Study: *Devising a lesson-observation system at Greybourne College of FE*

In response to a recommendation from the Local LSC to strengthen its own self-assessment procedures, Greybourne College has recently produced this draft pro-forma that it intends to pilot for evaluating the quality of lessons. The new form incorporates many elements from the Common Inspection Framework and is illustrated below.

Name of teacher:	FT or PT:	Course:	Student Attendance Present:
			No. on register
Guidelines – observers will take account of the extent to which:		Comments of observer	
Teaching, learning and assessment *the teacher* • manages learning to take account of the range of students' needs			

- demonstrated good specialist knowledge
- promotes good working relationships and equal opportunity
- monitors and evaluates students' performance and sets appropriate assessments

the student
- develops knowledge, skills and understanding
- extends his/her knowledge and skills through completing assessment

Resources

the teacher
- has appropriate specialist knowledge and competence

the students
- have access to suitable accommodation, equipment and learning resources

Achievement and standards

the students
- make progress during the lesson in relation to their prior attainments and learning goals
- demonstrate understanding and competence in their written and other work

Feedback to teacher (the observer should highlight the main strengths and the most important areas for development)

Strengths:

Areas for development:

Grade:

ACTIVITY

Any assessment of classroom performance would be incomplete if it failed to take account of the outcomes of successful learning, i.e. students' achievements, because they provide a tangible measure of how much learning has taken place. Assessments of teaching and learning also have to take into account how resources are managed to support learning. This applies to the role of information and communications technology (ICT) and other basic resources, for example accommodation and specialist equipment. One of the strengths of the above form is that it does have sections for comments on these areas. By completing the activity below, you will be in a better position to judge whether the proposed observation form allows the observer to assess these aspects appropriately.

Make use of the above observation form for evaluating a couple of sessions, perhaps those of colleagues from your ITT course. Then with a colleague consider the pros and cons of the observation form. Has it enabled you to capture the relevant evidence on teaching, learning and achievement? Is it too short for capturing the evidence? What have you missed? Make some amendments to the form and then find a colleague to discuss your proposals.

COURSE VALIDATION, MONITORING AND REVIEW

Evaluating the success of individual teaching sessions is one critical element of the quality assurance process. Many aspects of the student's experience, both inside and outside the classroom, are the consequence of decisions made by the course team and senior college managers. As the discussion in Chapter 1 indicated, course teams play a central role in the co-ordination and management of courses (GNVQ, GCE A-levels, etc.) in further and adult education. In this section, the role of the course team in quality assurance is explored through a discussion of the processes of validation, monitoring and review of courses. The four dimensions – accessibility, teaching and learning, students' achievements and validity – outlined at the start of this chapter are critical elements of these processes.

Validation and revalidation

Validation is the process of gaining approval for a new course, and revalidation is the process of gaining approval for a replacement or modified course. Both validation and revalidation involve the course team in working together to agree the aims of the course and how they are going to organise, teach and assess it. The proposals of the course team are usually presented in a course submission document that is scrutinised by an external validating body such as the Open College Network (OCN) or Edexcel (BTEC). Where the course submission is for a degree or a higher national diploma programme, the course documentation is usually subject to validation procedures determined by a university.

The procedures associated with validation and course approval are akin to that of product verification in a commercial environment. Through the process of course development leading to validation, the course team are taking collective responsibility for planning and assuring the quality of the product (the course) that they are intending to offer to students. In order to achieve approval for a course proposal, the course team must demonstrate that they can meet the quality criteria of the awarding body.

Achieving course approval: some key questions

For the awarding body, validation is a demonstration that the college has the necessary resources and commitment to deliver and assess its qualification. Often standard pro formas will be issued for the course team to complete. Whilst the format of these will differ, the course team will usually have to provide answers to the following questions:

- Why is the course/programme needed?
- What does it contain – aims, objectives and syllabus content?
- How will it be structured – modules, work experience, length?
- What teaching and learning methods will be employed?
- How will it be assessed and verified?
- How will it be managed?
- What quality assurance procedures will apply for guaranteeing standards?
- What human and physical resources will be available?

Validation is most straightforward in situations where the structure, content and assessment of the course is prescribed by the examining or awarding body. This applies to most courses within the National Qualification Framework, that is GCSE and GCE A-levels, NVQs and GNVQs. Validation is more complex where the course team have more autonomy in deciding the aims, level, structure and content of the course. This applies to most higher educational courses and some further education courses such as those validated by the Open College Network.

Internal validation

As an aspect of their quality control system, many colleges will expect the course team to present their submission document to a validation panel for approval, before it is sent to an external awarding body. The validation panel will normally contain both internal and external members. A typical panel might comprise the following members:

- *chairperson*, normally a senior manager from the college, for example the vice-principal
- *an internal subject expert*, usually from a different department or section of the college
- *an external subject expert*, from another college offering a similar course
- *an external industrial member*, to assess the vocational relevance of the course
- *a committee clerk*, to record the proceedings and validation decision.

A typical programme for a validation event would involve the panel in meeting the following groups:

- *the course team*, to consider the proposed curriculum
- *senior college managers*, to discuss strategic and resource issues

- *past and/or present students*, to consider their evaluations of the course
- *employers/community groups*, to examine the vocational relevance of the course.

Following scrutiny of the documentation and the series of meetings, described above, the validation panel would make a decision either to approve the course proposal, often with attached conditions, or to reject it. In cases where an external validation was also required, the submission would then be sent on to the relevant awarding body. Where colleges are regarded by external awarding bodies as having rigorous internal validation procedures, it is common to grant them delegated authority for approving qualification proposals. This is an expression of confidence by the awarding body in the college's own quality systems.

Activity

Contact the manager responsible for quality assurance procedures at the college at which you are working or where you are doing teaching practice. Ask for a copy of the quality assurance manual and any specific documentation on validation and approval procedures. Once you have had a chance to assimilate these documents, arrange an interview with him or her so that you can explore these procedures. You might also find it useful to attend a validation event to get a fuller flavour of how validation operates.

Monitoring and review

Whilst validation is normally an event that occurs every four or five years, monitoring is a continuous process involving the course team in collecting day-to-day evidence about the effectiveness of the course. This evidence will include both qualitative information, for example students' comments and feedback during course meetings, and quantitative information, for example data on attendance, retention and pass rates. At regular intervals, usually once per term, the course team will review this evidence and make judgements about the success of the course using the four dimensions of quality – accessibility, teaching and learning, students' achievements and validity – which were outlined in the first part of the chapter. Such reviews will be carefully recorded by the course leader and team and presented, usually in an annual evaluative report.

Monitoring information is commonly collected at four key stages of the student's progress through a college. These stages are *pre-entry*, *entry*, *on-programme* and *exit*. Examples of the types of monitoring data commonly collected, at each stage, are presented in Table 10.2.

Table 10.2   *Collecting monitoring data at different stages of the course*

Stage	Monitoring information	Sources of evidence
Pre-entry	Number of applications Breakdown in terms of gender, ethnicity, postcode, etc. Course publicity and marketing	Application forms Postcode analysis FEFC individualised student records Prospectus
Entry	Records of enrolment College and course induction Entry qualifications and student performance in assessment for basic skills	Student feedback on efficiency of enrolment and introduction – waiting times, quality of advice/guidance Students' record of achievement, their qualifications and results in screening for literacy, numeracy and information technology
On-programme	Teaching and learning methods Resources Students' achievements	Staff and student perceptions of success of teaching methods, including evaluation through observation of teaching Quality of accommodation, suitability of staff and specialist equipment Analysis of results in assessment, data on student attendance and retention
Exit	Pass and success rates Student destinations	Measures of student retention and achievement over course as a whole, including value added Analysis of numbers progressing to further education and employment

---

Case Study: *Monitoring data collected at Greybourne College of FE*

The quality assurance unit at Greybourne College of FE has developed detailed procedures for the annual monitoring and review of courses that are outlined in a comprehensive Quality Manual. Each course team is required to maintain a course log containing monitoring information based on the four stages of the course described above.

This information has to be recorded under the following sections:

- course aims and objectives
- regulations governing in-course assessment and examinations
- the student handbook
- records of course team meetings, including action points

- feedback from student questionnaires
- external verifier's and examining body reports
- analysis of progress of student cohorts from start to finish of course showing student retention, pass and success rates
- records of staff development
- feedback from employers, higher education and other external agencies
- the annual course report and action plan.

It is the duty of the course leader to maintain the course log as a resource for all course team members. The course log is also expected to be available for internal audit by the college's quality assurance unit and for external scrutiny by verifiers and inspectors. Once per year, the course team are required to produce an annual course report drawing upon the course log. The purpose of the annual course report is to provide a summative record of the team's overall evaluation of the course. All course reports are expected to contain a clear action plan with targets for improving the course during the next academic year. At the end of the year all course reports have to be submitted to the quality unit, where each report is considered. The quality unit then provides an overall summary of key college-wide issues for the college academic board.

This fictitious case study provides a typical example of the types of monitoring data you will encounter in real colleges. Bearing this in mind, you might find it useful to investigate how a course with which you are familiar is evaluated. Try the following activity.

ACTIVITY

Obtain a copy of the most recent annual evaluation report for a course on which you have taught (either during teaching practice or in your role as a full- or part-time teacher). Look through it carefully and assess what it is telling you about the quality of the course using the four dimensions of accessibility, teaching and learning, students' achievements and validity, which were described earlier in this chapter. Once you have done this, arrange a meeting with the course leader and attempt to compare your evaluations about the success of the course with those of the course leader.

QUALITY ASSURANCE AT AN INSTITUTIONAL LEVEL

The previous sections of this chapter have attempted to demonstrate that the quality of individual teaching and the success of the course team in managing and monitoring the course are central aspects of the systems of quality assurance. As a teacher in further or adult education, your main focus will be upon evaluation at this level.

You will appreciate that quality assurance procedures go beyond the level of the individual teacher and course team. The emphasis upon a wider institutional level is important because it rightly draws attention to procedures such as student guidance, governance and management, which all ultimately have an impact on how successfully providers meet the needs of students and the wider community. Many institutional systems have developed in response to external demands from inspection, from the awarding and examining bodies and from other agencies, such as the DfES.

Self-assessment and inspection

External inspection

There are currently two national inspectorates involved in the external assessment of the quality of providers in the post-compulsory sector:

- The Office for Standards in Education (Ofsted) was given responsibility for the inspection of colleges by the Learning and Skills Act 2000 and commenced a new cycle of inspections in April 2001. Prior to this period, FEFC had been responsible for the inspection of colleges under powers granted by the 1992 Further and Higher Education Act. You will find that inspection reports, for the college where you are teaching, provide a useful history of the organisation and much evaluative material on quality and standards of teaching, learning and students' achievements.
- The Adult Learning Inspectorate, also established by the Learning and Skills Act 2000, works closely with Ofsted on college inspections and is itself responsible for inspections of adult and community education and work-based learning. Both inspectorates make use of the same inspection guidelines known as the 'Common Inspection Framework' (Ofsted and ALI, 2001).

Self-assessment and inspection

Usually the starting point for inspection is the organisation's own procedures for assessing and enhancing the quality of its own provision. Ofsted, the LLSC and the ALI require colleges and training providers to produce a self-assessment report that contains their own evaluation of their strengths and weaknesses under the headings of the inspection frameworks.

Five broad questions, drawn from the Common Inspection Framework, will often provide the skeleton for self-assessment reports. These are as follows:

- How well do learners achieve?
- How effective are teaching, training and learning?
- How well do programmes and activities meet the needs and interests of learners?
- How well are learners guided and supported?
- How effective are leadership and management in raising achievement and supporting all learners?

The development of self-assessment is strongly developed in further education, where the former FEFC inspectorate produced helpful guidelines (FEFC, 1997a) to assist colleges with fostering a self-critical and rigorous approach. More recently, the LSC (LSC, 2001) produced its own guidelines for providers on self-assessment and development plans. The challenge for staff working on self-assessment is to demonstrate the robustness and accuracy of their own evaluation. A major challenge is to demonstrate that self-assessment is firmly grounded in a careful scrutiny of evidence. This evidence will be drawn from several sources, including:

- the analysis of labour market needs as part of the college's strategic planning
- findings from surveys of students and employers
- the college's own evaluations of the success of teaching and learning based upon the observation of lessons
- evidence from the annual course review and evaluation reports
- the analysis of student attendance, retention, pass rates and value added
- findings from surveys of staff
- analysis of surveys of employers
- performance measured against the college's own and national targets
- benchmarks attempting to compare the college's performance over time with similar colleges.

The emphasis upon self-assessment is based upon the belief that standards of provision are most likely to improve when organisations make the pursuit of quality central to their own missions by setting high standards and devising procedures for measuring them and monitoring their achievement. The necessity of target setting and monitoring has been constantly reinforced by government. For example, the DfES Success for All programme (DfES, 2003) contains four major themes for improving the performance of providers in the LSC sector and each theme has related targets for colleges. The development of targets and benchmarks is discussed further on page 241.

ACTIVITY

Inspection reports are publicly available documents. Summaries of Ofsted and ALI reports are available on the internet (see web sites – listed in Appendix 5). Obtain the most recent inspection report published for your college or training organisation. Consider the conclusions that the inspectors have arrived at and compare these with your own initial impressions of the quality of provision.

Quality frameworks and the awarding and examining bodies

The examining and awarding bodies such as Edexcel, City & Guilds and the Association of Accounting Technicians play an important role in defining and moderating standards. Where courses are wholly or mainly assessed through external examinations, quality control is maintained through the external control of assessment. This applies to many GCE A-levels and many professional courses. For these programmes, an important guide to standards is provided by the chief examiner's report. In this document feedback is given on candidates' performance in examinations.

For most vocational courses, such as NVQ programmes, that have a large element of continuous assessment, the awarding bodies appoint moderators or external verifiers to visit the college and check the standards of student work and the internal assessment and verification procedures (see Chapter 3 for a discussion of internal and external verification). The external verifier will normally visit the college on two or three occasions each year to meet the course team and students. An important part of the verifier's brief is to check internal processes of quality control and assessment. She or he is responsible for evaluating the effectiveness of the internal moderation of assessment.

MEASURING PERFORMANCE: TARGETS AND BENCHMARKS

The employment of quantitative measures – targets, benchmarks and performance indicators – is an important aspect of the evaluation of quality and effectiveness. For example, the annual publication of tables by the Department for Education and Skills (DfES) showing the results achieved by 16–18-year-old students at schools and colleges (the league tables) has become an important event in the national educational calendar. LSC also publishes a range of measures for success and national benchmarks on student retention and achievement, which has enabled college managers to gauge their performance against that of other colleges.

In this section, the use of measures of student achievement is first discussed at course level. Then there is a brief outline of the range of quantitative measures used to assess the effectiveness of performance at a college-wide level.

Measures of students' achievements at course level

Four basic measures of student progress and achievement are commonly used by course teams to measure success:

- student attendance
- student retention
- pass rates
- success rates.

In addition to the above, the use of value-added measures has become increasingly common for GCE A-level and other level 3 courses where reliable national data are available. All of these measures are discussed below.

Student attendance

Many colleges devote considerable staff time, involving both teaching and support staff, to recording student attendance. Electronic recording of attendance is becoming more and more common because it allows for much quicker analysis of attendance patterns than is possible with manual registers. Students carry swipe cards to record their presence in classes. Data are transmitted to a central database and sophisticated analysis is possible. For example, it is possible to determine the attendance patterns of individual students according to which classes they miss by teacher, by subjects and by day. This allows tutors to follow up persistent non-attendance and take action to prevent students dropping out of courses. This is especially important for full-time students in the 14–19 age range, where the college plays a more custodial role. Usually tutors or support staff will follow up persistent absence as early as possible to counsel students and to determine the reasons for non-attendance. Many studies (Martinez, 1998) have demonstrated that it is possible to prevent students withdrawing from courses by identifying non-attenders early and offering them careful guidance.

Student retention

Student retention is a measure of the percentage of students still attending a course in relation to the number who started it. It is usually calculated by using selected census points during the year. As far as colleges are concerned, LSC census data are collected on 1 November, 1 February and 1 May each academic year. The most common measure of retention is a calculation of the percentage of students attending in May as a proportion of those who were enrolled in the previous November. College managers, including course leaders, pay close attention to retention figures because funding is partly linked to the number of students who are retained on courses and go on to complete them. Poor retention figures for a particular course or subject are also likely to give rise to questions about the effectiveness of teaching and learning. Research indicates that the causes of student withdrawal in further education are diverse and complex. Often financial factors are critical. Experienced college managers will be aware of these issues and take them into account when examining levels of retention.

Pass rates

Pass rates provide a measure of the proportion of students who gain the target qualification by successfully completing the formal assessment. This may simply mean they have passed the examinations at the end of the programme. Pass rates are most commonly used for GCE A/AS-levels and GCSE subjects and also for some professional examinations. They are a somewhat limited measure of quality because they only measure the performance of students who are still attending at the end of a course and who decide to enter for the examination. The annual league tables published by the DfES are based mainly on pass rates for GCSE and GCE examinations. Many of the criticisms of these tables stem from the fact that they do not take into account retention and value-added measures.

Success rates

Success rates are a powerful measure that combine student retention and pass rates in a single tool. In a classic study, *Unfinished Business* (HMSO, 1993), success rates were used to demonstrate the high wastage rates for 16–19 students across post-16 education. The success rate for a course expresses the pass rate as a percentage of the students who started the course. This single measure allows course leaders to assess

ACTIVITY

The following information for a two-year GCE A-level course shows the number of students starting, completing and passing the course. The data for starts is based upon 1 November of the first year of the course and the data for completion is based upon the census date of 1 May of the second year. The start figure is 100 students to make all the calculations simple. Using the data below, calculate the retention, pass and success rates for this group of students. What does this tell you about these measures?

No. of students enrolled 1 Nov. Year 1	No. of students enrolled 1 May Year 2	No. of students entered for examination	Number passing
100	70	50	40

the effectiveness of the course in terms of students' achievements. The above activity demonstrates the differences between student retention, pass and success rates.

The use of value-added measures

Some schools and colleges supplement the basic measures outlined above with data on value added. One of the problems with crude measures of retention and achievement is that they do not indicate the distance travelled by students. That is, they do not relate their final achievement to their starting point. Value-added measures take account of students' existing qualifications, that is their prior achievements, and measure achievement in terms of the gap between student attainments at entry and exit. There are now robust systems for measuring value added for students progressing from GCSE to GCE A-level programmes. Measuring value added for vocational courses is a less developed science.

The advanced level information service (ALIS), offered by the University of Newcastle, is widely used by school and sixth form colleges. It is based upon predicting students' performance at GCE A-level and AVCE from their achievements at GCSE and then comparing actual grades achieved with predicted grades. Students' average scores at GCSE have been found to be a good predictor of GCE A-level performance. A student's average score is derived by giving each GCSE a numeric value, A = 7, B = 6, C = 5, and so on, and then calculating the average score per GCSE. The predicted GCE A-level grade(s) for an individual student, or indeed a cohort of students, can be calculated and then compared with actual grades to check whether performance is better or worse than anticipated.

When value-added measures are used consistently over a period of time, usually three years, they provide an accurate picture of the success of a college, or individual departments, in adding value to students' achievements. The ALIS is based upon a large national database and an individual college or course team can use the data on each GCE A-level subject to compare their performance with that of other institutions. In the following activity, you are asked to research how value-added measures can be used by colleges to set targets for individual students to help them improve their performance.

ACTIVITY

Greybourne Sixth Form College has been using value added (the ALIS system) as part of its quality assurance system for over five years. ALIS data are used by senior management to assess the performance of the individual subject-based departments at the college. A decision has been taken to extend the use of value added by using the data to set targets for individual students. It is proposed that each student's predicted GCE A-level grades would be calculated using their GCSE scores and this information would be communicated to them to improve their actual performance.

You have been asked by your head of department to research how other sixth form colleges use value-added systems in this way. He has suggested that you select a sample of inspection reports of sixth form colleges to obtain an initial impression of how value-added data are used in target setting. Present your findings and recommendations in a brief report.

Measures of institutional performance

There are also performance indicators and benchmarks, published annually by LSC, for assessing quality and effectiveness at a college-wide level. These enable colleges to compare their achievements with those of similar institutions. For example, a sixth form college will be able to compare its overall retention levels on GCE A- and AS-level courses with other sixth form colleges.

'Measuring success' across the LSC sector

LSC is developing measures that can be employed across colleges, adult education and other providers (LSC, 2004):

- The learner success rate – as outlined earlier, success rates are a powerful device when used for evaluating individual qualifications. Asking how many of the students who started the qualification obtained the award has an intrinsic attraction. It also enables the evaluator to gain a quick picture of student retention and pass rates using a single headline figure. Success rates can also be derived for a collection of qualifications and indeed for a college, or other provider, as a whole. If used in this way, the success rate will express the number of qualifications achieved as a percentage of the number of learners who started the courses.
- Value-added and distance-travelled measures – reference was made earlier to the ALIS system, historically associated with measuring value added on level 3 qualifications such as GCEs. Like value added, distance travelled is an attempt to compare the achievement of learners at the end of a course with their attainments at entry. It is more common with qualifications that are hard to calibrate, for example NVQs or leisure courses taken by adults.

- Employer engagement – at a national level the DfES is keen on measuring the extent to which colleges and other providers respond to national needs for skills training. Each college has to agree targets with its local LSC in a three-year development plan.
- Value for Money (VFM) – although VFM has precise meanings within accounting and finance, in FE and adult education, it has become closely associated with cutting costs. This is unfortunate as VFM implies a comparison based upon examining the relationship between inputs (for example funding levels) and outputs (qualifications achieved?). In public services, it also implies assessing the degree to which services meet their original objectives.

ACTIVITY

Have a browse through the DfES web site (www.successforall.gov.uk) and collect as much information as you can find on the concept of 'distance travelled'. Now think about some of the adults that you have encountered and taught. What practical difficulties do you think would arise in attempting to precisely measure 'the distance travelled' by some of these adults?

Benchmarks

Apart from these broad performance indicators, LSC also currently publishes annually a detailed set of benchmarks for student retention and achievement. The purpose of these is to enable individual colleges to set targets based upon assessing their own performance against similar colleges in the sector. Benchmarks are available for different types of college, such as general and specialist FE colleges. They are also available by qualification type – GCE A-level, GNVQ, etc., and by college deprivation category. That is, they take account of the extent of deprivation in the catchment area that the college serves.

Using these, it is possible for a college to take account of its unique mix of students and courses and to evaluate its performance. This process of target-setting in relation to national benchmarks is central to the management of quality improvement in the current climate. External bodies place great emphasis upon how rigorously colleges monitor their effectiveness using such targets and benchmarks.

Review Questions

1. As a result of working through this chapter, explain the difference between the concepts of quality and quality assurance.
2. How important are the criteria of accessibility and validity to the evaluation of the quality of a course?
3. Outline three factors that are commonly taken into account when assessing the quality of teaching and learning.
4. Distinguish between the processes of course validation and course review.

5 How is self-assessment of the quality of provision linked to external inspection?

6 Explain the differences between student attendance, student retention and success rates. How useful is each of these measures in assessing the quality of a programme?

SUMMARY

- The concepts of accessibility, teaching and learning, students' achievements and validity provide useful starting points for understanding what we mean by quality in education.
- Quality assurance can be approached from the point of view of the individual teacher, the course team and the whole institution.
- Self-assessment is an important tool for critically evaluating professional practice at any of these three levels.
- The use of targets, benchmarks and performance indicators has become fundamental to assessing the standards of provision in FE and adult education.

Suggested Further Reading

LSC (2001) *Self Assessment and Development Plans*, Coventry: LSC
    A more specific outline of the roles of self-assessment and inspection in development.

Sallis, E. (1992) *Total Quality Management in Education*, London: Kogan Page
    A wide-ranging discussion of quality assurance.

11 CONTINUING PROFESSIONAL DEVELOPMENT

Objectives

After reading this chapter, you should be able to:
- describe the background and context of professional development in general
- describe the professional development framework for further education in particular
- define professional development and understand why it is necessary in the context of further and adult education
- provide examples of typical developmental needs and strategies in relation to teaching roles
- relate professional development to current developments in lifelong learning.

The days when initial training in a profession was regarded as sufficient to last an entire working life have long gone. Nowadays, to be a professional means having continually to up-date your knowledge, skills and attitudes in every aspect of your work as a teacher, trainer, or as a manager of learning. This is particularly true of the further and adult education sectors, given the enormous changes that have characterised the last decade.

This chapter outlines the background and meaning of professional development, identifying the typical *developmental needs* of teachers in both their classroom and their wider management of learning roles. *Developmental strategies* to help meet these needs are outlined, and finally the whole process is related to current ideas of lifelong learning and skills, which are now very important for professionals in every walk of life.

It is important at the outset to distinguish between continuing professional development (CPD) and initial teacher training (ITT) Although these processes share many characteristics and features, they nevertheless represent different stages of professionalism and the distinct learning and practice needs of such stages. For example, the idea of professionalism as standing for a 'community of practice', introduced in Chapter 2 of this book, clearly stands for the shared meanings, experiences, discourses and practices of those who are already professional practitioners. Initial training and qualification, especially in a profession with such diversity of recruitment, poses different theoretical and practical issues.

This chapter is concerned with continuing professional development, and not directly with initial teacher training, so the model of development presented is not necessarily relevant to such training.

When this book was first published in 2000, the model of continuing professional development presented was that of the Further Education National Training Organisation (FENTO). At the beginning of 2005, however, FENTO, together with the National Training Organisation (NTO) system itself, was replaced by new authorities with responsibility for initial teacher training and continuing professional development in the post-compulsory education sector. The authority that replaces FENTO is called Lifelong Learning UK (LLUK) and it is the Sector Skills Council (SSC) for lifelong learning, such councils having replaced the original National Training Organisation system.

These developments have as much significance for initial training as for continuing professional development, and they will be described in more detail later at the end of this chapter. However, as a result, the FENTO model of CPD, as opposed to ITT, remains valid in the absence of any more up-to-date alternative. Thus the FENTO model remains a model of practice relevant to teachers in the whole of the lifelong learning and skills sector. This model will now be described in the historical perspective of FENTO and the National Training Organisation system and, later in the chapter, the current system emerging, particularly in relation to initial teacher training, will be introduced.

THE BACKGROUND OF PROFESSIONAL DEVELOPMENT

This first section introduces the reasons why continuing professional development has become a necessity for every kind of professional worker: it is therefore about the trends and developments that teachers and adult educators experience in common with, for example, doctors, lawyers, social workers, nurses, and so on. What all these occupations have is a *knowledge base* underpinning professional practice.

So what are the common trends in society that are making continuing professional development a necessity rather than the option it once was?

The context of professional development

Here are some of the reasons why, in all professional occupations, the need for continuing professional development (CPD) is critical:

- The need for training leading to initial *qualifications*, and subsequent continuing upgrading of skills and knowledge, has become a universal feature of all professional careers.
- Competition for rewarding careers in the professions, as well as the pressures upon *employment* likely to be faced in the light of technological and social change, mean that those who do not undertake CPD are less likely to enjoy successful careers.
- The growth of *knowledge* itself has led to more and more emphasis being placed upon levels of skill and understanding, and to considerable upward pressure in the levels of professional qualification.
- The growth of *competition*, both national and international, means that for individuals, as well as for national economies, the continual development of knowledge and skills has become vital for survival.
- New forms of *accountability*, to the public, to the learner, and to the professional body itself, mean that forms of observing, measuring and monitoring performance have become major features of the professional career of the teacher at all levels in the system.

These developments, in knowledge, employment, qualifications, competition, accountability, and so on, form the background against which the need for professional development has to be understood.

ACTIVITY

Make a list of the professional development needs you think you are likely to experience in your own career. You will be able to come back to them later, after having been introduced to the national standards that are now being produced. You might also like to attempt a preliminary definition of what you understand by professional continuing development.

National Training Organisations

In response to the developments in technology and society outlined above, the Government set up training organisations for around 70 industries and occupations, including further education itself.

This means that for most of the vocational qualifications being taught in the colleges there was a relevant National Training Organisation (NTO). Thus, there were NTOs for a wide range of occupations and industries, including banks and building societies, plumbing, chemical manufacturing, construction trades, distributive trades, electrical trades, engineering, food and drink, hairdressing, hospitality, information technology, the motor industry, science and technology. In other words, the trades and occupations for which colleges provide vocational qualifications were likely to be covered by a relevant NTO. It was envisaged that:

Each NTO should become the automatically preferred point of reference for strategic leadership and practical guidance about skills and qualifications needs for a defined employment sector and/or range of occupations, and how the learning needs of people can be met through training and education.

DfEE (1998b: 5)

NTOs provided a vehicle for employers to take a strategic view of training, and were 'dedicated to meeting the current and future skill needs of their employment sectors'. The network of NTOs was also part of the Government's strategy for lifelong learning:

This . . . puts lifelong learning at the heart of government policy. It underpins a more competitive economy and greater opportunities for all. It provides a challenge for the NTO network to take a leading role in brokering employment interests to influence what is learnt, how it is learnt and how achievement is recognised.

DfEE (1998b: 5)

In the last section of this chapter we will return to the lifelong learning context in which all professional development and continuing professional education is now being located.

NTOs were therefore a partnership between employers and the education and training system, and were intended to play a key role in achieving the Government's national learning targets, as well as its policy on equal opportunities. The Department for Education and Employment (DfEE) therefore identified four priorities:

- taking action on skill needs and shortages
- making lifelong learning a reality
- serving the whole UK
- building a stronger NTO network.

The first two of these were clearly relevant to the education and training system as a whole, and to the colleges and adult education providers in particular. Every NTO was required to produce what is called a Skills Foresight analysis with regard to its sector of employment:

> *Skills Foresight is a structured way of thinking about future skills needs and how best to meet them. The emphasis must increasingly be on spotting skills needs early and reacting quickly. This requires keeping in touch with the sector labour market, collecting skills intelligence in a conscious and planned manner, and directly engaging employers in the process. A clear analysis of skill requirements and training supply underpins the setting of an informed strategy for the sector, and forms the foundation for credible employer advice to Government and partners in the education and training system.*
>
> DfEE (1998b: 10)

You will notice from this quotation that the emphasis was upon 'collecting skills intelligence in a conscious and planned manner' and upon 'a clear analysis of skill requirements and training supply'. Although the quotation is concerned with national training policy, you should be able to see how the emphasis on information, planning and analysis is just the same as it needs to be in the case of individual professional development.

ACTIVITY

Return to the first activity (page 249), where you were invited to list your own likely professional needs, and think about them again in relation to the principles of the Skills Foresight analysis described above: what are the *information*, *planning* and *analysis* tasks associated with *identifying* your own professional development needs, and in thinking about *strategies* to try to meet them?

Make a list of the *tasks* you might need to perform in relation to your needs. To what extent do you think your needs for professional development will reflect progression in your career as a teacher in further or adult education?

The Further Education National Training Organisation

The NTO that was of the greatest relevance to teachers and managers working in colleges was the Further Education National Training Organisation (FENTO). This was not the only national body that established professional standards in education and training. Teacher training for qualified teacher status, for example, was monitored by the Teacher Training Agency, and its *Standards for the Award of Qualified Teacher*

Status (TTA, 1997) represented 'the threshold for entry into the profession and the first stage of the professional framework for teachers'. Qualified teacher status for further education colleges did not then exist, but the establishment of FENTO constituted the first step in the direction of mandatory qualified status for further education teachers. There were similar proposals for continuing professional development in higher education, in the form of The Higher Education Training Organisation (THETO) and in the Institute for Learning and Teaching in Higher Education, which was a recommendation of the Dearing Report of 1997.

FENTO itself was established in 1998, replacing the Further Education Staff Development Forum (FESDF), and its members represented colleges, industry, local and government bodies, trade unions and educational bodies in the UK (FENTO, 1998). Its remit covered governors and all full- and part-time staff in the further education sector, and this included managers and senior postholders, as well as every other category of administrative and support staff.

Responsibility for standards for work-based trainers belonged to the Employment National Training Organisation (ENTO), which was responsible for the TDLB Assessor and Verifier awards. Many staff in further education have had to gain these awards in order to teach on NVQ and GNVQ courses. They constitute the main form of training for work-based assessors, and were strongly advocated by the then Training and Enterprise Councils (TECS).

Before considering the national occupational standards for teachers that were being established, we need to consider the elements of continuing professional development as these emerge from the FENTO documents, because these still constitute the prevailing model for such development.

ACTIVITY

Before looking at the professional development process as described in the model, you may find it useful to reconsider your own definition of continuing professional development, which you were invited to construct as part of the first activity in this chapter.

The professional development process

It has already been seen that the principles of the Skills Foresight analysis involved tasks of information, planning and analysis, in order to identify professional development needs and formulate strategies to meet them. In the activity that followed (page 250), you were invited to list the kinds of task you would have to perform in relation to your own needs and strategies. Now consider your list in the light of the following quotation from the FENTO document:

> *Teachers and teaching teams need to contribute effectively to the continuous improvement of quality by evaluating their own practice, by identifying opportunities for personal and professional development, and by participating in programmes of professional development. Teachers should recognise the importance of, and engage*

in, critical reflection upon professional practice, within the context of the internal and external factors influencing FE.

FENTO (1999a)

The document goes on to list those areas in which teachers in colleges need to have what is described as *generic knowledge*. These are:

- the organisation's aims, objectives and policies, and the nature of the service it provides
- appropriate sources of evidence on which to draw when evaluating their own work
- methods of evaluating their own experience against the requirements of the job
- ways of reflecting upon their own teaching experience and the experience of learners
- current issues and trends within vocational and educational training and development
- appropriate sources of professional support
- the nature and role of further education within the current vocational and educational structure and within the wider community
- likely future developments within further education and their implications for teachers' own practice and that of the institution
- the mission and aims of the organisation and how to contribute to the decision-making processes within it.

ACTIVITY

As a result of reading this account of the generic knowledge that underpins all professional development in further and adult education, provide examples of the kinds of information, analysis and planning tasks that were identified in your earlier activities. You need *information* about sources of professional support, *analysis* of your teaching experience and the learning experience of your students, and *planning* for likely future developments.

The FENTO model stresses the three key functions of:

- evaluation
- planning
- development.

Evaluation

Evaluation and critical reflection on your own practice is one of the most important principles behind every form of professional development. So how *do* you evaluate your own practice? The model provided by FENTO suggests that, in order to evaluate their own practice, teachers should:

- identify where and how their subject or vocational area fits within the organisation and the wider further education sector

- consider their own professional practice in relation to the major influences upon further education
- develop opportunities for good practice while recognising the full range of factors and constraints operating within further education
- identify the extent and nature of their current knowledge and skills in relation to the demands of the job
- conduct a critical evaluation of their own teaching by eliciting, valuing and using feedback from learners, other teachers, managers and external evaluators
- evaluate their own key skills against what is required in their teaching
- evaluate the quality of their relationships with learners, colleagues and other stakeholders
- assess their own contribution to the achievement of the organisation's objectives
- create and use opportunities to question their own practice and to seek audits of their competence from others, as appropriate
- use evaluations to improve their own and their team's effectiveness.

At the beginning of this chapter, it was suggested that, in the case of every professional occupation, there is a knowledge base underpinning practice. In our own case, this was referred to as *generic knowledge* for the information, analysis and planning tasks required by professional development.

Activity

Now consider the points listed in the FENTO model of evaluation of practice, and against each task write down the kinds of generic knowledge that you would need as a teacher in order to carry out the evaluation of the task.

The FENTO model describes this as 'critical understanding and essential knowledge', and it provides examples of what teachers need to know about in order to perform these evaluation tasks. Here are some examples:

- their current role and the knowledge and skills required to carry it out
- the contribution that learners make to teachers' evaluation and their own teaching
- vocationalism and its role within further education
- ways of addressing teachers' own development needs
- the impact of teachers' own values, beliefs and life experiences on learners and learning
- ways of analysing evaluation data.

The above points are examples of the things you need to *know* in order to evaluate your own practice, and they are part of the *knowledge base* of good professional practice.

Planning

One of the most fundamental elements of professional development is the process of planning in order to ensure that your practice keeps pace with all the developments likely to affect it: in technology, knowledge, the college sector, business and industry, and so on. Later in this chapter we will be looking at the kinds of *strategies* needed to meet your development needs once these have been identified. According to our model, in order to plan for future practice, teachers must:

- identify developments in vocational and education fields relevant to their own areas of work and to further and adult education in general
- consider the relevance of current developments to their own practice within existing and potential roles
- monitor curriculum developments in their own subject and keep up-to-date with new topics and new areas of work
- take account of subject developments in the content of programmes and in teaching
- consider and implement appropriate changes in programme design and delivery that best reflect current vocational and educational developments
- take into account the resource constraints influencing intended developments and make best use of the opportunities available.

ACTIVITY

As in the case of evaluation, consider what kinds of *generic* or *essential* knowledge are needed in order to plan for future practice, and check your list against the list in the FENTO model given below.

In order to plan future practice, teachers need to know about:

- current developments within their own areas of professional competence and the relevance of these to teaching
- changes in further and adult education, and the likely impact of these on their own practice
- the relevance of current developments to learning
- ways of negotiating changes to current programmes of learning
- how to plan their own personal development and how personal development fits into wider organisational strategies
- the resource constraints applicable to personal and professional development.

All of these above points are examples of generic or essential knowledge needed to be an effective planner. They are therefore all very general and abstract, so here are the same examples in terms of more concrete examples:

- changes to the funding and organisation of colleges arising from the review of post-compulsory education, or the growth of management tasks carried out by teachers
- new guidelines from government or industry that require new forms of student record-keeping, health and safety measures, or inspection, approval and validation of new courses
- changes in course structures, such as modularisation, or assessment, or the development of new systems of accreditation, experiential learning, access provision or work-based learning

- technological developments that might have relevance to a range of subjects, such as possibilities for design or modelling, or the internet and the presentation of images, research or communication
- changing student populations and learning needs, most likely in relation to patterns of recruitment and changing patterns of employment
- sources of information, or support for professional and personal development, such as the availability of training or access to professional and vocational qualifications.

These are examples of the kinds of things you need to know about or find out in order to plan for future practice as a teacher in further and adult education.

Development

As this chapter is intended to demonstrate, continuing professional development (CPD) is now a requirement of every profession, and that of the further and adult education teacher or trainer is no exception. This is why the FENTO model is described here, to provide a general framework within which to identify your own developmental needs and strategies. In order to achieve this, all teachers should:

- identify where their own knowledge and skills need to be updated
- identify effective ways of maintaining their subject expertise and keeping it up-to-date
- engage in research and study related to professional practice
- set realistic goals and targets for their own development
- take up professional development opportunities relevant to their work and to institutional priorities.

ACTIVITY

You should now be able to think of the kinds of generic or essential knowledge needed in order to engage in continuing professional development as a teacher. Make a list of practical examples of the kinds of things you would need to know about in order to accomplish the development tasks listed above.

Your list should have included some theory, some skill development, some sources of information, some research, and so on.

We have now reviewed in outline the FENTO model of professional development in terms of its elements of reflective practice, evaluation, planning and development. The next section of this chapter describes the *processes* involved in professional development for teachers, trainers and managers in further and adult education.

NEEDS, STRATEGIES AND EVALUATION

One of the most important sources for understanding what professional development in this field means are reports from the Inspectorate and other sector-wide bodies. In terms of the changing background to professional development, therefore, the following trends were identified by FENTO and other national investigations:

- wider participation in further education, with a wider range of student learning needs
- greater flexibility in the organisation of programmes
- new kinds of qualifications and assessment systems
- new and more facilitative roles for teachers.

This is the background against which teachers in the sector are expected to develop their professional knowledge, competence and skills. Although in the past it was not compulsory for further education teachers to have qualified teacher status, the majority do have some kind of teaching qualification. However, with compulsory qualified teacher status currently being introduced, the need for continual professional development, in addition to initial qualification, will be equally important for individual teachers, and colleges have, in the past, taken steps to encourage this.

For example, many colleges adopted the Investors in People (IiP) standard, and are working towards a learning organisation model of professional development. The national standard of IiP was developed during 1990 by the National Training Task Force, together with business and industry, and supported by the then Department of Employment and the Training and Enterprise Councils (TECS). It set a level of good practice for training and development for employees in relation to the goals of the organisations in which they work.

The Investors in People standard is based on four key principles:

- commitment to invest in employee training to achieve business goals
- planning how individuals' and workforce skills could be developed
- taking action to develop and use skills in a continuing programme to meet organisational objectives
- evaluating the outcomes of training and development for individuals' progress towards meeting goals.

These principles represent a cyclical process, and are broken down into a number of indicators, against which organisations are assessed for recognition in the scheme. In order to achieve the necessary standard, organisations have to undertake the following:

- understand the standard and its strategic implications
- review current practice against the standard
- make a commitment to the standard and communicate this to employees
- plan and take action for change
- assemble evidence for assessment against the standard
- achieve recognition as an Investor in People
- work to ensure continuous improvement and development.

There are clearly advantages for colleges, as there are for businesses, in adopting a national standard of good practice for staff development, and the scheme has accordingly been viewed as a benchmark of good practice and widely adopted.

The college background

The national survey, *Standards and their Assurance in Vocational Qualifications* (FEFC, 1997f), identified teachers' expertise as a major factor in the standards being achieved by their students, together with problems encountered by teachers in updating their professional development. There have been major changes that have implications for staff development in the colleges:

> *National vocational qualification (NVQ) competence-based assessment has created new styles of learning and an increased need to track students' progress effectively through regular assessment. Greater flexibility in the organisation of learning programmes has led to students spending more time studying on their own, using learning centres, open-access computer facilities or assessment centres. Support staff have an important role to play in these new-style learning environments. Saturday colleges and roll-on roll-off programmes have created their own demands for flexibly deployed, multi-skilled staff. The teacher as the facilitator of learning or as a mentor for staff development, is using very different skills from those of the traditional lecturer. Students range from those with severe learning difficulties to those following graduate or professional courses, all of whom require and expect some recognition of their personal learning needs.*
>
> FEFC (1999b: 2)

ACTIVITY

In the light of the above quotation, make a list of the skills of the teacher as the facilitator of learning, and identify the ways in which they are 'very different' from those of the traditional lecturer.

The rest of this section will consider the points made in the Inspectorate's reports that have a direct bearing on improving teaching and learning, from the point of view of the colleges themselves.

Colleges have to provide evidence of the quality of teaching and learning they provide. Classroom observation has identified the most common weaknesses in teaching and learning as follows:

- unclear schemes of work
- a failure to identify intended learning outcomes
- a failure to check that learning is taking place during lessons
- ineffective management of classroom activities
- a failure of staff to evaluate the effectiveness of the lessons they teach
- inadequate marking and grading of essays and assignments.

> ### ACTIVITY
>
> In the case of each of these common weaknesses:
>
> a) Provide an example of what you think it means. For example, what might be unclear about a scheme of work, or what would be a case of ineffective classroom management?
> b) What strategies would you use to try to overcome the problem?
> c) Where might you look for advice and support?

The most obvious sources of support for your professional practice lie within the college itself, in the form of staff development officers, professional tutors, and line managers in the area of curriculum, but other sources can be discovered in the changing system that will be introduced later in this chapter when the successors to FENTO, FEDA and NTOs are described, mostly under the aegis of the Lifelong Learning UK Sector Skills Council.

Ways of measuring teacher performance

In Chapter 10, you were introduced to ways in which classroom performance can be measured from the point of view of quality assurance. In this section, the process will be considered again in relation to professional development in general. Most colleges and adult education services measure the performance of their staff through:

- staff reviews
- appraisals
- observations of teaching.

Case Study: *Reviewing teaching and learning in Greybourne Adult and Community Education Service*

In Greybourne Adult and Community Education Service, all part-time tutors are observed teaching as part of the review and staff development process. The LEA reviews teaching practice across the adult education centres, and all centre managers are encouraged to conduct lesson observations as part of their review process. The emphasis is on improving classroom practice and the standard of lesson planning and, in particular, on encouraging innovative approaches with adult learners, and the management of different levels of student ability.

What was described as the 'closed culture' of the classroom is changing, therefore, and observations for staff development purposes are increasingly carried out by peers, managers, professional tutors or staff development officers. In most cases, the observers are trained, the results inform the staff development programme, and feedback is given to the teacher.

ACTIVITY

Assume that you are conducting classroom observations as part of the peer review for staff development programmes. Describe the kind of preparation you would need to make for observing another teacher in the classroom situation, assuming that the class falls within the same general subject or curriculum area as your own. In particular, give examples of what you would consider as the innovative use of teaching materials or the management of a range of students' learning needs. You may find the discussion of the evaluation of teaching and learning in Chapter 10 useful when completing this task.

In attempting this activity, you will need to remember that effective classroom observation requires careful preparation. You should therefore bear in mind the need to construct the *criteria* of good classroom practice, and the *standards* by which effective teaching is measured. Later in this chapter, we will review these criteria and standards in the light of the national standards that were embodied in the FENTO model of continuing professional development.

Many professional activities of teachers in further education colleges are *team activities*, and being an effective member of a professional team has become one of the most important aspects of professionalism in teaching and managing learning. In this way, all professions might be described as communities of practice. And this is true not only of curriculum development, but also of the assessment of teacher performance. Increasingly, professional development is coming to be seen as a wider process of personal development, and this is why many aspects of it are based upon teams, or peer groups, and involve reflective kinds of practices. This was shown to be part of the model of professional development described above, where the importance of engaging in critical reflection was stressed.

Strategic plans and human resource development

At the same time that professional development is increasingly focused on the personal development of teachers, each college is required to produce strategic plans for its development as an institution. There is sometimes a tension between personal professional development and that arising from the priorities determined by managers. In other words, those arising from the mission or goals of the organisation, and personal development arising from the choice of individual staff. For example, choosing to study a modern foreign language for recreational purposes.

ACTIVITY

Investigate the ways in which continuing professional development is organised within your own college. You will find the annual staff development plan a useful source. What are the relative priorities given to professional development to achieve organisational goals and personal development?

A staff development plan such as this is essentially a management tool to ensure that professional development is delivered. As we have seen, however, professional development can also be regarded as a form of wider personal development. In other words, as the teacher's role changes from one of traditional or pedagogic teaching towards being more of a facilitator or enabler of learning, new skills and attitudes are needed. Being critically reflective is one of these necessary changes.

So there are different 'cultures' of development. Here are three examples:

- *personal professional development*, which focuses upon the *whole person*, perhaps in terms of the capacity for critical reflection or for the development of facilitative attitudes towards learning
- *human resource development*, which focuses upon the *knowledge* and *skills* of the teacher or manager as a resource contributing to the cost-benefit analysis of the college's strategic plan. This means that staff have relevant knowledge about qualification and assessment systems and specialised subject developments, and are generally up-to-date in curriculum matters
- *functional or 'fit-for-purpose' development*, which focuses more narrowly upon *skills* and *competence*. This means the ability to perform the functions of teacher or manager of learning properly, but without the dimension of personal development or critical reflection that other perspectives include.

ACTIVITY

Following on from your investigations in the last activity into the way in which continuing professional development is organised in your own college, try to analyse the ways in which it may reflect the three 'cultures' described above, in differing proportions.

Most colleges have programmes that reflect all these elements in some way or another. However, not all of them have the kind of comprehensive system of professional development that would include:

- self-assessment
- monitoring of teacher performance
- appraisal
- development and training
- staff support.

So it has to be emphasised that observations of teaching alone cannot provide a complete system of professional development, and that, to be effective in the new conditions of teaching, something more comprehensive is required.

Case Study: *Professional development at Greybourne Sixth Form College*

Greybourne Sixth Form College has a comprehensive system of staff development. Each year, staff development plans are drawn up by individual departments. These identify lists of costed priorities for staff development. In most departments the top priority is for subject updating for individual teachers. At a college-wide level, all new teaching and support staff are required to attend an induction programme. This runs throughout their first term at the college and includes an introduction to the internal organisation and its policies. There is strong emphasis upon equal opportunities and on ensuring staff are familiar with the resources available to support them in their jobs. Each new member of staff is allocated a personal mentor during their first year in college.

ACTIVITY

The above case study suggests that Greybourne Sixth Form College has a comprehensive system of staff development. Compare this with the staff development procedures of your own college or adult education service.

You will have noticed that the professional development programme at Greybourne Sixth Form College includes procedures for induction and for mentoring new staff. The majority of colleges provide an induction programme, and some do this for part-time and support staff, as well as for full-time teachers, who may themselves be serving a probationary period or employed on a short-term contract. Mentoring for new staff also exists in many colleges. Induction and mentoring are important aspects of professional development, and we need to consider them briefly before going on to examine the national standards, and the developmental needs and strategies that they call for on the part of every teacher.

Induction and mentoring

As we saw above, most colleges provide an induction programme for new staff. In a comprehensive induction, staff will be introduced to the working of the college as a whole. These are supported by induction packs and staff handbooks, which are a valuable source of information about the sources of support for professional development that are available in the college, not only to new members of the staff.

ACTIVITY

Review your own experience of induction and mentoring, and make a list of what you consider to be the:

a) *contents* of an effective induction programme
b) *functions* of an effective mentor.

Mentoring has become a major technique of human resource management. It has been defined as:

> *Off-line help by one person to another in making significant transitions in knowledge, work or thinking.*
>
> Megginson and Clutterbuck (1997: 13)

'Off-line' here means that, in management terms, mentoring is not normally seen as the job of a line manager:

> *A mentor is usually more senior or experienced than the learner, but there are also cases of peer mentoring that work very successfully. On occasion in formal schemes and more often in natural, spontaneous or informal mentoring relationships, the mentor is also the line manager. Where we find line managers successfully acting as mentors, they seem to have a highly developed capacity to separate out the two functions.*
>
> Megginson and Clutterbuck (1997: 14)

ACTIVITY

In the light of your own experience of the mentoring relationship, reflect on the functions of the mentor and the line manager, and why these may have to be separated out for effective mentoring, according to Megginson and Clutterbuck.

In colleges, the functions usually are separated out:

> *Mentoring is usually undertaken within the curriculum area and where it is most effective, the new teacher has support in developing schemes of work, basic classroom management and alternative ways of teaching as well as being introduced to aspects of college life.*
>
> FEFC (1999b: 8)

In other words, the mentoring relationship usually involves staff working in common curriculum or subject areas. This too is an important aspect of professional development for staff in colleges. For most staff in further and adult education, the primary orientation will be to particular subjects or occupational areas. The standard FEFC division listed ten programme areas as follows:

- Mathematics, Science and Computing
- Agriculture
- Construction
- Engineering
- Business
- Hotel and Catering/Leisure and Tourism
- Health and Care/Hairdressing and Beauty Therapy

- Art and Design/Performing Arts
- Humanities
- Basic Education.

In all of these key areas of the curriculum there are important sources of subject updating for teachers. As was seen in the case of the old National Training Organisations, most of these sources are external to the college system itself. The most readily available sources are professional associations. Thus, for example, in the area of Construction the following may be sources of subject updating for teachers:

- British Association of Construction Heads
- Construction Industry Training Board
- Association of Plumbing Teachers
- Association of Painting Craft Teachers
- Guild of Bricklayers
- Chartered Institute of Building.

In the case of Hotel and Catering, the following are relevant sources of subject updating:

- National Association of Heads of Catering
- National Association of Master Bakers (Training Section)
- Hotel and Catering International Management Association
- Hospitality Training Foundation.

All of the programme areas of the curriculum are provided with relevant professional associations that are important for subject updating as part of the professional development process for teachers.

ACTIVITY

In relation to your own subject area or areas in the curriculum, use the kinds of sources of information indicated above to discover the professional organisations or associations most likely to be of help in updating your subject area knowledge.

So far in this chapter, the general principles and organisation of professional development have been outlined, in the context of the models that were developed by the DfEE, the Inspectorate, FENTO and other agencies. The remainder of the chapter will describe the national standards for teaching and supporting learning that have been established, and describe some of the strategies that are open to individual teachers to meet them. Finally, the whole process will be related to the policies for lifelong learning that governments have since initiated.

THE NATIONAL STANDARDS FOR TEACHING AND SUPPORTING LEARNING

These standards are intended to apply to the whole of the further education sector in England and Wales. They represent the fundamental key to understanding your own developmental needs as a teacher in further and adult education, and you should familiarise yourself with them in detail, since they can only be summarised here. The purpose of the standards is to:

- provide an agreed set of standards that can be used to inform the design of accredited awards for FE teachers, validated within the national qualifications framework, or by higher education institutions or other awarding bodies
- provide standards that can be used to inform professional development activity within FE
- assist institution-based activities such as recruitment, appraisal and the identification of training needs.

The second of these purposes, therefore, provides the basis for individual teachers to identify their learning needs, and the national standards also represent the criteria against which observation, inspection and appraisal of performance will be measured. They will also be used as the standards for awards and professional qualifications.

The standards themselves address the professional development needs of teachers, rather than their subject-related expertise, and reflect broad values of reflective practice and scholarship. You may recall that generic knowledge was stressed as an important aspect of professional development, and as something that underpinned all teachers' developmental needs. The national standards also make this point:

> *The ability of teachers to reflect on their practice and to employ appropriate methods is a crucial one which any set of standards should seek to promote. Reflective practice and scholarship should also underpin the wider professional role of the teacher in managing the learning process, developing the curriculum and guiding and supporting the learner . . .*
>
> FENTO (1999a: 3)

The standards reflect a view of the key purpose of the teacher:

> *The key purpose of the FE teacher and those directly involved in supporting learning is to provide high quality teaching, to create effective opportunities for learning and to enable all learners to achieve to the best of their ability.*
>
> FENTO (1999a: 5)

So the standards reflect the 'major areas of activity' that follow from the key purpose of the teacher as defined above.

The standards also remind us of the underlying principles of the FENTO model of professionalism, which were set out earlier in this chapter: reflection, planning, evaluation and development. Thus, teachers should:

> *reflect critically on their practice and evaluate the effectiveness of teaching and learning, the curriculum, and the learners' progress. They should also have a clear*

understanding of how their subject contributes to the overall educational experience of their learners.

FENTO (1999a: 5)

The national standards are organised into key areas of teaching, each of which is then broken down into a list of teaching tasks, together with the knowledge and critical understanding necessary to perform them effectively.

Key areas of teaching

The national standards identify seven key areas of teaching as follows:

A Assessing learners' needs
B Planning and preparing teaching
C Developing and using a range of teaching and learning techniques
D Managing the learning process
E Providing learners with support
F Assessing the outcomes of learning and learners' achievements
G Reflecting on and evaluating one's own performance and planning future practice.

These areas can be expressed in the form of a diagram as shown in Figure 11.1.

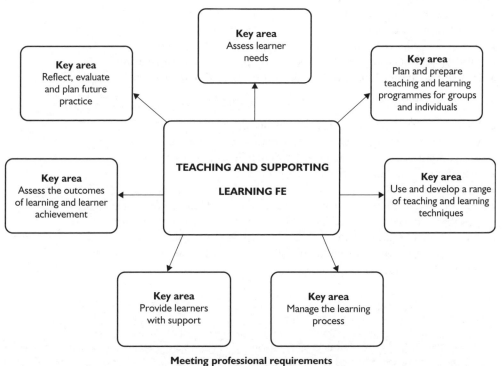

Meeting professional requirements
An underpinning area of professional competence which supports and informs all other teaching activities

Figure 11.1 *Key areas of teaching (FENTO, 1999a)*

Each key area of teaching is subdivided into a number of more specialised tasks or functions. For example, *A: Assessing learners' needs* is broken down into:

A1   Identify and plan for the needs of potential learners
A2   Make an initial assessment of learners' needs.

C: Developing and using a range of teaching and learning techniques is broken down into:

C1   Promote and encourage individual learning
C2   Facilitate learning in groups
C3   Facilitate learning through experience.

In addition to this breakdown of the key areas of teaching, for every task or function there is a description of the kinds of knowledge and critical understanding that teachers need to carry them out effectively.

In the space available, it is only possible to look at one of the key areas of teaching in detail, that of B1, which is concerned with the first stage in planning and preparing teaching.

B1: *Identify the required outcomes of the learning programme*
In order to do this teachers:

- interpret curriculum requirements in terms of syllabuses, objectives and schemes of work for learning programmes
- produce learning outcomes from programmes of study
- establish precise learning objectives and content
- define the subject/technical knowledge and skills required
- fulfil validating and awarding body requirements, where relevant
- ensure that basic skills and key skills are integral to provision, as required.

This requires knowledge and a critical understanding of:

- how to select appropriate learning programmes
- ways of establishing learning outcomes for programmes of study
- the content required to achieve particular learning outcomes
- programme validation criteria and procedures
- ways of ensuring that basic skills and key skills are integral to learning outcomes
- how to derive individual learning programmes from required learning outcomes
- possible progression routes and their implications for the learner
- how to analyse and evaluate skills, knowledge and values within a curriculum area
- the importance of inclusive learning and ways of ensuring that teachers meet the needs of all students.

ACTIVITY

In the case of your own subject area or areas, review your teaching in the light of the above checklist of activities and knowledge. Identify areas you feel may be in need of further attention.

You should now have some idea of what are the key areas of teaching on which the national standards are based, and of the kinds of tasks and knowledge required to perform them satisfactorily.

ACTIVITY

Returning to the FENTO model of professional development, which you will remember was based on reflective practice, evaluation, planning and development, give examples of strategies that could be adopted to help you to perform the key teaching tasks effectively.

DEVELOPMENT STRATEGIES

This chapter has introduced several sources of support for professional development, mostly from the point of view of the college and the further education sector, for example induction, development officers, professional tutors, observation, inspection and appraisal, together with external resources for subject updating. The national standards provide the kind of detailed description of what is expected by way of good practice in teaching and learner support.

In addition, there are strategies that teachers can adopt for themselves as part of the professional development process. Many of these are, of course, built into the initial training and professional continuing development programmes for teachers in further and adult education. The following section will briefly review some of the commonest of these.

Reflective journals

Both the FENTO model of professional development and the national standards stress the importance of systematic reflection, and there are various forms that reflection can take. It could, for example, be shared in a peer or tutor group setting. But the keeping of a journal to record events in teaching, with the possibility of reflecting upon them after an interval of time, is one of the most common. A reflective journal is a written record of *experience* that can provide the evidence for identifying developmental needs, together with elements of critical understanding and the formulation of strategies to overcome problems, gain new knowledge and practise new skills. The use of an unfamiliar teaching method, for example, may provide a range of evidence to evaluate its use: feedback from learners or colleagues, the assessment of student learning, and so on, leading to formal evaluation. Such a journal will contain subjective or introspective reflection that is for private use only, but it can constitute a very important record of personal and professional development.

Such a reflective journal may help you to identify strengths and weaknesses and to become more aware of developmental needs, together with your own preferred teaching styles in relation to others of which you are aware. Although it is usually best to record incidents as soon as possible after they have happened, the journal constitutes a permanent record of your thoughts, feelings and responses, and is a source to which you are able to return, reflecting upon your development as a teacher.

Action plans

These are targets that you set for yourself, having identified a learning need in relation to the various forms of feedback you may receive, and the national standards of good teaching practice. Unlike a reflective journal, an action plan may be something drawn up with others, such as a peer group or a mentor or anyone who is likely to be concerned with your development as a teacher, such as a tutor or supervisor. Above all, such a plan will incorporate a *strategy* for meeting developmental needs, which in turn makes it possible to evaluate progress made or obstacles encountered. Action plans have something in common with *learning contracts*, which are similarly statements of intent to acquire new knowledge or skills or to address particular needs and problems.

A typical completed action plan might look like the one in Table 11.1. Such a plan might be typical of students in an initial teacher training situation, but it is capable of being adapted for use by the most experienced of teachers, having access to the kinds of support that have been outlined in this chapter.

An action plan consists of five basic stages:

1 Learning need
2 Statement of learning objectives
3 Strategies to achieve objectives
4 Evaluation
5 Further action.

As was suggested, such an action plan may form a document, or a kind of contract, to be negotiated with a tutor or a mentor or even in a peer group setting.

Significant incidents

A significant incident (sometimes called a critical incident) is an event that often triggers off the identification of a developmental need, or the kind of event that features in reflective journals and stimulates developmental strategies. The event itself may be of a positive or a negative kind, but it is, by definition, one that had some kind of impact and drew your attention to some aspect of teaching that caused a strong personal reaction. Significant events may be formally or publicly presented, but they may be reserved for the more private reflective journal. Either way, they represent an important source of need identification and strategy formulation for professional development.

ACTIVITY

Think of a significant event in your recent teaching experience and try to identify the reasons why it was significant, and consider ways in which it might be useful in formulating strategies to meet your developmental needs as a teacher.

Table 11.1 *An example of an action plan (University of Surrey School of Educational Studies PGCEA Handbook)*

Learning need	Learning objectives (These should be clear and specific)	Strategies to achieve objectives	The extent to which objectives have been achieved	Further action required (if any)
I need to gain insight into difficult students and their management in the classroom situation.	Clarify what I mean by 'difficult' student. List the personal characteristics and student behaviours that I experience as difficult. Examine my own responses to students to determine my current strategies for dealing with difficult situations. Consider the extent to which my behaviour may affect the situations I find difficult. Learn about what might cause students to behave in these ways. Find out what strategies might help me to be more effective in managing the 'difficult' student.	Invite supervisory tutor and colleagues to help me reflect on situations when I have felt inadequate in dealing with students who I have found difficult. Observe lessons focusing on how teachers handle difficult students. Consult teachers in my practice placement and my peers to find out how they deal with difficult classroom situations. Undertake a review of the literature relating to difficult students and their management. Identify some of the strategies I could use with a difficult student.	Compiled a table of strategies detailing when they might be appropriate and what I need to be able to do to use them. Tested out strategies and found that they were effective in managing difficult students. Invited supervisors to sit in on any situations where I anticipate having to handle difficult students and ask for feedback.	To develop a wider range of strategies to manage difficult students.

These are some of the ways in which developmental strategies may be formed, in addition to the other sources of support that have been mentioned in this chapter. All of them are based on the assumption that learning, whether of a professional kind or any other, is a *process* without end.

The view that learning is, indeed, a *lifelong process*, and one that can never be regarded as final or complete, is one that has now been incorporated into government policy for education and skills, and this chapter will conclude with a brief account of the relation between professional development and lifelong learning as this has been reformulated in recent policy developments. First, however, it is necessary to trace the FENTO model of CPD in these developments.

Critique of the FENTO model

An Ofsted Report published in 2003 evaluated the model of the FENTO standards in these terms: 'While the FENTO standards provide a useful outline of the capabilities required of experienced FE teachers, they do not clearly define the standards required of new teachers . . . They are therefore of limited value.'

In other words, the FENTO standards are suitable in the case of continuing professional development, but not in that of initial teacher training.

In the meantime, however, the focus of policy had shifted away from the traditional, largely college-based and category-related provision, towards a more holistic concept of lifelong learning and skills in which many divisions, such as FE and AE, or college-, work- or community-based provision are beginning to be eroded. Also, there was an increasingly strong focus on the creation of a fully professionalised workforce in the lifelong learning and skills sector, and a growing emphasis upon the entry qualification status that is necessary for all other professions. Out of these developments, new structures and frameworks have been developed within which the FENTO model of CPD now operates.

> ## ACTIVITY
>
> From your own experience, what reasons would you give for agreeing with the Ofsted report that the FENTO standards might be suitable for continuing professional development, but not so relevant for initial teacher training?

LIFELONG LEARNING: FROM POLICY TO PRACTICE

The Department for Education and Employment (DfEE) became the Department for Education and Skills (DfES) in recognition of the fact that skills are now a condition of employment. We have seen earlier that policy has shifted towards a concept of lifelong learning on the part of individual learners, as opposed to the traditional categories of both learners and providers. There has also been a growing emphasis upon skills and achievement, wider social inclusion, learner-centred provision, and further attempts to bridge the traditional status divide between academic and vocational or skills learning.

Based on findings of the Ofsted survey inspection carried out during 2002–2003, the DfES began to formulate new policies for the future of initial teacher education for the Learning and Skills Sector, the name adopted for the traditional post-compulsory education and training provision. These policies focused on the training of teachers in colleges, the very mixed nature of recruitment to the sector, and the fact that only a proportion of teachers were formally trained to teach. Although Ofsted found good practice, this took place within some fundamental weaknesses, such as the theory–practice link, lack of support for new teachers, and the need to improve subject teaching.

Since 2001, the FENTO standards had virtually achieved mandatory status and were reflected in initial training. As the Ofsted report said, however: 'The FENTO standards are not an appropriate tool for judging the final attainments of trainees. Also, the standards are too wide-ranging to define the curricula for initial teacher training.'

As a result of these reports, the functions of FENTO were taken over by the Lifelong Learning Sector Skills Council, which will now be the most influential source for teacher training and professional development in the sector.

Similarly, the functions of the Further Education Funding Council (FEFC) have been taken over by the Learning and Skills Council (LSC). The LSC, together with its local LSCs, is responsible for planning and funding vocational education and training across the lifelong learning sector. Likewise, the Further Education Development Agency (FEDA) has become the Learning and Skills Development Agency (LSDA).

Of particular relevance for both initial teacher training and continuing professional development is the Success for All programme, set up jointly by the DfES and the LSC. This programme is concerned with quality and responsiveness across the new learning and skills sector, and its major themes include both initial teacher training and continuing professional development. The reform of ITT for the Learning and Skills Sector centres around the award of Qualified Teacher Learning and Skills (QTLS), but the policy also includes provision for CPD for practitioners once qualified: 'Throughout their careers, teachers will go on updating their subject and teaching skills and knowledge, as the context in which they work changes' (DfES Standards Unit, 2004).

A feature of the ITT process for trainee teachers will be registration with the Institute for Learning (IfL), which will 'award QTLS to those completing training, and register them as holding a "full licence to practise." Each teacher will need to renew their licence on a regular basis by completing an annual tariff of appropriate continuing professional development.'

So CPD will in future be mandatory for teachers in the sector, and they will be licensed to practise in the same way as other professional workers. The Institute for Learning is the professional body for teachers in the post-compulsory education and training sector, and will be responsible for

- researching the CPD needs of its members
- establishing a CPD framework to support members' professional development
- investigating good CPD practice across the sector
- canvassing members' opinions on key issues
- providing news and research.

With effect from the beginning of 2005, the functions of FENTO with regard to standards were taken over by Lifelong Learning (UK). This is the Sector Skills Council for Lifelong Learning, and it is responsible for workforce planning and development in the sector, as well as being central to the Skills for Business network that constitutes the link to employers.

The new infrastructure within which both ITT and CPD will therefore function can be summed up as follows:

- Department for Education and Skills (DfES) replaces Department for Education and Employment (DfEE) to determine overall policy
- Lifelong Learning UK (LLUK) replaces Further Education National Training Organisation (FENTO) to set standards for both ITT and CPD
- Learning and Skills Council (LSC) replaces the Further Education Funding Council (FEFC) to fund the sector
- The Institute for Learning (IfL) will constitute the professional body to represent teachers' interests in both ITT and CPD, and will award both QTLS and the licence to practise to established teachers
- DfES Standards Regional Network will implement the Success for All agenda and support regional and local initiatives in ITT, Centres of Excellence in Teacher Training (CETTs), mentoring, teaching practice, and so on.

The concept of CPD has changed, therefore, and has come into line with the general concept of professionalism:

- entry to the profession is controlled by an autonomous professional organisation
- only qualified teachers will have a licence to practise
- CPD is mandatory.

All of these developments have taken place, however, within a policy and structure of lifelong learning, so that the traditional categories of further and adult education have been subsumed under a wider concept of lifelong learning and skills.

Review Questions

1 List what you consider to be the most important reasons why continuing professional development should be mandatory for every teacher in the post-compulsory sector.
2 What would you say were the most important three priorities in the professional development process?
3 Reflecting upon your attempt at the first activity in this chapter (page 249), what would now be your own list of professional needs, and can you see them changing in the light of the recent developments just described?
4 Give some examples of the kind of strategies and sources of support you already use in order to meet perceived developmental needs. In the light of the changes described, in what ways do you now think these sources might be widened?
5 What would you see as the main role of the colleges in implementing government policy for lifelong learning and skills?

SUMMARY

- Continuing professional development has become of central importance to every kind of professional career: in the case of the lifelong learning sector it will in future be mandatory.
- The Learning and Skills Councils have been set up to co-ordinate the Government's policies for training, education and employment.
- Lifelong Learning UK, as the relevant Sector Skills Council, will be responsible for establishing standards and models of both initial teacher training and continuing professional development.
- The historic FENTO model outlined in this chapter reflects system- and college-based strategies for organising professional development.
- Continuing professional development, like the initial training and QTLS award, will be the responsibility of the Institute for Learning, which is the professional body for teachers in post-compulsory education and training.
- Continuing professional development in further and adult education has therefore been put into the wider context of government policy for lifelong learning and skills.

Suggested Further Reading

Although the following are mostly concerned with the schools context of education, they deal with many generic issues of continuing professional development in education generally.

Armitage, A. *et al.* (2003) *Teaching and Training in Post-Compulsory Education*, Maidenhead: OU Press
  This includes chapters on teaching and learning, assessment, resources, course planning etc. Describes the growth of vocationalism and key issues in the background of post-compulsory education. Includes exercises, theoretical references, and examples of students' work.

Craft, A. (1996) *Continuing Professional Development*, London: Routledge in association with the Open University
  Deals with theory and practice issues, evaluation and planning of CPD, effectiveness, appraisal, developmental needs and methodology.

Glover, D. and Law, S. (1996) *Managing Professional Development in Education: Issues in Policy and Practice*, London: Kogan Page
  This book covers national and institutional policy developments in professional development, together with descriptions of initiatives, costing and evaluation, illustrated with case studies.

Guskey, T.R. and Huberman, M. (eds) (1995) *Professional Development in Education: New Paradigms and Practices*, New York: Teachers College Press
  This edited collection of papers provides an international symposium on professional development, covering a range of perspectives on issues, theory and practice.

Hillier, Y. and Thompson, A. (eds) (2005) *Readings in Post-Compulsory Education*, London: Continuum International Publishing Group
  An edited collection of readings in major issues affecting the post-compulsory education sector, including managing change, student retention, information technology, basic skills, etc.

Wallace, S. (2001) *Teaching and Supporting Learning in Further Education: Meeting the FENTO Standards*, Exeter: Learning Matters
  Also geared to the FENTO standards, this covers the background to the standards, together with strategies such as journals and evaluation. Also, planning and preparing for learning programmes, needs assessment, achievement and outcomes, managing learning, key skills etc.

APPENDIX 1: GREYBOURNE COLLEGE OF FE

MISSION STATEMENT

The College aims to satisfy fully the needs of our customers and the community through lifelong education and training.

COLLEGE POLICIES

We are commited to:

- the Equal Opportunities Policy
- the College Charter
- Investors in People.

GUIDE TO QUALIFICATIONS

A-level	Level	A-level	Level	A-level	Level
Accounts A/AS-level	3	Film Studies A-level	3	Physics A/AS-level	3
Art A/AS-level	3	French A-level	3	Politics A-level	3
Biology & Human Biology A/AS-level	3	General Studies A/AS-level	3	Psychology A-level	3
Business Studies A/AS-level	3	Geography A-level	3	Russian A-level	3
Chemistry A/AS-level	3	German A-level	3	Sociology A/AS-level	3
Communication Studies A-level	3	Graphic Design A-level	3	Spanish A-level	3
Computing A/AS-level	3	History A-level	3	Sports Studies/Physical Education A-level	3
Economics A-level	3	Law A/AS-level	3	Textiles A-level	3
English Literature A-level	3	Mathematics A/AS-level	3	Theatre Studies A-level	3
Environmental Science AS-level	3	Media Studies A-level	3		
European Studies AS-level	3	Photography A-level	3		

GCSE	Level	GCSE	Level	GCSE	Level
Biology GCSE	2	German GCSE	2	Physics GCSE	2
Chemistry GCSE	2	History GCSE	2	Psychology GCSE	2
English GCSE	2	Human Physiology & Health GCSE	2	Sociology GCSE	2
French GCSE	2	Information Technology GCSE	2	Spanish GCSE	2
Geography GCSE	2	Mathematics GCSE	2		
Art & media					
Art & Design Foundation Studies Edexcel/BTEC	3	Diploma in Contemporary Music NCFE	3	Media Communications & Production GNVQ Intermediate	2
Art & Design GNVQ Intermediate Edexcel/BTEC	2	Fine Bookbinding & Conservation Certificate/Diploma SOCF	3	Media National Diploma Edexcel/BTEC	3
Art & Design GNVQ Advanced	3	Foundation Certificate in Contemporary Music SOCF	2	Performing Arts & Entertainment Industries GNVQ Advanced	3
Art & Design SOCF	2/3	Graphic Design GNVQ Advanced Edexcel/BTEC	3	Photography/Design National Diploma Edexcel/BTEC	3
Art & Design/Fine Bookbinding & Conservation Higher National Certificate	4	Graphic Design NationalDiploma Edexcel/BTEC	3	Printing & Graphics Communications Certificate C & G	2
Cultural Venue Operations and Support NVQ 2	2	Higher Diploma in Contemporary Music NCFE	4	Solo & Duo Acting	2
Business & IT					
Administration & Secretarial Procedures Higher Diploma RSA	4	Business Higher National Diploma Edexcel/BTEC	4	Information Technology NVQ 2 RSA	2
Administration NVQ 2 RSA	2	Computing Higher National Diploma	4	Private Secretary's Certificate PSC/SSC	3
Business GNVQ Intermediate	2	Information Technology GNVQ Intermediate	2	Rapid Hi-Tech Secretarial	3

Business AVCE	3	Information Technology AVCE	3	Secretarial with A-level	3
Care & health					
Caring Services (Social Care) Higher National Diploma Edexcel/BTEC	4	Gateway Programme Entry level GNVQ Foundation	1	Personal Development Programme The Prince's Trust	1
Certificate in Child Care & Education CCE-CACHE	2	Health & Social Care GNVQ Intermediate Edexcel/BTEC	2	Skillpower Programme	Entry level
Childhood Studies (Nursery Nursing) National Diploma Edexcel/BTEC	3	Health & Social Care GNVQ Advanced Edexcel/BTEC	3	Vocational Access Programme	Entry level
English as a Foreign Language EFL	1	Nursery Nursing Diploma NNEB-CACHE	3		
Hair & beauty					
Beauty Therapy NVQ	1	Beauty Therapy NVQ	3	Hairdressing Certificate NVQ	2
Beauty Therapy Certificate NVQ	2	Hairdressing: Introduction to Salon Services NVQ	1	Total Look Hairdressing with Beauty Therapy C&G	2
Hospitality & food					
Hospitality & Catering GNVQ Advanced	3	Hotel Reception/ Customer Service NVQ	2	Professional Catering NVQ	2
Hotel Catering & Institutional Management Higher National Diploma	4				
Technology					
Bricklaying NVQ	2	Electrical Installation NVQ	2	Interior Design CENTRA	2
Building Crafts Occupations NVQ	1	Electronics Foundation C&G	1	Motor Vehicle Studies/ Engineering National Diploma Edexcel/BTEC	3
Building Studies Higher National Diploma Edexcel/BTEC	4	Electronics/Electrical Power (Engineering) Higher National Diploma/Certificate	4	Painting & Decorating NVQ	2

Carpentry & Joinery NVQ	2	Engineering Foundation NVQ	2	Plumbing NVQ	2
Construction & the Built Environment GNVQ Intermediate Edexcel/BTEC	2	Engineering GNVQ Intermediate Edexcel/BTEC	2	Technical Design	2
Construction & the Built Environment GNVQ Advanced Edexcel/BTEC	3	Engineering GNVQ Advanced Edexcel/BTEC	3	Vehicle Maintenance NVQ	1
Electrical Electronics (Engineering) National Diploma Edexcel/BTEC	3	Engineering Higher National Diploma/Certificate Edexcel/BTEC	4		
Tourism & Leisure					
ABTAC Travel Services NVQ	2	Leisure & Tourism GNVQ Advanced Edexcel/BTEC	3	Travel & Tourism Management Higher National Diploma Edexcel/BTEC	4
ABTAC Travel Services NVQ	3	Leisure Management Higher National Diploma Edexcel/BTEC	4		
Leisure & Tourism GNVQ Intermediate Edexcel/BTEC	2	Sports Foundation Award	2		

APPENDIX 2:
GREYBOURNE SIXTH FORM COLLEGE

A/AS-level	Level	A/AS-level	Level	A/AS-level	Level
Accounting	3	Geography	3	Modern Languages:	
Art:	3	Government &	3	– French	3
Ceramics,	3	Politics		– German	3
Graphics,	3	Graphical	3	– Spanish	3
Fine Art,	3	Communication		Music:	
Textiles	3	History	3	– General	3
Biology	3	Law	3	– Practical Music	3
Business Studies	3	Mathematics:	3	AS Music	3
Chemistry	3	– with Mechanics	3	Performing Arts	3
Computing	3	– with Statistics	3	Photography	3
Design & Technology	3	– Further		Physical Education	3
Economics	3	Mathematics	3	Physics	3
English Language	3	– AS Mathematics	3	Psychology	3
English Literature	3	– AS Statistics	3	Religious Studies	3
Film Studies	3	Media Studies	3	Sociology	3
General Studies	3			Theatre Studies	3
AVCE					
Art & Design	3	Health & Social Care	3	Leisure & Tourism	3
Business	3				
Intermediate GNVQ					
Business	2	Health & Social Care	2	Leisure & Tourism	2

Appendix 3:
Greybourne Adult and Community Education Service

Mission statement

The Adult Education and Community Service works in partnership with groups and individuals in the town – regardless of age, gender, lifestyle, race, religion, previous educational experience or ability – to provide community-based, high-quality adult learning opportunities and support, responsive to local need.

Service objectives

- To provide a co-ordinated range of learning opportunities promoting: individual personal development; intellectual, creative, artistic and physical skills; and effective participation in society.
- To develop a flexible service responsive to the expressed needs of individuals, groups and localities by the provision of effective mechanisms for consultation.
- To provide a comprehensive service by working in close co-operation with other providers within the statutory, non-statutory and voluntary sectors to ensure the provision of clear educational progression routes.
- To encourage participation by facilitating access in terms of the timing, modes of attendance, location of provision, etc., and by identifying and meeting the needs of potentially disadvantaged groups of adult learners, for example adults with disabilities, adults with literacy and numeracy needs, women, older adults, minority ethnic groups and unemployed people.
- To underpin the provision with appropriate support services, particularly in relation to educational guidance for adults.

GUIDE TO QUALIFICATIONS

Subject area	Description (selected examples)
Office/Business	Introduction to computing, Computer awareness, Running a small business
Languages	Conversational French, Improvers' Spanish, Urdu
Humanities	Local history, Creative writing, Family history, History of transport
Physical Education/ Sport/Fitness	Aerobics, Yoga, Men's keep fit, Tap dancing, Western dancing, Badminton, Tai Chi
Practical Crafts/Skills	Simple fabric prints, Machine knitting, Painting and drawing, Car maintenance, Guitar, Decoupage, Decorative stencilling, Pottery, Stained glass crafts
Role Education	Stress management, Assertiveness training, Parenting, Public speaking, Counselling, Financial planning, Sign language
Independent Living and Communication Skills	Courses to teach independent living and communication skills to persons with learning difficulties
Basic Education	Literacy, Numeracy, and English as an Additional Language courses – open learning, full-time/short courses, self-study, careers advice and guidance
Accredited Vocational	RSA CLAIT, C&G Fashion, RYA Coastal Navigation, Sign Language, OCNW courses
Access to FE/HE	Access courses through the Open College Networks

APPENDIX 4:
AN ABC OF THE POST-COMPULSORY CURRICULUM

ABC 'A Basis for Credit', the title of a 1992 FEU project and associated publications concerned with developing a credit, accumulation and transfer framework for post-compulsory education

academic appeals student appeals against assessment decisions, based upon a formally approved academic appeals procedure

academic board a group of academic staff (usually) elected to regulate academic affairs, and accountable to senior management or governing bodies in a college

access the opportunities provided by the educational system to individuals for entry and progression beyond compulsory schooling

Access courses designed to help disadvantaged adults gain entry to professional preparation or accreditation

accreditation the process leading to the recognition of successful student achievement through the granting of an award

Adult and Community Learning (ACL) a sector funded by the LSDA, concerned with adult lifelong learning

affective domain learning that involves attitudes, feelings and emotions

andragogy the theory of adult learning, which stresses the value of approaches that build upon the existing experience of the learner

APL the accreditation of prior learning, a generic term that encompasses both the assessment and recognition of prior experiential learning (APEL) and the accreditation of prior certificated learning (APL)

appraisal a system for assessing, and providing guidance on, the professional development of staff

assessment the process by which evidence of student learning and achievement is obtained and evaluated against agreed criteria

basic skills traditionally associated with the 'three Rs' – reading, writing and arithmetic – but increasingly today also associated with communication skills, information technology skills and problem-solving

brainstorming an intensive discussion in which the quantity of ideas produced is more important than their quality

BTEC Business and Technology Education Council, one of the national awarding bodies; now part of Edexcel

buzz-group a small group of usually two to six members, established for a short time to discuss a problem or issue

capability an all-round human quality, the integration of knowledge, skills and competencies expressed in learner confidence

case studies detailed histories of real situations or incidents often used to relate and apply concepts and problem-solving skills to work contexts

Certificate of Pre-Vocational Education (CPVE) an early foundation level award aimed at preparing students for future occupational roles – it has been replaced by other awards, such as GNVQ Foundation level

City & Guilds (C&G)   founded in 1878, specialising in developing vocational, general and leisure qualifications; awards certificates in a broad range of subjects, many of which are NVQs and GNVQs; now part of AQA

cognitive domain   learning that involves mental processes

competence   the ability to perform tasks in real or simulated work roles

course   a curriculum, usually based upon a number of compulsory elements that is studied in a set sequence, over a set period of time

course committee   a formally constituted group consisting of tutors, students and employers who have responsibility for managing and developing the course; meetings of the course committee usually have an agenda and are minuted

course leader   the member of teaching staff responsible for co-ordinating teaching and assessment by the members of the team of staff delivering the elements of a course

course monitoring and review   the process of collecting and reviewing information to inform the evaluation of the success of the course in achieving its objectives for promoting student learning and achievement

course team   the group of teaching staff who work together to manage teaching and learning on the course

credit   a measure of the volume and level of learning achieved on a module or discrete element of a course or programme

credit accumulation and transfer (CAT)   the process by which qualifications and past achievements are awarded educational credit so that students can transfer from one course or programme to another without undue loss of time

credit value   a numerical value given to a unit to signify its worth in relation to other units; learners can accumulate credits to a credit achievement target

criterion referencing   systems of assessment, such as NCVQ, which are based upon an explicit definition of the expected outcomes of assessment

curriculum design   the process of developing vocational courses and programmes akin to product development in commercial organisations

debate   a teaching method that allows the presentation of sharply contrasting viewpoints

desktop publishing   the use of computer application programs to produce text-based materials to a high typographical standard

didactic teaching   a teacher-led approach that focuses on the transmission of knowledge from the teacher to the students

difficulty index   the difficulty of a test item, measured by the percentage of candidates answering correctly; usually items with very low and very high difficulty are omitted from final versions of a test

discrimination index   a measure of the success with which a test item discriminates between 'good' and 'bad' candidates on the test as a whole; thus, items that are answered well by 'bad' candidates and poorly by 'good' candidates are usually omitted from final versions of a test

discovery learning   a student-centred method that encourages learners to establish concepts and principles for themselves

distracters   plausible but incorrect answers in a multiple-choice test

Education for capability   an initiative sponsored by the Royal Society of Arts, concerned with promoting approaches that develop learner capability, such as the capacity for independent learning, in post-compulsory education

Educational Resource Information Centre (ERIC)   an American-based, internet-delivered system that abstracts journal articles on aspects of educational research

EFL   English as a Foreign Language

ENB   English National Board, the professional body responsible for validating nursing, midwifery and some other health-related qualifications in England

entry   the stage in a learner's career at which they enter a college or other educational institution, usually through enrolment and registration for an award

ESOL   English for Speakers of Other Languages

evaluation   measurement of the worth of an educational programme (in contrast to assessment, which measures student attainment)

exit   the stage in a learner's career when they leave a college or other educational institution, usually upon successful completion of a course

FENTO standards   Further Education National Training Organisation standards for teaching and supporting learning, consisting of three main elements: professional knowledge and understanding, skills and attributes, and key areas of teaching

flexible learning   a generic term commonly associated with open access to learning programmes and student-centred learning methods

formative assessment   assessment used to provide students with feedback about the success of their work, not usually associated with formal assessment or grading (summative assessment)

franchising   a formal agreement whereby one institution, often a college or university, allows another institution to deliver a learning programme that it has validated

full-time equivalent (FTE)   calculation of the size of the student body; in a college, for example, where 22 hours was considered a full student timetable, a part-time student taking 11 hours of study would count as half a full-time student

Further Education Funding Council (FEFC)   founded in 1992 under the Further and Higher Education Act, the FEFC replaced local education authorities as the funding body for further education; responsibility for adult education is divided between the FEFC and local authorities. In 2001 it was replaced by the LSC

Further Education Resources for Learning (Ferl)   an internet-based information service

general credit   credit or exemption offered to applicants in acknowledgement of past learning and achievements, usually in connection with the first stage or entry level to a course

General National Vocational Qualifications (GNVQ)   a series of qualifications, mainly for full-time students in schools and colleges, designed to provide a vocational alternative to GCEs

guidance   the totality of institutional processes aimed at supporting the student in his or her studies, choice of programme and career route

Higher Education Funding Council (HEFC)   the national organisation responsible for funding universities and higher education and for external quality assurance of the sector

independent learning   approaches to learning where the learner takes responsibility for their own learning

individualised learning   programmes that allow learners to study in their own time and at their own pace, often delivered by resource-based learning materials

integration   the linking together of elements of vocational programmes, through devices such as cross-modular or integrated assignments

internal validation   the process through which new or revised course proposals are approved internally, before being scrutinised by an awarding body

job competence   see competence

key skills   transferable life skills, often referred to as common skills, such as numeracy and communication, which form the foundation for the learner's success in work and education; many vocational qualifications contain compulsory key skills units

Learning and Skills Council (LSC)   established in April 2001, to take over the responsibilities of the FEFC and TECs, for the planning and funding of FE, ACL and WBL

learning outcomes   detailed statements of what the student is expected to achieve as a result of successfully completing a module or other component of the curriculum

learning programme   a modular and flexible structure of learning based upon open access and many exit points, permitting the learner a wide range of choices over what, when and how they study

level   a broad measure of the overall demand of a qualification

lifelong learning   a commitment to creating educational opportunities for individuals to learn and study, throughout their lives

LLUK   Lifelong Learning UK, the Sector Skills Council created in 2004 to replace FENTO

local learning partnerships   partnerships between institutions involved in post-16 and adult learning provision to create more coherent local arrangements for learning, careers advice and guidance, student support, etc.

moderation   the alignment of assessment standards

moderator   an external assessor appointed by a national awarding body to monitor standards achieved on a set of vocational courses

module   a unit of learning or assessment

monitoring   the systematic evaluation of a college's course provision often through the use of performance indicators

National Council for Vocational Qualifications (NCVQ)   the national organisation, established in 1986, responsible for rationalising vocational qualifications in the UK, now subsumed into the Qualifications and Curriculum Authority (QCA)

National Education and Training Targets (NETTS)   a set of agreed objectives for increasing participation in the vocational education and training system and for raising standards

National Institute of Adult Continuing Education (NIACE)   promotes the study and advancement of adult education in the UK

national occupational standards   standards of occupational competence developed by a standard-setting body and approved by the regulatory bodies

National Open College Network (NOCN)   a body that offers awards to adult learners, particularly those people for whom more traditional qualifications are inaccessible or inappropriate; NOCN operates through 31 local Open College Networks (OCNs) based across the UK

National Training Organisation (NTO)   an organisation recognised by the Government to act on behalf of employers in key sectors of industry, commerce and the public sector; the NTO for the further education sector was FENTO and is now LLUK (see above)

National Vocational Qualification (NVQ)   an award accredited by NCVQ as conforming to the standards set by an approved lead body

notional learning time   an estimate of the number of hours it would take the average learner to achieve the unit or credit

occupational standards   levels of competence established and defined by employers

peer group assessment   assessment process in which a student's peers can award or withhold marks according to a set of pre-agreed criteria (for example, the student's degree of participation within the group)

performance criteria   the specific criteria associated with the assessment of NVQ and GNVQ units and elements

portfolio of evidence   a collection of assignments, projects and other evidence to demonstrate the successful achievement against learning outcomes and/or performance criteria

pre-entry   the stage prior to enrolling or registering for a qualification

professional associations   national organisations that represent the interests of their members (for example, nurses, chartered secretaries) and also determine qualification routes related to entry to the profession

profile   a means of recording achievement

programme leader   see course leader

programme team   see course team

psychomotor domain   learning that involves physical movement

qualification   a certificate of achievement or competence specifying awarding body, qualification type and title

Qualifications and Curriculum Authority (QCA)   created through merger of the National Council for Vocational Qualifications (NCVQ) and the School Curriculum and Assessment Authority (SCAA). Duties include developing a coherent national framework of qualifications; accrediting and ensuring the quality of all publicly funded qualifications offered in schools, colleges and workplaces; promoting quality and coherence in education and training to increase lifelong learning opportunities and the creation of a learning society

quality assurance   the processes and procedures developed by organisations to ensure that quality of delivery is maintained

quality control   implementation of a system of quality assurance to check and verify that appropriate standards have been maintained

Quality in Learning and Teaching (QUILT)   a staff development initiative that includes the development of ILT materials

record of achievement (ROA)   a file with evidence of students' achievements, including reports incorporating tutor and student comments, with a substantial element of self-evaluation and action-planning

referral   a situation in which a student marginally fails to achieve a pass level in an assignment or end-of-course assessment

reliability   the ability of an assessment tool to consistently measure what it is supposed to measure

resource-based learning (RBL)   learning in which the subject matter is delivered more by materials (for example, text-based, audio or video) than directly by a teacher

Sector Skills Councils   employer-based organisations responsible for setting standards for a group of occupations. Lifelong Learning UK (LLUK) is the SSC with responsibility for FE, WBL and ACL

self-assessment   assessment in which the students make an evaluation of their own performance

self-assessment report   a formal evaluative report prepared by a college or other provider, normally for the purposes of inspection, on its key strengths and weaknesses

simulation   a learning tool that is based upon a simple representation of reality to enable the learner to determine the critical variables in a complex situation

skills strategy   the national strategy for raising the levels of skills and qualifications in the working population

standard-setting body   an organisation, usually a sector skills council (SSC), recognised by a regulatory authority as responsible for formulating standards of competence for an employment sector

student-centred learning   approaches to learning designed to encourage students to take responsibility for their own self-development

student handbook   a guide written for students that provides a simple summary of the structure, content and assessment of a course or learning programme

summative assessment   the formal assessment process leading to grading and the determination of whether a student passes or fails a course

synoptic assessment   assessment that tests a candidate's understanding of the connections between different elements of a subject

teacher-centred learning   learning in which the objectives of learning and the content of most classroom interaction is initiated and perpetuated by the teacher

Training and Enterprise Councils (TECs)   known as LECs in Scotland or Local Enterprise Councils, until 2001 TECs managed a range of government-sponsored programmes and assisted local firms in staff training and development

unit   the smallest part of a qualification that can be separately certificated

unitisation   the process of structuring the framework of a qualification in terms of units as basic building blocks rather than full qualifications

unit of competence   a component of an NVQ award, which in turn is broken down into elements of competence

University of the Third Age (U3A)   established in the UK in 1982 to provide educational opportunities for older members of society (those over 50)

validation   the process of gaining approval from an awarding body for a new or modified course or programme

validity   the extent to which an assessment tool measures what it is supposed to measure

verification   the monitoring of the process of assessment to ensure that consistent standards are maintained, undertaken in the NVQ model by internal and external verifiers

work-based assessment   the measurement of performance in the workplace, usually by a workplace assessor

work-based learning (WBL)   training programmes where the learner is based in the workplace

Workers' Education Association (WEA)   founded in 1903 to develop the intellectual capacity of working men (*sic*)

APPENDIX 5:
USEFUL ADDRESSES AND WEB SITES

Adult Learning Inspectorate
Web: http://ali.gov.uk

AoC NILTA Ltd
5th Floor, Centre Point
103 New Oxford Street
London WC1A 1RG
Tel: 020 7827 4629
Fax: 020 7827 4650
Web: http://www.nilta.org.uk

AQA (formerly AEB, NEAB and City & Guilds)
Web: http://www.aqa.org.uk/

Association of Colleges (AOC)
5th Floor
Centre Point
103 New Oxford Street
London
WC1A 1DD
Tel: 020 7827 4600
Fax: 020 7827 4650
Web: http://www.aoc.co.uk/

Association of Scottish Colleges
Argyll Court
The Castle Business Park
Stirling
FK9 4TY
Tel: 01786 892100
Fax: 01786 892109
E-mail: enquiries@ascol.org.uk
Web: http://www.ascol.org.uk/

Basic Skills Agency (BSA)
7th Floor
Commonwealth House
1–19 New Oxford Street
London
WC1A 1NU
Tel: 020 7405 4017
Fax: 020 7440 6626
E-mail: enquiries@basic-skills.co.uk
Web: http://www.basic-skills.co.uk

BBC Learning
Web: http://www.bbc/co.uk/learning

British Council
10 Spring Gardens
London
SW1A 2BN
Tel: 020 7930 8466
Fax: 020 7839 6347
Minicom: 0161 957 7188
General enquiries E-mail: general.enquiries@britishcouncil.org
Web: http://www.britishcouncil.org/

British Educational Communications and Technology Agency (Becta)
Milburn Hill Rd
Science Park
Coventry
CV4 7JJ
Tel: 024 7641 6994
Fax: 024 7641 1418
Web: http://www.becta.org.uk/

Chartered Institute of Personnel and Development
151 The Broadway
London
SW19 1JQ
Phone: 020 8612 6200
Fax: 020 8612 6201
Web: http://www.cipd.co.uk/

City & Guilds (C&G)
1 Giltspur Street
London
EC1A 9DD
Tel: 020 7294 2800
Fax: 020 7294 2400
E-mail: enquiry@city-and-guilds.co.uk
Web: http://www.city-and-guilds.co.uk

Commission for Racial Equality (CRE)
St Dunstan's House
201–211 Borough High Street
London SE1 1GZ
Tel: 020 7939 0000
Fax: 020 7939 0001
E-mail: info@cre.gov.uk
Web: http://www.cre.gov.uk/

Department for Education and Skills (DfES)
Sanctuary Buildings
Great Smith Street
London
SW1P 3BT
Tel: 0870 0012345
Email: info@dfes.gsi.gov.uk
Web: http://www.dfes.gov.uk/

Edexcel
(See web site for regional centres)
One90 High Holborn
London
WC1V 7BH
Customer Services
Tel: 0870 240 9800
Web: http://www.edexcel.org.uk/

Further Education National Consortium (FENC)
Web: http://www.fenc.org.uk/

Further Education Resources for Learning (Ferl)
Web: http://ferl.becta.org.uk/

Institute for Learning (IfL)
4th Floor
32 Farringdon Street
London
EC4A 4HJ
Telephone: 020 7332 9540
Web: http://www.ifl.ac.uk/

Learning and Skills Council (LSC)
Cheylesmore House
Quinton Road
Coventry
CV1 2WT
Tel: 0845 019 4170
Fax: 024 7682 3675
Web: http://www.lsc.gov.uk

Learning and Skills Development Agency (LSDA)
Regent Arcade House
19–25 Argyll Street
London
W1F 7LS
Switchboard: 020 7297 9000
Fax: 020 7297 9001

Lifelong Learning UK
http://www.lifelonglearning.co.uk/

National Association of Teachers in Further and Higher Education (NATFHE)
27 Britannia Street
London
WC1X 9JP
Tel: 020 7837 3636
Fax: 020 7837 4403
Minicom 020 7278 0470
E-mail: hq@natfhe.org.uk
Web: http://www.natfhe.org.uk/

National Institute of Adult Continuing Education (NIACE)
20 Princess Road West
Leicester
LE1 6TP
Tel: 0116 204 4200/4201
Fax: 0116 285 4514
Minicom: 0116 2556049
E-mail: enquiries@niace.org.uk
Web: http://www.niace.org.uk

National Open College Network (NOCN)
9 St James Court
Friar Gate
Derby
DE1 1BT
Tel: 01332 268080
Fax: 01332 268081
E-mail: nocn@nocn.org.uk
Web: http://www.nocn.org.uk

National Union of Students (NUS)
Nelson Mandela House
461 Holloway Road
London
N7 6LJ
Tel: 020 7272 8900
Fax: 020 7263 5713
Email: nusuk@nus.org.uk
Web: http://www.nus.org.uk/

OCR (formerly Oxford and Cambridge and RSE Examination Board)
9 Hills Road
Cambridge
CB2 1GG
Tel: 01223 552552
Fax: 01223 552553
E-mail: helpdesk@ocr.org.uk
Web: http://www.ocr.org.uk/

Office for Standards in Education (Ofsted)
Alexandra House
33 Kingsway
London
WC2B 6SE
Tel: 020 7421 6800
Web: http://www/ofsted.gov.uk/

Qualifications and Curriculum Authority (QCA)
29 Bolton Street
London
W1Y 7PD
Tel: 020 7509 5555
E-mail: info@qca.org.uk
Web: http://www.open.gov.uk/qca/

Sector Skills Development Agency
3 Callflex Business Park
Golden Smithies Lane
Wath-upon-Dearne
South Yorkshire
S63 7ER
Tel: 01709 765444
Email: info@ssda.org.uk
Web: http://www.ssda.org.uk/

University for Industry
Ufl Ltd
The Innovation Centre
217 Portobello Street
Sheffield
S1 4DP
Tel: 0114 224 2999
Fax: 0114 270 0034
E-mail: @ufi.cwc.com
Web: http://www.ufiltd.co.uk/

Workers' Education Association (WEA)
Temple House
17 Victoria Park Square
London
E2 9PB
Tel: 020 8983 1515
Fax: 020 8983 4840
Web: http://www.wea.org.uk/

APPENDIX 6: REFERENCES

Ainley, P. and Bailey, B. (1997) *The Business of Learning: Staff and Student Experiences of Further Education*, London: Cassell

Anderson, D., Brown, S. and Race, P. (1997) *500 Tips for Further and Continuing Education Lecturers*, London: Kogan Page

Armsby, A. (1994) 'Convergence of learning resource services in further education' in Armsby, A., Drage, R., Anderson, D., Riley, J., Warrington, S., Martin, D., Adams, M., Copsey, D., Jones, H. and Mauger, S. *Managing the Growth of College Learning Resource Services*, Bristol: The Staff College

Ashcroft, K. and James, D. (eds) (1999) *The Creative Professional: Learning to Teach 14–19 year olds*, London: Falmer Press

Bales, R.F. (1950) *Interaction Process Analysis: A Method for the Study of Small Groups*, London: University of Chicago Press

Ball, C. (1991) *Learning Pays: The Role of Post-compulsory Education and Training*, London: RSA

Basic Skills Agency (1994) *Older and Younger: The Basic Skills of Different Age Groups*, London: Basic Skills Agency

Bernstein, B. (1971–5) *Class, Codes and Control* (3 vols), London: Routledge & Kegan Paul

Bligh, D. (1971) *What's the Use of Lectures?* Harmondsworth: Penguin

Bloom, B.S. (1956–64) *Taxonomy of Educational Objectives* (2 vols), London: Longman

Boud, D. (1992) 'In the midst of experience: Developing a model to aid learners and facilitators' in Mulligan, J. and Griffin, C. *Empowerment through Experiential Learning*, London: Kogan Page

Boud, D. (1995) *Enhancing Learning through Self Assessment*, London: Kogan Page

Boud, D., Keogh, R. and Walker, D. (1985) *Reflection: Turning Experience into Learning*, London: Kogan Page

Bruner, J. (1974) *Toward a Theory of Instruction*, Cambridge, Mass.: Harvard University Press

Buzan, A. (1974) *Use Your Head*, London: BBC Publications

Calder, J. (1994) *Programme Evaluation and Quality*, London: Kogan Page

Calder, J. and McCollum, A. (1997) *Open and Flexible Learning in Vocational Education and Training*, London: Kogan Page

Coleman, J.S. (1990) *Foundations of Social Theory*, Cambridge, Mass.: Harvard University Press

Cooper, C.L. and Rousseau, D.M. (1996) *Trends in Organizational Behaviour*, Vol. 3, Chichester: John Wiley & Sons Ltd

Craft, A. (1996) *Continuing Professional Development*, London: Routledge in association with the Open University

Davies, W.J.K. (1989) *Open and Flexible Learning Centres*, London: National Council for Educational Technology

Dearing, R. (1996) *Review of Qualifications for 16–19-year-olds* – Full Report, London: Schools Curriculum and Assessment Authority (now QCA)

DfEE (1998a) *NVQs and SVQs at a Glance*, London: DfEE

DfEE (1998b) *National Training Organisations: Prospectus 1999–2000*, London: DfEE

DfEE (1998c) *The Learning Age: A Renaissance for a New Britain* (Green Paper CM 3790), London: The Stationery Office

DfEE (1999a) *Learning to Succeed: School Sixth Form Funding*, London: DfEE

DfEE (1999b) *Qualifying for Success*, London: DfEE

DfES (2003) *Success for All – Delivery Plan*, London: DfES

DfES (2004) *14–19 Curriculum and Qualifications Reform: Final Report of the Working Group on 14–19 Reform*, London: DfES

DfES (2005) *14–19 Education and Skills*, London: DfES

DfES Standards Unit (2004) *Equipping our Teachers for the Future: Reforming Initial Teacher Training for the Learning and Skills Sector*, London: DfES

Dewey, J. (1938) *Experience and Education*, New York: Macmillan

Ecclestone, K. (1996) *How to Assess the Vocational Curriculum*, London: Kogan Page

Ellington, H. and Race, P. (1994) *Producing Teaching Materials: A Handbook for Teachers and Trainers*, 2nd edition, London: Kogan Page

Ellington, H., Percival, F. and Race, P. (1993) *Handbook of Educational Technology*, 3rd edition, London: Kogan Page

English National Board for Nursing, Midwifery and Health Visiting (1992) *Adding up the Past – APL/APEL: Guidelines for Good Practice*, London: ENB

Erikson, E.H. (1965) *Childhood and Society*, Harmondsworth: Penguin

Ferl (2004) http://ferl.becta.org.uk. Accessed 22 June 2005

Further Education Development Agency (1995a) *Supporting Adult Part-time Learners in Further Education Colleges*, London: FEDA

Further Education Development Agency (1995b) *Learning Styles*, London: FEDA

Further Education Funding Council (1992) *Funding Learning*, Coventry: FEFC

Further Education Funding Council (1994) *Guide for College Governors*, Coventry: FEFC

Further Education Funding Council (1996a) *Students' Destinations: College Procedures and Practices*, Coventry: FEFC

Further Education Funding Council (1996b) *Committee on Students with Learning Difficulties – Inclusive Learning* (Tomlinson Report), London: HMSO

Further Education Funding Council (1996c) *The Assessment of Vocational Qualifications in the Further Education Sector*, Coventry: FEFC

Further Education Funding Council (1996d) *Learning Works*, Coventry: FEFC

Further Education Funding Council (1996e) *Report of the Learning and Technology Committee* (Higginson Report), Coventry: FEFC

Further Education Funding Council (1997a) *Self-Assessment and Inspection*, Coventry: FEFC

Further Education Funding Council (1997b) *Learning Works* (Kennedy Report), Coventry: FEFC

Further Education Funding Council (1997c) *Validating Self-Assessment*, Circular 97/12, Coventry: FEFC

Further Education Funding Council (1997d) *Statistical Bulletin*, Coventry: FEFC

Further Education Funding Council (1997e) *Franchising and Collaborative Provision in the FE Sector*, Coventry: FEFC

Further Education Funding Council (1997f) *Standards and Their Assurance in Vocational Qualifications*, Coventry: FEFC

Further Education Funding Council (1998) *Accrediting Colleges*, Coventry: FEFC

Further Education Funding Council (1999a) *Networking Lifelong Learning: An ILT Development Strategy for FE*, Coventry: FEFC

Further Education Funding Council (1999b) *Professional Development in Further Education: National Report from the Inspectorate 1998–99*, Coventry: FEFC

Further Education National Training Organisation (1998) *FENTO: The New Further Education National Training Organisation*, London: FENTO

Further Education National Training Organisation (1999a) *Standards for Teaching and Supporting Learning in Further Education in England and Wales*, London: Association of Colleges

Further Education National Training Organisation (1999b) *Information Pack*, London: FENTO

Further Education Unit (1992) *Flexible Colleges: Access to Learning and Qualifications in FE*, Part I, London: FEU (now FEDA)

Further Education Unit (1994a) *Maximising Potential Through Individual Action Planning*, London: FEU (now FEDA)

Further Education Unit (1994b) *Managing the Delivery of Guidance in Colleges*, London: FEU (now FEDA)

Gagné, R.M. (1977) *The Conditions of Learning*, 3rd edition, New York: Holt, Rinehart & Winston

Gagné, R.M., Briggs, L.J. and Wager, W.W. (1992) *Principles of Instructional Design*, 4th edition, New York: Holt, Rinehart & Winston

Gardner, H. (1993) *Frames of Mind: The Theory of Multiple Intelligencies*, London: Fontana Press

Glover, D. and Law, S. (1996) *Managing Professional Development in Education: Issues in Policy and Practice*, London: Kogan Page

Griffiths, M. (1994) *Transition to Adulthood: The Role of Education for Young People with Severe Learning Difficulties*, London: David Fulton Publishers

Guskey, T.R. and Huberman, M. (eds) (1995) *Professional Development in Education: New Paradigms and Practices*, New York: Teachers College Press

Hall, B. (1997) *Web-Based Training Cookbook*, New York: John Wiley & Sons, Inc.

Handy, C. (1993) *The Age of Unreason*, London: Business Books Ltd

Hirst, P.H. and Peters, R.S. (1970) *The Logic of Education*, London: Routledge & Kegan Paul

HMSO (1993) *Unfinished Business*, London: HMSO

Hoggett, P. (1987) 'Modernisation, political strategy and the welfare state: An organisational perspective', *Studies in Decentralisation and Quasi Markets 2*, University of Bristol

Holmberg, B. (1977) *Distance Education*, London: Kogan Page

Honey, P. and Mumford, A. (2000) *The Learning Styles Questionnaire: 80 Item Version*, Maidenhead: Peter Honey

Jaques, D. (1991) *Learning in Groups*, 2nd edition, London: Kogan Page

Jarvis, P. (1992) *Paradoxes of Learning*, San Francisco: Jossey-Bass

Jarvis, P. (1995) *Adult and Continuing Education: Theory and Practice*, 2nd edition, London: Routledge

Jarvis, P., Holford, J. and Griffin, C. (2003) *The Theory and Practice of Learning*, 2nd edition, London: Kogan Page.

JISC (2002) Requirements for a Virtual Learning Environment, www.jisc.ac.uk/index.cfm?name=mle_related_vle. Accessed 29 January 2005

Kelly, A.V. (1999) *The Curriculum: Theory and Practice*, 4th edition, London: Paul Chapman

Kimball, L. (1995) 'Ten ways to make online learning groups work', *Educational Leadership*, Vol. 52, part 22, pp. 54–6

Knowles, M. (1978) *The Adult Learner: A Neglected Species*, 2nd edition, Houston: Gulf Publishing Co.

Knowles, M. (1986) *Using Learning Contracts*, San Francisco: Jossey-Bass

Kolb, D. (1984) *Experiential Learning*, Englewood Cliffs, N.J.: Prentice Hall

Kolb, D. and Fry, R. (1975) 'Towards an applied theory of experiential learning' in Cooper, C.L. (ed.) *Theories of Group Processes*, London: John Wiley

Kyriacou, C. (1998) *Essential Teaching Skills*, 2nd edition, Cheltenham: Stanley Thornes

Lave, J. and Wenger, E. (1991) *Situated Learning: Legitimate Peripheral Participation*, Cambridge: Cambridge University Press

Lawton, D. (1975) *Class, Culture and the Curriculum*, London: Routledge & Kegan Paul

Lockwood, F. (1992) *Activities in Self-Instructional Texts*, London: Kogan Page

Lockwood, F. (1998) *The Design and Production of Self-Instructional Materials*, London: Kogan Page

Lowe, R. (1993) *Successful Instructional Diagrams*, London: Kogan Page

LSC (2001) *Self Assessment and Development Plans*, Coventry: LSC

LSC (2003) *Measuring Success in the Learning and Skills Sector – A consultation and discussion document on new measures of success for FE colleges, work-based learning providers, adult learning providers and school sixth forms from 2005*. Co LSC (2004). Circular 04/02 – Plan-led funding for FE, Coventry: LSC

Lucas, N. (2004) *Teaching in Further Education – New Perspectives for a Changing Context*, London: University of London, Institute of Education

Maier, P., Barnett, L., Warren, A. and Brunner, D. (1998) *Using Technology in Teaching and Learning*, 2nd edition, London: Kogan Page

Martinez, P. (1998) *Improving Student Retention: A Guide to Successful Strategies*, London: Further Education and Development Authority

Maslow, A. (1954) *Motivation and Personality*, New York: Harper & Row

Maslow, A. (1968) *Towards a Psychology of Being*, 2nd edition, New York: Van Nostrand

McLean, R. (1980) *Typography*, Thames & Hudson

Megginson, D. and Clutterbuck, D. (1997) *Mentoring in Action*, London: Kogan Page

Mehrens, W.A. and Lehmann, I.J. (1984) *Measurement and Evaluation in Education and Psychology*, 3rd edition, New York: Holt, Rinehart & Winston

Miller, A. (1998) 'Business and community mentoring in schools' Research Briefs. *Research Report 43*, London: DfEE

Muller, D. and Funnell, P. (1991) *Delivering Quality in Vocational Education*, London: Kogan Page

Myers, D.G. (1998) *Psychology*, 5th edition, New York: Worth Publishers

Nasta, T. (1993) *Change through Networking in Vocational Education*, London: Kogan Page

Nasta, T. (1994) *How to Design a Vocational Curriculum*, London: Kogan Page

NCET (1996) *GNVQ: Integrating IT*, NCET Publications

North, V. with Buzan, T. (1996) *Get Ahead: Mind Map Your Way to Success*, Poole: Buzan Centres

Ofstead and the Adult Learning Inspectorate (ALI) (2001) *The Common Inspection Framework for Inspecting Post-16 Education and Training*, London: Ofsted/ALI

Ofsted (2003) *The Initial Training of Further Education Teachers – A Survey*, London: Ofsted

Parsons, D. and Berry-Lound, D. (2004) *Qualifications of Staff in LSC-funded Provision*, London: DfES

Pavlov, I. (1928) *Lectures on Conditioned Reflexes*, London: Martin Lawrence

Peters, R.S. (ed.) (1973) *The Philosophy of Education*, London: Oxford University Press

Peters, T. (1988) *Thriving on Chaos: Handbook for a Management Revolution*, London: Macmillan

Petty, G. (1998) *Teaching Today*, 2nd edition, Cheltenham: Stanley Thornes

Piaget, J. (1929) *The Child's Conception of the World*, London: Routledge & Kegan Paul

Rogers, C. (1969) *Freedom to Learn*, Columbus, Ohio: Charles E. Merrill

Rogers, J. (1989) *Adults Learning*, 3rd edition, Milton Keynes: Open University Press

Rosenthal, R. and Jacobson, L. (1968) *Pygmalion in the Classroom: Teacher Expectations and Pupils' Intellectual Ability*, New York: Holt, Rinehart & Winston

Rowntree, D. (1990) *Teaching Through Self-Instruction: How to Develop Open Learning Materials*, Revised edition, London: Kogan Page

Rowntree, D. (1994) *Preparing Materials for Open, Distance and Flexible Learning*, London: Kogan Page

Rowntree, D. (1997) *Making Materials-Based Learning Work*, London: Kogan Page

Rumble, G. (1997) *The Costs and Economics of Open and Distance Learning*, London: Kogan Page

Sallis, E. (1992) *Total Quality Management in Education*, London: Kogan Page

Schon, D. (1983) *The Reflective Practitioner: How Professionals Think in Action*, New York: Basic Books

Select Committee on Education and Employment (1998) *Sixth Report on Further Education*, London: House of Commons

Skinner, B.F. (1974) *About Behaviourism*, London: Cape

Standing Conference on Educational Development (1992) *Being a Personal Tutor*, Birmingham: SCED

Tansley, P. (1989) *Course Teams: The Way Forward in FE?* Windsor: Nelson

Teacher Training Agency (1997) *Standards for the Award of Qualified Teacher Status*, London: TTA

Thorndike, E.L. (1931) *Human Learning*, Cambridge, Mass: MIT Press

Toyne, P. (1979) *Credit Accumulation and Transfer Systems*, London: Department for Education and Science (now DfEE)

Tomlinson, M. (2004) *14–19 Curriculum and Qualifications Reform – Final Report of the Working Group on 14–19 Reform*, Annesley: DfES

Training Standards Council (1998) *Raising the Standard: Guidelines for Self-Assessment and Inspection of Government-Funded Training*, London: TSC

Tyler, R.W. (1949) *Basic Principles of Curriculum and Instruction*, Chicago: University of Chicago Press

Vygotsky, L. (1978) *Mind in Society*, Cambridge, Mass.: Harvard University Press

Walters, K. and Quilter, R. (2003) *Sink or Swim? Guidance and Support in Adult and Community Learning*, London: LSDA

Watson, J.B. (1930) *Behaviorism*, New York: W.W. Norton

Wenger, E., McDermott, R. and Snyder, W.M. (2002) *Cultivating Communities of Practice: A Guide to Managing Knowledge*, Boston, Mass.: Harvard Business School Press

Wheldall, K. and Merrett, F. (1989) *Positive Teaching in the Secondary School*, London: Paul Chapman Publishing

Wolf, A. (1995) *Competence Based Assessment*, Buckingham: Open University Press

Wragg, E.C. (1994) *An Introduction to Classroom Observation*, London: Routledge

Young. M.F.D. (ed.) (1971) *Knowledge and Control*, London: Collier-Macmillan

INDEX